# DELINQUENCY, CRIME AND SOCIETY
### HV 9058 S9 1972

A11066171001

## DATE DUE

| | | | |
|---|---|---|---|
| NO 30 '92 | | | |
| DE 9 '94 | | | |
| MR 24 '95 | | | |
| AP 26 '96 | | | |
| NO 8 '96 | | | |
| DE 5 '96 | | | |
| AU | | | |
| MY 9 '97 | | | |
| MY 29 '97 | | | |
| OC 7 '98 | | | |
| DE 5 '99 | | | |
| OC 23 '00 | | | |
| | | | |
| | | | |
| | | | |

DEMCO 38-296

D0961762

# Delinquency, Crime, and Society

*Contributors*

Daniel J. Abbott
Marshall B. Clinard
Donald R. Cressey
Harold Finestone
Daniel Glaser
Solomon Kobrin
Hans W. Mattick
Walter B. Miller
Emil Peluso
Joseph E. Puntil
Albert J. Reiss, Jr.
James F. Short, Jr.
William Simon
S. Kirson Weinberg
Marvin E. Wolfgang

# Delinquency, Crime, and Society

Edited by
James F. Short, Jr.

The University of Chicago Press
*Chicago and London*

Riverside Community College
Library
4800 Magnolia Avenue
Riverside, California 92506

JUL '92

JAMES F. SHORT, JR., is a professor of
sociology and director of the Social Research
Center at Washington State University. He is
the coauthor of *Group Process and Gang Delinquency,*
the editor of *The Social Fabric of the Metropolis,*
and coeditor of *Ernest W. Burgess on Crime, Family,
and Delinquency,* all published by the University
of Chicago Press.

The University of Chicago Press, Chicago 60637
The University of Chicago Press, Ltd., London

© 1976 *by The University of Chicago*
*All rights reserved. Published* 1976
*Phoenix Edition* 1978
*Printed in the United States of America*

82 81 80 79 78    5 4 3 2

*Library of Congress Cataloging in Publication Data*

Symposium on Juvenile Delinquency, University
  of Chicago, 1972
  Delinquency, crime, and society.

  Seven of the 12 papers are revisions of papers
first presented at the symposium, held to honor
H. D. McKay, and sponsored by the Institute for
Juvenile Research and the Chicago Area Project.
  1. Juvenile delinquency—Congresses.  2. McKay,
Henry Donald, 1899–  3. Shaw, Clifford Robe,
1896–  I. Short, James F.  II. McKay, Henry
Donald, 1899–  III. Illinois. Institute for
Juvenile Research, Chicago.  IV. Chicago Area
Project.  V. Title.
HV9058.S9 1972      364.36      75-27895
ISBN 0-226-75469-3 pbk.

Riverside Community College
Library
4800 Magnolia Avenue
Riverside, California 92506

# Contents

# Preface

The papers for chapters 3, 5, 6, 7, 8, 9, and 10 in this volume were prepared initially for a symposium honoring Henry D. McKay, held at the University of Chicago in the late fall of 1972. The symposium was sponsored by the Institute for Juvenile Research, a division of the Illinois Department of Mental Health, and the Chicago Area Project, a pioneering citizens action group originally developed by Clifford Shaw and Henry McKay. The general charge given speakers was to reflect on the state of knowledge concerning crime and juvenile delinquency in light of McKay's work and of emerging perspectives in research and theory concerning these phenomena. Speakers addressed various aspects of the general charge, and they spoke to it in terms of their own special interests and competencies.

The charge was broad, for as Albert J. Reiss notes in his chapter, "there is scarcely a problem in modern criminology that has not been illuminated by the pioneering investigations of Henry D. McKay." Inevitably, the papers address the research and the ideas of the "Shaw and McKay tradition," reflecting both the long-standing friendship and collaboration of McKay and Clifford R. Shaw and the enormous influence of their work on research, theory, and social action concerning crime and delinquency.

The volume includes thoroughly revised versions of the symposium papers and contributions by several scholars who did not address that gathering. The implicit charge to all contributors was that their papers should advance knowledge, as the most fitting tribute to the man we wished to honor. The volume, therefore, is more than a *Festschrift*, for it addresses critical and emerging issues in the study of crime and delinquency and their control. But it is a *Festschrift* as well, for the personal and/or professional debt to Henry McKay by all contributors was an important factor in our participation in the enterprise. Necessarily, it is equally a tribute to Clifford Shaw.

The desire to recognize the lifelong personal and scholarly contributions of a friend and colleague, Henry McKay, doubtless occurred to many of us, but the present effort was first suggested by William Simon and was warmly supported by the entire staff of the Institute for Juvenile Research, and by Anthony Sorrentino, Chicago Area Project executive vice-president. To implement the symposium and testimonial dinner, a sponsoring committee was organized, chaired by Elliott Donnelley, chairman, Chicago Area Project Board of Directors, and Professor Morris Janowitz, Department of Sociology, University of Chicago. A long and impressive list of sponsoring committee members, over one hundred individuals, were recruited to assist in the overall implementation of the symposium and dinner, and to each we are grateful. Among this group, special thanks are due a smaller working group, consisting of Peter Hunt (Urban Dynamic-Inter-City-Fund), chairman; Julian Schwartz (former executive director of the Chicago Area Project), treasurer; Emil Peluso, secretary; William Simon and Joseph Puntil, symposium chairmen; Merton Krause, symposium session chairman (all research-staff members of the Institute for Juvenile Research); Anthony Sorrentino (executive vice-president, Chicago Area Project Board), banquet chairman; and Ken Lingle, symposium host. Other members of the working group were: the Honorable Hubert Will (judge, U.S. District Court), Ben S. Meeker, (U.S. Probation and Parole Office), Charles Livermore (Department of Planning, City of Chicago), Betty Begg (commissioner, Department of Corrections, City of Chicago), Michael Spiotto (deputy commissioner, Chicago Police Department), Michael Delaney (former director of the Youth Division of the Chicago Police Department), Margaret Walters (secretary, Illinois Academy of Criminology), Russell Hogrefe (executive director, Chicago Youth Centers), Brochie Dilworth (executive director, Gads Hill Center), Professor Charles Shireman (School of Social Service Administration, University of Chicago), John A. Troike (Chicago Youth Centers), and Richard Jaffe (director, Institute for Social Action).

As in any enterprise of this sort, secretarial staffs deserve to be singled out for their contributions: from the Institute for Juvenile

Research, Karen Sintic, Estelle Marvel, Fran Behan, Mary Jo Broderick, and Betty Sharton; from the Social Research Center of Washington State University, Linda Love and Martha Copp; and from the Stanford Law School, Gladys Smith.

Special thanks are due Ken Lingle for his contribution through the Harris Bank Foundation for financial assistance toward this publication. As editor, I am especially grateful to the sponsoring committee for the opportunity to serve in this capacity and to my coauthors for their contributions and their cooperation. I am certain that I speak for all of us and for countless others who have benefited from his contributions, his counsel, and his friendship, in acknowledging the greatest debt of all to Henry.

JFS

## Introduction

## On Criminology
## and Criminologists:
## Continuity, Change,
## and Criticism

*James F. Short, Jr.*

As a field, criminology has many "schools" of thought, research traditions, and conflicting interpretations of the nature of the behavior we study and of what should (and should not) be done about it. Yet there is continuity and a cumulative character to much of our work. Today's healthy theoretical ferment and methodological controversy reflect similar conflicts in criminology's parent disciplines, as well as profound debate on fundamental issues confronting local, national, and international societies.

Among the research traditions most basic to both continuity and change in criminological thought, perhaps none has been so important to research, theory, and social action with respect to crime and delinquency as that associated with Clifford R. Shaw and Henry D. McKay and the "Chicago school" of urban sociology. So great has been its impact that, though the basic findings seemed clear more than forty years ago, controversy over the validity of these findings continues, and even the most recent theoretical formulations draw upon them for support or in criticism. Yet little systematic attention has been given to assessment of some of the more important empirical questions raised by this tradition, nor has the theoretical development of the tradition been systematically analyzed and placed in contemporary perspective.

This book is devoted to just such issues. Appropriately, since our initial purpose in coming together for a symposium, and later in preparing this volume, was to honor one member of the Shaw and McKay collaboration—Henry D. McKay—most of the contributors to this book are "Old Chicagoans" in the sense that they were intellectually nurtured at the University of Chicago and in that city's streets and institutions. Some address themselves to assessing ideas generated by the work of McKay and Shaw, building new empirical and theoretical contributions in their own right. Others report their own field research, drawing upon that work to resolve problems of interpretation. Still others set out to test, in very different cultural contexts, research findings and theories advanced by McKay and Shaw from their studies in Chicago during the early to mid-twentieth century. One draws primarily on his long experience as participant in, and student of, the American prison system.

The book is not limited to scholarship within the Chicago tradition. Contributions are included from research traditions that have long personal and professional associations with Henry McKay and Clifford Shaw. These contributions reflect both quantitative and qualitative approaches, as does the work of the sociologists, past and present, from the Illinois Institute for Juvenile Research (IJR).

The Chicago tradition, much in evidence in these papers, is represented by a small fraction of students and associates of Henry McKay over the years. Indeed, this volume is in a sense a "progress report" on continuing work in that tradition, as modified by other perspectives and new data. Methodologically, most of us remain confirmed empiricists, though hardly wedded to any one method. In this, too, our acknowledged forebears are McKay and Shaw.

The contents of the book reflect two basic concerns: the explanation of crime and delinquency; and the analysis of social control of crime and delinquency. The dichotomy is by no means clear, for as McKay and Shaw clearly recognized, explanation necessarily involves agents and agencies of control. Chapters, therefore, are not organized in these terms but in terms of basic theoretical and empirical issues (Part I), studies of youth gangs (Part II), attempts to replicate findings and interpretations of Shaw and McKay in two African settings (Part III), and studies focused primarily or in major degree on social policy implications of research and theory (Part IV).

## Basic Theoretical and Empirical Issues

Most of the chapters focus on one or another theoretical or empirical issue raised explicitly in the work of Henry McKay and Clifford Shaw. Harold Finestone begins by carefully tracing the evolution of the theoretical perspectives with which Shaw and McKay approached their data and which, in turn, guided their empirical inquiries. Beginning with an emphasis on social change (influenced especially by W. I. Thomas) on the development of delinquent traditions and processes associated with becoming delinquent, Shaw and McKay moved toward a functionalist position which emphasized relationships between delinquency and relatively stable features of social structure. In so doing, they came independently to conclusions elaborated in Merton's classic statement of the relationships between culturally structured success goals and socially structured limitations on approved opportunities for the achievement of those goals (Merton 1938; Shaw and McKay 1942). This position has seen its richest development with respect to delinquency in the theoretical work of Cohen (1955) and Cloward and Ohlin (1960), in Miller's (1958) counter-argument that features of lower-class culture are sufficient to explain much delinquency, and in research designed to test hypotheses derived from these statements (Short 1964; Short and Strodtbeck 1965, 1974; Short, Rivera and Tennyson 1965; Rivera and Short 1967a and 1967b; Kobrin, Puntil, and Peluso 1967; Elliott and Voss 1974; Horowitz and Schwartz 1974).

As a result of both empirical and theoretical challenges to functionalist interpretations, Finestone suggests that the study of delinquency within the Shaw and McKay tradition is moving into "a third stage," the interactionist approach. In so doing, this tradition moves also toward an allied theoretical perspective, that of the conflict theorists (Coser 1956; Turk 1969; Quinney 1970; Chambliss 1974). Each of these perspectives takes as a central task explanation of social differentiation and its consequences.

Finestone suggests that the developing present stage of delinquency theory requires concepts that are transitive, that can be interpreted in both sociological and social psychological terms. Different levels of explanation must be bridged and integrated: macro- (social structure, culture) and micro- (group process, interpersonal interaction) sociological levels; individual (biological, psychological), microsociological, and macrosociological levels (Cohen and Short 1971). Images of the delinquent held at each stage of development of the Shaw and McKay tradition permit such bridging, though little research has been done to promote theoretical integration. The delinquent has been portrayed as "disaffiliated" (in social change and social disorganization terms), as "frustrated social climber" (in the functional stage), and as "aggrieved citizen" (the emerging interactionist conflict stage). But the insights into the relationship between young people and society captured by images such as these necessarily are incomplete. What is required is synthesis and integration between two levels of explanation. The most promising steps in this direction appear to be formulations which combine study of cultural and structural aspects of social differentiation with systematic study of individual and collective aspects of delinquency. Beginnings have been made (see Reiss 1952; Baittle and Kobrin 1964; Sherif and Sherif 1965; Cohen 1965; Short and Strodtbeck 1965, 1974; Gordon 1967; Klein and Crawford 1967; Cartwright, Howard, and Reuterman 1971; Toby 1974). But concern for integration must be explicit, systematic, and sustained in theory and in research design and its implementation—conditions rarely, if ever, achieved.

The difficulties posed by this challenge are highlighted in Chapter 2, written by three members of the current IJR staff. William Simon, Joseph E. Puntil, and Emil Peluso stress both continuities and discontinuities with the earlier IJR tradition, as well as social changes and changed perspectives on adolescents and their social worlds. Preliminary findings from recent ethnographic studies and survey interviews throughout Illinois are briefly reviewed, indicating essential similarities as well as contrasts in adolescent behavior patterning across a broad range of social classes and community contexts. These findings are interpreted in part as manifestations of an ever-changing national culture. Despite enormous quantities of data and improved technologies of data reduction, however, the critical link "between social structure and group life and individual destinies" remains illusive.

Indeed, even basic empirical issues fundamental to such theoretical linkage remain to be settled, as Albert J. Reiss, Jr., demonstrates with his searching inquiry into conclusions reached by Shaw and McKay, "that delinquency is endemic in certain neighborhoods and that the probability of becoming delinquent is greater for persons in lower than high income status groups." These conclusions have been challenged by recent research, including findings of the current IJR group.

Reiss examines in a variety of ways the long-standing controversy concerning the social-class distribution of delinquency. Neither findings nor methods used in self-reported studies of delinquency have been consistent, he points out, and such studies have tended to examine less serious offenses. Many studies, including the present IJR survey, focus on prevalence rather than incidence of delinquency, thus obscuring important aspects of behavior patterning. Self-report studies have failed to examine systematically both onset of and desistance from behaviors studied, and they have not permitted cohort analysis because they lack longitudinal focus. These limitations are stringent, but, in view of the fact that only one cohort study of delinquency has been carried out using any type of data (Wolfgang, Figlio, and Sellin 1972; and Wolfgang, in this volume), careful attention to such limitations is required if methods and findings of different studies are to be made comparable and therefore cumulative.

Reiss examines studies of police discretion, the relative serious-ness of offenses committed by juveniles in different social strata, the class distribution of delinquent gangs, and patterns of criminal victimization. He concludes that "the social control of crime by agents of law enforcement may be more determined by . . . relationships between victims, offenders and events than by the organization of discretion of official agents of social control." (See also Reiss 1974.)

It is clear from the current IJR research and Reiss's thoughtful treatment that nearly half a century after initial publication of the Shaw and McKay work (1929), neither the empirical questions raised nor their theoretical interpretation can be regarded as settled.

Competition between viewpoints and levels of theoretical focus, and between relative emphasis on change and continuity, is consequential beyond academic argument. It is on the basis of such arguments and understandings that social policies are formulated and implemented. Yet it is clear that major issues remain unresolved and are likely to remain so. If these chapters raise more questions than they answer, they reflect the state of the field, and they suggest the difficulties as well as the im-portance of the points at issue.

One would like to believe that the empirical issues left unresolved by inquiries such as these can be reconciled by more careful and continuous inquiry. Perhaps the *exceptions* to the similarities in delinquent behavior across classes and communities observed by the IJR group are those which a finer-grained microview of social life in varying contexts would reveal to be crucial to differences which occur so dramatically in official and victimization data. It is hoped that, with the knowledge and research tools now available, these and other questions may be more definitively addressed in the future. Still, it is well to note that the change and complexity which characterize social life are likely always to confound even the most sophisticated data, analyses, and arguments.

## Cultural and Institutional Contexts of Delinquency

The group nature of delinquency was a consistent theme in the work of Shaw and McKay (Shaw and McKay 1931; McKay 1949). Recent studies of gangs have confirmed the "versatile activity repertoire" of most youth gangs and their shifting organizational and behavioral character in response to external and internal forces. In Part II, Walter Miller and James Short focus on forces of change external to gangs which are related to gang adaptations and stability.

Miller's and Short's interpretations of gangs in the "urban crisis era" of the 1960s are mutually supportive. That period experienced the full impact of several social movements and other broad social and cultural developments with special significance for youth, particularly minority youth in the United States: civil rights and youth movements, extensive rioting in large urban ghettos, a new emphasis on cultural pluralism and participatory democracy, the "politicization" of many social issues, and rapid social change spurred by technological and demographic changes. Despite these momentous social changes, youth gangs exhibit a large measure of continuity and stability in culture, structure, and behavior. Much of the widely publicized appearance of change was either temporary or superficial. Miller and Short stress the importance of forces external to gangs in publicly defining the nature of the "gang problem" and in shaping public response. Official (especially police) and media practices were crucial in this respect. They were important, also, in creating the social context within which a few supergangs emerged, as well as for the specific directions taken by such gangs in behavior and ideology (see also Kalberg and Suttles 1974; Spergel 1969, 1973). Miller examines evidence concerning gang participation in the urban riots of the 1960s. Short explores the context within which a variety of economic and community improvement enterprises were undertaken by and on behalf of the supergangs. While these treatments do not solve the theoretical problem posed in Finestone's chapter, it is clear that such matters cannot be fully understood as the product of a single level of explanation. Miller and Short tap both micro- and macrosociological levels in viewing gangs (in Finestone's phrasing) "both as a society in which some adolescents have their most meaningful personal and social experiences and as a social organization with very important relations with other institutions in the community." The individual (psychological) level is largely neglected in these papers, though the importance of a variety of social abilities and disabilities has been stressed by several writers (Short and Strodtbeck 1965, 1974; Gordon 1966; Klein and Crawford 1967; Caplan 1973; Horowitz and Schwartz 1974).

In Part III portions of the Shaw and McKay work are replicated in two African countries, Ghana and Uganda. S. Kirson Weinberg compares factors related to delinquency in Accra, a cosmopolitan metropolis in Ghana, with findings reported in the early Shaw and McKay studies and in more recent studies in this country. While his discussion ranges broadly, data for conclusive tests are rare. The Shaw and McKay generalizations concerning the concentrations of officially defined delinquency in slum areas are sustained, though the location of such areas varies under different conditions of technological development and governmental policy. Delinquency is also found to vary among ethnic (tribal) groups in Accra according to their experience in the urban milieu, as suggested by the early Shaw and McKay work. Similarly, peer-group experience is found to be crucially related to the extent and nature of delinquency in Accra, as in the United States.

The relation of family organization to delinquency is very much a function of cultural pattern. The situation is especially complex in Ghana, where the traditional polygamous and matrilineal family pattern exists side by side with the Western, Christian-influenced monogamous conjugal pattern. Lacking systematic evidence, Weinberg suggests that parent-child conflict results in greater peer-group influence in the slums of Accra, much as in the United States.

The usefulness of subcultural variations in delinquency, except as ideal types or for heuristic purposes, is a continuing subject of debate. Weinberg finds no evidence of either the conflict or retreatist orientations discussed in the United States (Cloward and Ohlin 1960) among peer groups in Accra. He does find useful a distinction between those delinquent activities (chiefly stealing) which are oriented toward subsistence or hedonic gratifications and those which are more career oriented.

Weinberg closes his essay with observations concerning replications of Shaw and McKay research in a variety of cultural settings. He suggests that this work is an important beginning for more systematic cross-cultural inquiry.

Just such an inquiry is presented in Chapter 7, by Marshall B. Clinard and Daniel J. Abbott. Their carefully designed study compares two slum communities in Kampala, Uganda—one with an exceptionally high crime rate, the other with a low rate. Interviews with residents of these two areas disclosed no difference in disapproval of theft. Clinard and Abbott suggest that the disparity in crime rates between the two communities results from differences in "both cultural and communicative integration." Reflective of the former, the low-rate community "was tribally homogeneous and its older generation selected their close friends from a limited variety of cultural backgrounds." Higher communicative integration in the low-rate community was reflected in the fact that, especially among adults who were over twenty-five years old, "There was more visiting, less mobility, and greater participation in local community organizations, including religious groups." The high-rate area was characterized by less stable family relationships and greater individual isolation.

Clinard and Abbott conclude that, despite erosion of traditional authority that occurs with urbanization and industrialization, older persons continue to play a vital role in determining the character of urban slum communities. Higher socioeconomic status was not associated with more effective social control in these communities, and "fairly rapid" population change did not "destroy cohesivenesss automatically."

While the latter finding may call into question the importance of community stability for delinquency control, as Clinard and Abbott suggest, it may also be the case that continuity of tribal cultures (which was much higher in the low-rate community) is of overriding importance in this "developing country," in contrast to more fully developed urban industrial societies. Such an interpretation seems especially likely in view of the further conclusion that "internal relations and patterns of behavior within the local community" were more important than were relations outside the local community in controlling crime. While conclusive evidence is lacking, length of residence appears to be a key variable at both individual and aggregate levels in the explanation of such phenomena as community attachment and social control in England and in the United States (see Kasarda and Janowitz 1974; McKay 1969).

## Research, Theory, and Social Policy

The final section of the book addresses the complex relationships between research, theory, and social policies designed to control crime and delinquency. The first paper in this section, by Donald R. Cressey, applies the "delinquency area" notion to the problem of corporate crime. This is followed by three chapters (by Solomon Kobrin, Daniel Glaser, and Marvin E. Wolfgang) that focus on ideas and programs oriented toward juvenile delinquents. In the final chapter, Hans Mattick reflects on his experience with maximum-security prisons and jails and the often contradictory goals and ideals that plague this method of handling criminals.

Others have noted similarities, as well as differences, in the criminality of upper- and underworlds (Sutherland 1949; Geis 1974). Cressey notes that neither the corporate world nor the slum is effectively organized against crime; that, in fact, basic to the organization of each is "an ideology conducive to widespread law violation, including the notion that some crime is not crime, 'really.'" But in the politics of crime control the slum is no match for the large corporation. The history of antitrust legislation and its enforcement has resulted in a system of socialism for the rich and capitalism for the poor, says Cressey, developing a theme which emerged from Sutherland's (1949) pioneering work on white-collar crime. Cressey notes that the corporate world, despite fascinating variations, appears to be "a high delinquency neighborhood, and the need for democratic organization of this world . . . is great." Indeed, he concludes that "what is at stake is democracy, not free enterprise, which long ago disappeared." Cressey calls for systematic analysis of structural conditions that are conducive to violations of antitrust laws. One of these, clearly, is "political organization, on a corporate base, for keeping interest groups, especially consumer groups, from making antitrust violation a focus of popular concern." The need for more effective consumer organization against illegal restraint of trade is clear, as another recent treatment of the topic also emphasizes (Geis 1974).

Following this call for additional research and action concerning upperworld crime, the book returns to "ordinary" crime, the subject of most traditional criminological inquiry. Here the problem is quite different from that posed by illegal restraint of trade. For here the problem is *lack* of power and *lack* of integration with conventional society. The aim of recent preventive and rehabilitative programs, therefore, is to avoid the alienation of youth from conventional institutions and to promote integration of young and old toward common purposes.

Solomon Kobrin, himself both product and carrier of the Shaw and McKay tradition of delinquency studies, moves outside that tradition to address the problems and limits of labeling theory as it has been applied to juvenile delinquency. That theory, which enlarges "the area taken into consideration in the study of deviant phenomena by including in it activities of others than the allegedly deviant actor" (Becker 1973), has had enormous influence on thinking and social policy concerning juvenile delinquency.

Kobrin focuses his discussion on current programs designed explicitly to avoid the stigmatizing consequences of youthful contact with the juvenile justice system. These "diversion" programs attempt to avoid the authority-laden, coercive atmosphere that "clings to courts and their functionaries," thereby making it possible for reform aims to be pursued "without risking the danger of the stigmatizing label." As is so often the case, however, the translation of a theoretical analysis (in this case the labeling insight) into social policy has many pitfalls. The labeling response is, after all, as Kobrin remarks, "an irrepressible feature of human interaction in that persons perceive and identify one another by employing culturally standardized cognitive categories" (see also Feldman, 1974). The problem posed is not simply that of the ability of persons involved in diversion programs to suspend negative labeling. To the extent that the behavior over which control is sought is predatory and personally threatening (crimes *mala in se*), the sociologist must inquire as to the impact on the social fabric of changing (or seeming to change) the labeling of such behavior.

Kobrin suggests that diversion programs are unlikely to avoid the labeling process insofar as they tend "to foster the segregation of delinquents, to neglect the use of group experiences in favor of individual treatment methods, and to employ coercion in maintaining program membership." He concludes that "intervention efforts keyed to a reversal of negative labeling promise limited success," and that closer attention needs to be given to institutional processes "associated with bureaucratization and its often arbitrary and sometimes mindless narrowing of the 'value space' within which the firm attachment of the young to institutional goals . . . may take place." The Kobrin and Glaser papers converge in targeting the public schools as the "primary institutional home of the young in advanced industrial societies in which change may be both appropriate and feasible." The importance of the school in relation to juvenile delinquency is strongly supported by recent research (Polk and Schafer 1972; Elliott and Voss 1974). It should be noted, nevertheless, that schools increasingly retreat from their traditional role in loco parentis, and student participation in many schools may be declining (Meyer et al 1971; Dornbusch 1974). This retreat creates major educational problems and weakens the ability of the school to serve as an effective institutional setting for delinquency prevention. Indeed, the evidence suggests that dropping out of school may reduce both "delinquent behavior and the likelihood of official police contact" (Elliott and Voss 1974, p. 306).

Meyer and his associates (1971) report that "the relation between the high school student and his school has come to be recognized by both parties as a very limited one" (p. 26). Problems which previously might have been conceived as matters properly the subject of school discipline now tend to be defined as "problems of *youth in society*," rather than as school problems. Much problematic youth behavior is perceived to be related to "political, economic, ethnic, cultural, and age-group interests and tastes." While such conduct creates problems for the school, "neither the students nor the school administrators see them as primarily relevant to the school." Both respond by working out "*ad hoc* arrangements to permit the school organization to go on, while the problems are acted out elsewhere" (p. 26). It is important to recognize that these *ad hoc* arrangements do not represent a commitment to involve either students or local community adults in program planning and school operation. Glaser's chapter suggests ways in which adolescents may be helped to bridge the gap between childhood and adulthood, in part through more effective involvement of both students and adults in school–related programs.

Glaser's chapter combines intellectual autobiography with a sociology of knowledge. The dual attraction for the Chicago sociologists of "the ivory tower of academia" and "the workaday world of high crime rate neighborhoods" led to the development of "the most important idea in the field of crime prevention and correction," namely, the use of the marginal worker in delinquency programs. The product of a different social world, the marginal worker can "blend the language, norms and values of subcultural settings which may be in conflict, yet in need of one another." McKay and Shaw were marginal workers, standing as it were with one foot in crime prevention activity and one in social science. Glaser emphasizes the need for marginal workers of many types and the importance of generalizing the relationship between research and social policy.

Glaser traces the idea of marginal workers to the "law of sociocultural relativity," probably the most powerful proposition in sociology and anthropology. This "law" holds that "social separation produces cultural differentiation." Citing evidence that the social separation (and therefore the cultural differentiation) between youth and adults is today at a high level, Glaser argues that the greatest need in crime preventive and correctional programs is for persons and programs which effectively bridge relationships between youth and adult worlds. The importance of this basic notion is indicated by the fact that marginal workers (variously called detached workers, extension youth workers, gang workers, or street workers), while successful in monitoring some types of delinquent activities such as gang fights, typically fail to prevent other types of serious delinquent behavior such as theft and drug use. Glaser attributes the failure to the tendency in such programs to concentrate on "fun and games activities rather than on decreasing the social separation of delinquents from people in the legitimate roles which youth must adopt if they are to achieve independence in a noncriminal way of life." He ends his chapter by discussing imaginative new ways in which delinquency control activities might employ this basic principle, including additional use of marginal workers.

Marvin E. Wolfgang, together with his mentor and frequent collaborator, Thorsten Sellin, has been responsible for another major research tradition which has ranged widely over the field of criminology. His chapter in this volume is based on two pioneering bodies of work in that tradition, one concerned with measuring juvenile delinquency and the other with study of delinquency in a birth cohort in Philadelphia. Focusing on "the dynamic flow of delinquency" in the cohort through age twenty-six, Wolfgang concludes that "maximum efficiency and effectiveness of an intervention program should occur prior to age eighteen" and after "the third recorded offense, unless the first or second are of a very serious quality." Accumulated seriousness scores would be maintained in the files of the system "to be used as a basis for determining the moment and gravity of sanctioning intervention." While additional research is needed "to fit the best treatment strategy to the personal reactions of the individual," Wolfgang suggests that a major advantage to such a system would be promotion of "clarity, both to the social agents of response and to the youthful deviants about where a young person stands in the social scale of adjudged harmfulness to the community." Noting that the juvenile justice system badly needs correction and that a point system such as he suggests would require great care to protect juveniles against abuses, Wolfgang also calls for "a juvenile public defender system and the admission into juvenile court of only serious cases."

In view of the power differentials noted earlier with respect to corporate and street crime, social scientists put forward proposals for control of the latter with some ambivalence. For, while street crime violates "the universal wish to preserve one's property against theft and one's body against invasion" (Nettler 1974, p. 3), there is, as Cressey notes, "more at stake in the regulation of corporations than there is in the regulation of street crimes." The danger to democracy is greatest from both sources—from corporate restraint of trade because it concentrates economic and political power, from street crime because the fears of the body politic may lead to toleration of, even demand for, increased restrictions on personal freedom and, in the extreme case, to a police state. The social fabric of a free society is damaged by both, but the damage is more insidious when respected members of the community undermine the basis for law and order by personal and corporate example.

Conflict in rule–creation and in rule–enforcement seems an inevitable by–product of social differentiation. The power of economic interests and moral entrepreneurs in law–making and in the "mobilization of bias" (Chambliss 1974) have been amply demonstrated. The difficulties of changing power differentials in law-making and enforcement, and of elevating public concern and outrage concerning corporate crime to the levels focused on street crime are enormous; and they are complicated by lack of knowledge of "the full costs and consequences of such a course once it is set" (Geis 1974, p. 275). At the very least, however, more effective consumer and voter organization would seem a good place to start. And, lest there be any doubt, the ideological thesis is, as Geis (1974) notes, "that society ought to outlaw acts which can, with logic, be shown directly to hurt, and deprive innocent people—armed robbery, pollution, burglary, insider transactions, false advertising, rape" (p. 280), and, of course, restraint of trade.

The book closes with Hans Mattick's "Reflections of a Former Prison Warden," a stinging indictment of the entire criminal justice system as arbitrary, discriminatory, and ineffective, in law and in practice. His most severe comments are reserved for the prison system. Of particular interest, in view of my immediately preceding remarks, are Mattick's comments on the important role of economic factors in the establishment of the prison system and in its continued development. From the beginning, though cloaked in the rhetoric of humanitarianism and rationalism, prisons afforded opportunities for political patronage and economic exploitation. Mattick does not deny the humanitarian motives of those who sought to replace an earlier system based on "death, corporal punishment, and banishment" for offenders, nor of those who have labored toward the goal of rehabilitation or sought to improve prison conditions. He argues, rather, that human values typically have been slighted in the political and professional decisions that have shaped correctional policy and practice. He concludes, as have many others in the past, that imprisonment "serves to confirm prisoners in their criminal careers and maladjusts them for their future life in the free community," while misleading and victimizing citizens in the general public by creating "the illusion that a serious social problem is being successfully addressed." He calls for the "systematic physical destruction of the older, Bastille-like monster prisons" and for fundamental alterations of the law and the entire criminal justice system.

The dilemma faced by those who seek fundamental change in "corrections" (a misnomer in itself, in view of past and present policy and achievement) is similar to that many of us face with respect to larger social, economic, and political systems. Most of us come down on the side of change with continuity, rather than revolutionary change and discontinuity. We do so in part because, in Mattick's terms, we deny the "luxury" (and the hypocrisy) of "preaching the doctrine of increasing misery as an efficient cause of future change if the preacher of the doctrine does not have to share the misery." We do so, also, because we doubt the possibility of utopian solutions and distrust the ability and the wisdom of those who would destroy cultures and social systems as a basis for establishing other cultures and social systems. Like Henry McKay and Clifford Shaw, we hope by means of our disciplines and our citizenship to continue dialogue concerning the nature of human behavior in its individual and collective aspects. And, like them, we hope to contribute toward diagnosis, understanding, and humane solution to some of that behavior's problematic aspects.

## References

Baittle, Brahm, and Solomon Kobrin
1964        "On the Relationships of a Characterological Type of Delinquent to the Milieu." *Psychiatry* 27 (February): 6–16.

Becker, Howard S., ed.
1973        *Outsiders: Studies on the Sociology of.Deviance*. 2d ed. New York: The Free Press.

Caplan, Nathan
1973        "Street Skills of Many Hard-to-employ Youths May Hinder Success in Job Training Programs." *ISR Newsletter* (Autumn): 5.

Cartwright, D. C., K. I. Howard, and N. A. Reuterman
1971        "Multivariate Analysis of Gang Delinquency: III. Age and Physique of Gangs and Clubs." *Multivariate Behavioral Research* 6 (January): 75–90.

Chambliss, William J.
1974        "The State, the Law, and the Definition of Behavior as Criminal or Delinquent." In Daniel

Glaser, ed., *Handbook of Criminology*. Chicago: Rand McNally, pp. 7–44.

Cloward, Richard, and Lloyd E. Ohlin
1960        *Delinquency and Opportunity: A Theory of Delinquent Gangs*. New York: The Free Press.

Cohen, A. K.
1955        *Delinquent Boys*. New York: The Free Press.
1965        *Deviance and Control*. Englewood Cliffs, N.J.: Prentice-Hall.

Cohen, A. K., and James F. Short, Jr.
1958        "Research in Delinquent Subcultures." *Journal of Sociological Issues* 14:20–27.
1971        "Crime and Juvenile Delinquency." Chapter 2 in R. K. Merton and R. Nisbet, eds., *Contemporary Social Problems*. 3d ed. New York: Harcourt, Brace, Jovanovich.

Coser, Lewis
1956        *The Functions of Social Conflict*. London: Routledge and Kegan Paul.

Dornbusch, Sanford M.
1974        "To Try or Not to Try." *Stanford Magazine*, 2 (Fall/Winter): 50–54.

Elliott, D. S., and H. L. Voss
1974        *Delinquency and Dropout*. Toronto: D. C. Heath and Company.

Feldman, Ronald A.
1974        "Social Labeling, Status Offenses, and Juvenile Justice." Boys Town, Nebraska: Center for the Study of Youth Development (manuscript).

Gordon, R. A.
1966        "Social Level, Disability, and Gang Interaction." *American Journal of Sociology* 73 (July): 42–62.

Geis, G.
1974        "Avocational Crime." In Daniel Glaser, ed., *Handbook of Criminology*. Chicago: Rand McNally, pp. 273–98.

Horowitz, Ruth, and Gary A. Schwartz
1974        "Normative Ambiguity and Gang Violence." *American Sociological Review* 39 (April): 238–51.

Hewitt, L. E., and R. L. Jenkins
1947        *Fundamental Patterns of Maladjustment: The Dynamics of Their Origin.* Springfield: State of Illinois.

Inkeles, Alex
1960        "Personality and Social Structure." In R. Merton, L. Broom, and L. Cottrell, Jr., eds., *Sociology Today.* New York: Basic Books, pp. 249–76.

Kalberg, Stephen, and Gerald D. Suttles
1974        "Gangs, the Police and Politicians in Chicago during 1964–1970." Paper for E. W. Burgess Memorial Symposium. University of Chicago.

Kasarda, John D., and Morris Janowitz
1974        "Community Attachment in Mass Society." *American Sociological Review* 39 (June): 328–39.

Klein, M. W., and L. Y. Crawford
1967        "Groups, Gangs and Cohesiveness." *Journal of Research in Crime and Delinquency* 4 (January): 63–75.

Kobrin, S., J. Puntil, and E. Peluso
1967        "Criteria of Status among Street Gangs." *Journal of Research in Crime and Delinquency* 4 (January) 98–118.

McKay, Henry D.
1949        "The Neighborhood and Child Conduct." *The Annals* 261 (January): 32–41.
1969        "Recent Rates of Delinquency and Commitment in Chicago: Distribution and Trends" and "Rates of Delinquents and Commitments: Discussion and Conclusion." In Clifford R. Shaw and Henry K. McKay, *Juvenile Delinquency and Urban Areas.* Rev. ed. Chicago: University of Chicago Press, pp. 329–58, 374–89.

Merton, Robert K.
1938        "Social Structure and Anomie." *American Sociological Review* 3 (October): 161–94 (revised and enlarged in Merton, *Social Theory and Social Structure.* New York: Free Press, 1957, pp. 677–82).

Meyer, John W., Chris Chase-Dunn, and James Inverarity
1971        "The Expansion of the Autonomy of Youth:

Responses of the Secondary School to Problems of Order in the 1960's." Stanford University: Laboratory for Social Research (mimeographed).

Miller, Walter J.
1958        "Lower Class Culture as a Generating Milieu of Gang Delinquency." *Journal of Social Issues* 14 (Summer): 5–19.

Nettler, Gwynn
1974        *Explaining Crime*. New York: McGraw-Hill.

Polk, Kenneth, and Walter E. Schafer, eds.
1972        *Schools and Delinquency*. Englewood Cliffs, N.J.: Prentice-Hall.

Quinney, Richard
1970        *The Social Reality of Crime*. Boston: Little, Brown.

Reiss, Albert J., Jr.
1952        "Social Correlates of Psychological Types of Delinquency." *American Sociological Review* 17:710–18.
1974        "Discretionary Justice." In Daniel Glaser, ed., *Handbook of Criminology*. Chicago: Rand-McNally, pp. 679–702.

Rivera, R. J., and James F. Short, Jr.
1967a       "Occupational Goals: A Comparative Analysis." In Malcolm W. Klein, ed., *Juvenile Gangs in Context: Theory, Research, and Action*. Englewood Cliffs, N.J.: Prentice-Hall, pp. 70–90.
1967b       "Significant Adults, Caretakers, and Structure of Opportunity, an Exploratory Study." *Journal of Research in Crime and Delinquency* 4 (January): 76–97.

Shaw, Clifford R., and Henry D. McKay
1929        *Delinquency Areas*. Chicago: University of Chicago Press.
1931        *Social Factors in Juvenile Delinquency*. Vol 2, National Commission on Law Observance and Enforcement, Report on the Causes of Crime. Washington, D.C.: U.S. Government Printing Office.
1942        *Juvenile Delinquency and Urban Areas*. Revised
1969        edition, ed. James F. Short, Jr. Chicago: University of Chicago Press.

Sherif, Muzafer, and Carolyn W. Sherif
1965        *Problems of Youth: Transition to Adulthood in a Changing World*. Chicago: Aldine.

Short, James F., Jr.
1964        "Gang Delinquency and Anomie." In M. B. Clinard, ed., *Anomie and Deviant Behavior*. New York: Free Press, pp. 98–127.

Short, James F., Jr., Ramon Rivera, and Ray A. Tennyson
1965        "Perceived Opportunities, Gang Membership, and Delinquency." *American Sociological Review* 30 (February): 56–67.

Short, James F., Jr., and Fred L. Strodtbeck
1965        *Group Process and Gang Delinquency*. Chicago:
1974        University of Chicago Press.

Spergel, Irving
1969        *Politics, Policies and the Youth Gang*. University of Chicago School of Social Service Administration (mimeographed).
1973        "Community-based Delinquency-prevention Programs: An Overview." *Social Service Review* (March): 16–31.

Sutherland, Edwin H.
1949        *White Collar Crime*. New York: Dryden. Reissued, with a foreword by Donald R. Cressey, by Holt, Rinehart and Winston, New York, 1961.

Toby, Jackson
1957        "The Differential Impact of Family Disorganization." *American Sociological Review* 22 (October): 505–12.
1974        "The Socialization and Control of Deviant Motivation." In Daniel Glaser, ed., *Handbook of Criminology*. Chicago: Rand McNally, pp. 85-100.

Turk, Austin T.
1969        *Criminality and Legal Order*. Chicago: Rand McNally.

Wolfgang, Marvin E., R. M. Figlio, and T. Sellin
1972        *Delinquency in a Birth Cohort*. Chicago: University of Chicago Press.

# I Basic Issues in the Study of Delinquency

# 1    The Delinquent
and Society
The Shaw and McKay
Tradition

*Harold Finestone*

## The Issues

Henry McKay has been preeminent in his efforts to develop a conception of juvenile delinquency which would accurately reflect its intrinsic connection with modern urban societies. He has been equally dedicated as a researcher and theorist, devoting himself over the years to gathering and interpreting a very comprehensive body of empirical data bearing upon this problem. We perhaps pay most fitting tribute to an intellectual contribution of such distinction by attempting to grasp it both in itself and in its capacity to stimulate significant subsequent efforts. The work of Henry McKay has been highly influential in this latter regard. Accordingly, it will be the purpose of this paper to depict his work, together with that of his collaborator, Clifford R. Shaw, as originating a tradition of research in delinquency which has been of considerable importance in American sociology. These men became pathfinders in the study of delinquency because they succeeded in formulating its central sociological issues in such a manner as to continue to stimulate and challenge subsequent generations of investigators.

Like all social phenomena, juvenile delinquency may be viewed from two aspects. It has both an epidemiological or sociological aspect and an individual or social psychological aspect. In its epidemiological aspect it tends to suggest such common-sense questions as the following. How widespread is the problem of delinquency in our society? Is it restricted to the poor or is it found at all income levels? Is it becoming more widespread at the present time? Is there something distinctive about the pattern of delinquency associated with our society? Does it tend to vary in different societies? In contrast to such questions are those which delinquency as an individual phenomenon tends to

Harold Finestone is a member of the Department of Sociology at the University of Minnesota.

suggest. Is it possible to explain how an individual becomes delinquent? Is there some specific principle manifesting itself in the delinquent's personal and social experience which can be identified? If such a principle can be identified, through what pattern and sequence of interpersonal experience does it become connected with the individual's participation in delinquency?

Sociologists, while acknowledging this distinction between the two aspects of delinquency, have not been in agreement over whether both types of issues should come within the scope of their discipline. Some, like Cohen (1959:462), have insisted that a sociological approach to deviant behavior would tend to exclude, as psychological, concern with a question such as the following: "How do people become the kind of individuals who commit criminal acts?" Others, like Cressey (1960:47), have maintained that theories of social behavior should be comprehensive enough to encompass both the collective and the individual aspects of such behavior:

> A theory explaining social behavior in general, or any specific kind of social behavior, should have two distinct but consistent aspects. First, there must be a statement that explains the statistical distribution of the behavior in time and space.... Second, there must be a statement that identifies, at least by implication, the process by which individuals come to exhibit the behavior in question.

## Social Control, Organization and Disorganization

The Shaw and McKay tradition may be depicted as a succession of efforts to resolve the issues posed by Cohen and Cressey. Is the sociology of delinquency to deal with both its epidemiological and its individual aspects? Is it to be concerned with delinquency in both its sociological and its social psychological aspects? How can a sociological theory be formulated so as to encompass both facets of the problem? For Shaw and McKay there was little uncertainty as to how this issue was to be resolved. Their data-gathering net was cast equally for data bearing upon the statistical distribution of delinquency in the urban community over time and for life–history data depicting in detail the process through which individuals became delinquents. Greatly abbreviated for purposes of discussion, their findings as derived

from both of these sources of data may be summarized as
follows:*

1. The rates of juvenile delinquents conformed to a regular
spatial pattern. They were highest in the inner–city areas and
tended to decline with distance from the center of the city.

2. The same spatial pattern was shown by many other indexes
of social problems.

3. The spatial pattern of rates of delinquents showed considerable long–term stability even though the nationality makeup of
the population in the inner–city areas changed greatly from
decade to decade.

4. Within the inner-city areas the process of becoming delinquent occurred within a network of interpersonal relationships
involving the family, the gang, and the neighborhood.

The epidemiological aspects of delinquency were addressed by
the ecological distributions of rates of delinquents and other
social indexes; the processes of becoming delinquent by the life
histories of individual delinquents. Each type of data was
regarded as complementary to the other. The ecological data
were used to depict the formal aspects of the community setting
and the life-history data to communicate the more intangible
nuances of the social life of the local community. In addition to
their joint use for illustrative and pedagogic purposes, each
warranted separate systematic collection for purposes of generating and testing theoretical formulations. Moreover, each kind
of data was suited for the investigation of different theoretical
problems. Thus, both Shaw and Burgess expressed the view that
the life histories were particularly compatible with the use of the
comparative method, through which means theories about the
process of becoming delinquent could be developed and tested.

Life-history data have theoretical as well as therapeutic value.
They not only serve as a means of making preliminary
explorations and orientations in relation to specific problems in
the field of criminological research but afford a basis for the
formulation of hypotheses with reference to the causal factors
involved in the development of delinquent-behavior patterns.
The validity of these hypotheses may in turn be tested by the

*This statement of findings has been abstracted from the whole body of Shaw
and McKay's work. However, the most convenient single source is provided by
Shaw and McKay (1931).

comparative study of other detailed case histories and by formal methods of statistical analysis (Shaw 1930:19).

A ... value of the life history that has not been generally recognized is that it indicates behavior processes and personality types which may be analyzed when a sufficient number of detailed life-histories have been accumulated for comparative study. It is to this use of the life-history that in my judgment we may look for an increase in our knowledge of personality and eventually for an increased control over human conduct (Burgess, in Shaw 1931:254).

Their careful gathering of data about epidemiological and individual aspects of delinquency was guided by a theoretical perspective which required both aspects. As Kobrin (1971:103) has indicated, Shaw and McKay's "approach to the problem was guided by ecological and social psychological theory, the former derived from the writings of Robert E. Park, the latter from those of W. I. Thomas." Of the two influences, here we are particularly interested in tracing that of Thomas, because of his attempt to integrate sociological and social psychological perspectives.

Thomas was noted for his position that a social theory adapted to the modern world should be formulated in terms of social change. In his view a scientific approach to the understanding of life in a complex civilized society "must be suited to the study of social change and transformation since this feature is outstanding in such a society" (Blumer 1939:70). Shaw and McKay accepted this premise as a basis for their work. They were also influenced by Thomas's position that the study of society should be concerned with the individual as well as with the social and cultural aspects of society.

If social theory is to become the basis of social technique and to solve these problems really, it is evident that it must include both kinds of data involved in them—namely, the objective cultural elements of social life and the subjective characteristics of the members of the social group—and that the two kinds of data must be taken as correlated (Thomas and Znaniecki 1927, 1:20).

The cause of a social or individual phenomenon is never another social or individual phenomenon alone, but always a combination of a social and an individual phenomenon (Thomas and Znaniecki 1927, 1:44).

Having accepted these basic premises, it is not surprising that Shaw and McKay should also have been influenced by Thomas's more specific conceptualizations. Thomas viewed social change as a process in which the relations between individuals and groups were undergoing a constant process of realignment (Thomas and Znaniecki 1927, 2:1127–32, 1303–6). It was a cyclic process in which individuals first became emancipated from their ties to traditional institutions and sought types of experience which these ties denied them. They then moved to reconstruct institutional ties on the basis of the new freedoms gained during the interim. As a consequence of such processes, the strength of the bond between the individual and the group, that is, the degree to which the group exercised control over the individual, was constantly varying. Social change would be initiated by a decline in the control exercised by traditional institutions over the individual. This phase of change was called social disorganization. For the group, it implied loss of the ability to act collectively; for the individual, the condition of untrammeled freedom to express his wishes and dispositions. Under certain conditions social disorganization would be followed by social reorganization. The reconstruction of bonds would then occur and the individual would again become subject to the control of traditional institutions. As processes, social disorganization and social reorganization could be analyzed from both group and individual perspectives. Social control manifested a Janus-like quality. Its sociological face was directed towards the group and its institutions and their ability to regulate the behavior of individuals. Its social psychological face was directed towards the individual and his wishes and the manner in which he responded to the efforts of the group to control his behavior.

To Shaw and McKay this conceptualization appeared to be highly appropriate to their subject matter. The processes of social disorganization and reorganization could be meaningfully applied to the passage of successive nationality groups through the spatial grid of the city. The entry of newcomers into inner-city areas was accompanied by a relatively high rate of delinquents, interpretable as an index of social disorganization. The ability of these immigrant groups to achieve social reorganization was manifested by their ability to move to more desirable residential areas and by the accompanying decline in their rates of delinquents (Shaw and McKay 1931:94–98). Juvenile delinquency, in short, was to be viewed as part of the natural history of the settlement process undergone by newcomers in urban communities. The life histories of individual delinquents suggested that these macrosocial processes involving the collective fate of various immigrant groups in the city had their personal counterpart in the life chances available to their native-born descendants. Thomas's concept of social disorganization appeared to fit the delinquency problem in inner-city areas in both its social and its individual aspects. Shaw and McKay took as their task the investigation of delinquency in inner-city areas within the setting of traditional institutional efforts to control the conduct of the younger generation, and the responses of the latter to such efforts.

In pursuing this task they turned to the analysis of both epidemiological data and life histories. Interpretation of the spatial distribution of rates of delinquents required that they seek to portray inner-city areas as the locus of complexly interrelated spatial, social, and cultural processes. The single most notable link between ecological and social factors was provided by the process of *change*. Spatially, the rapid expansion of the city from its center outwards converted inner-city areas into zones which were transitional from residential to either manufacturing or commercial land usage and, as a consequence, into the least desirable residential areas in the city. Culturally, the picture was equally dynamic. Every decade revealed considerable shifts in the nationality backgrounds of the inner-city population. Delinquency, since it was consistently highest in such areas, appeared to represent a point of convergence between ecological and cultural processes of change.

Social disorganization was equally discernible on both spatial and cultural levels. The inner city attracted a highly heterogeneous population. The same selective processes which made it relatively easy for the first generation of newcomers to the city to become aggregated in inner-city areas also permitted the location there of many illegitimate enterprises and deviant moral worlds. Such moral diversity within the inner-city areas meant that it was difficult if not impossible for immigrant communities to insulate themselves from illegitimate and criminal enterprises and influences. In the face of many centrifugal pulls, the traditional institutions, the family, the church, and the local community, became incapable of maintaining their solidarity. Their inability to organize effectively in defense of conventional values meant that they were unable to resist or limit the influence exercised upon their youth by the diverse value systems which became rooted in such areas. Continued high rates of delinquents in inner-city areas were a product of the joint operation of locational and cultural processes which maximized the moral diversity of population types at the same time as they weakened the collective efforts of conventional groups and institutions to protect their own integrity.

## Delinquent Traditions and Becoming Delinquent

We turn now to Shaw and McKay's treatment of the process of becoming delinquent, for which life histories were the major source of data. This process was viewed as the individual counterpart of the process of social disorganization. At this level it was assumed that social disorganization would be manifested as a breakdown in communication and understanding between youth and adult representatives of conventional institutions, such as parents, teachers, and judges. As the reciprocity of relationships between individual youth and adult institutional representatives declined, the individual inevitably worked free from the controls exercised by such conventional ties and became a candidate for novel relationships, novel forms of experience, and the assimilation of novel values.

*The Jack-Roller* depicts this process clearly (Shaw 1930). For the jack-roller, all his relationships with conventional adults lack understanding and mutual concern. He finds himself in a kind of social limbo and begins to feel sorry for himself. He craves the warmth and response which he feels are missing. He seeks companionship and role models among his older siblings and more experienced associates whom he encounters on the streets and in juvenile institutions. He gradually comes to identify himself with the flotsam and jetsam of "skid row" and comes to view himself as a derelict like them. He runs away from juvenile institutions and seeks to return home, only to be rebuffed again when he does so. A note of desperation and restlessness permeates his outlook as he finds himself unwanted and without a place in the community. His youthful life begins to unroll its course in a long sequence of transient, unstable interpersonal relationships. Through his street associations he learns to roll drunks on skid row. However, he meets with little success in such criminal activity, is apprehended and convicted after virtually every offense he commits. In late adolescence, finding himself locked in a reformatory cell, he recoils at the image of himself as a "criminal."

> The cell was bare, hard, and drab. As I sat on my bunk thinking, a great wave of feeling shook me, which I shall always remember, because of the great impression it made on me. There, for the first time in my life, I realized that I was a criminal. Before, I had been just a mischievous lad, a poor city waif, a petty thief, a habitual runaway; but now, as I sat in my cell of stone and iron, dressed in a gray uniform, with my head shaved, small skull cap, like all the other hardened criminals around me, some strange feeling came over me. Never before had I realized that I was a criminal (Shaw 1930:103).

As exemplified by *The Jack-Roller*, the process of becoming delinquent was characterized by the gradual severance of relationships between the adolescent and conventional institutions and by his increasing identification with similarly situated street-corner boys. McKay (1959) designated this process as one through which individual adolescents became detached from basic social institutions in inner-city areas. It was accompanied by the release of certain needs which traditional institutions could not meet, and which adolescents sought to fill by the formation of spontaneous associations with their peers. McKay (1959, no pagination) has stated this point of view as follows:

> If . . . disruption associated with change is associated with high rates of delinquents, the degree of disruption should be high in the inner-city areas. . . . The proposition presented here is that as a result of this disruption in the inner city most of the basic social institutions are so weak, inadequate, and inconsistent that they do not furnish an adequate framework for the control of the conduct of children. . . . In extreme form this absence of stabilizing influence is seen among the adolescent males who do not only have the freedom which comes from weak institutional structure, but tend also to be detached from whatever basic institutions there are. For this group, ties with family and church tend to be weak and only the school represents the thread which ties them to respectability.
>
> When the boy finishes school, or leaves school because he cannot get along there, this last thread is broken . . . . These boys without institutional ties tend, in the inner-city areas, to become identified with one another in groupings often called

gangs. . . . These corner groups and the social-athletic clubs into which some of them develop may be regarded as natural institutions which came into existence to meet the needs of the detached adolescent males.

Shaw and McKay (1942:437) eventually came to formulate the central issues with which they were concerned as follows:

Under what conditions do the conventional forces in the community become so weakened as to tolerate the development of a conflicting system of criminal values? Under what conditions is the conventional community capable of maintaining its integrity and exercising such control over the lives of its members as to check the development of the competing system?

## Structural Interpretation of Delinquency Tradition

Certain aspects of their data resisted analysis in terms of social change and social disorganization as ecological and cultural processes. The highly stable spatial pattern manifested in the rates of delinquents, with the highest rates appearing in the inner-city areas decade after decade, could not itself be interpreted as an instance of social change. Shaw and McKay suggested that this epidemiological pattern could be interpreted as the expression of a tradition of delinquency. This was regarded as a special cultural heritage of values, knowledge, and skills, which had originated in the inner-city areas and then had been transmitted from generation to generation by the adolescents who had resided there. The transmission of these delinquent values occurred through the interpersonal peer associations of inner-city youth, and was greatly facilitated by the gang context of these associations. Within this setting, the lines of transmission went from older to younger adolescents and from those belonging to the longer-settled nationality groups to those of the more recently settled. The central theoretical problem confronting Shaw and McKay had now subtly changed. Instead of seeking to relate juvenile delinquency to the processes of social change in the inner-city areas, they now had to account for a relatively stable structural feature of these areas, the delinquency tradition. Shaw and McKay (1942:439) proposed a functionalist interpretation which sought to explain the tradition of crime and delinquency in inner-city areas as one response of their residents to the economic and social values associated with the larger society.

Crime, in this situation, may be regarded as one of the means employed by people to acquire, or to attempt to acquire, the economic and social values generally idealized in our culture, which persons in other circumstances acquire by conventional means.... The power and affluence achieved, at least temporarily, by many persons involved in crime and illegal rackets are well known to the children and youth of the community and are important in determining the character of their ideals.

Not surprisingly, the new emphasis upon the role played by structural forces originating in the larger society was accompanied by a reduced emphasis upon the etiological significance of processes occurring in the local community. The most relevant feature of inner-city areas was no longer that they constituted the locus of processes of social change but that they comprised the local communities of lowest socioeconomic status in the city. Shaw and McKay also realized that the significance they now attributed to the tradition of delinquency implied a reduced theoretical emphasis upon the process of becoming delinquent. The latter was no longer to be regarded as an independent process manifesting its own generic principles and worthy of investigation in its own right. Becoming delinquent was now conceived as a fragmented process involving many types of unrelated personal and social contingencies, in which specific individuals came under the influence of the delinquency tradition. The process of becoming delinquent had become a residual category:

... many factors are important in determining whether a particular child will become involved in delinquency, even in those communities in which a system of delinquent and criminal values exists. Individual and personality differences, as well as differences in family relationships and in contacts with other institutions and groups, no doubt influence greatly his acceptance or rejection of opportunities to engage in delinquent activities. It may be said, however, that if the delinquency tradition were not present and the boys were not thus exposed to it, a preponderance of those who become delinquent in low-income areas would find their satisfactions in activities other than delinquency (Shaw and McKay 1942:440).

## The Functionalist Approach

Interpretations of their data had led Shaw and McKay to make a number of shifts in their theoretical perspective. From an emphasis upon the process of social change influenced by the perspective of W. I. Thomas, they had moved toward a functionalist position which emphasized the relationship between delinquency and relatively stable features of the social structure of the larger society. From an emphasis upon the priority of processes occurring within inner-city areas, they now assigned priority to the social strains arising out of the discrepancy between the low economic status of the local community and the economic and social values idealized in the culture of the larger society. From an emphasis upon the "push" factors toward delinquency represented by the social disorganization of traditional institutions, they came to stress the "pull" factors represented by access to an illegitimate opportunity structure. Turning their attention increasingly to the societal factors involved in delinquency, they tended to attribute less and less theoretical significance to the interpersonal process through which individuals became delinquent. During the course of this transition they proposed a functionalist interpretation of delinquency which adumbrated to a remarkable degree its subsequent development. They themselves, however, never ventured beyond a tentative preliminary statement of this position.

In spite of the fact that Shaw and McKay had selected for special attention the issue of explaining the "delinquency tradition," it is important to note that this was only one line of inquiry suggested by their work. For example, they apparently abandoned the search for the principles involved in the process of becoming delinquent, a theme later formulated by Sutherland (1939) in his theory of differential association. Thrasher's emphasis on the relationship between the gang and conflict processes also suggested alternative directions in which the Shaw and McKay tradition might have moved (Thrasher 1927).

Since the directions suggested by Shaw and McKay's pioneering work seem in retrospect to have been so manifold, the question suggests itself as to why subcultural theories of juvenile delinquency alone became so salient during the period following their major work. Bordua (1970:159) has noted: "There have been some profound changes in the way social theorists view the processes of gang formation and persistence. These, I believe, derive only partially, perhaps even unimportantly, from changes in the facts to be explained." At any given time in sociological research, the existing state of knowledge suggests several lines of inquiry. Among these lines a process of social selection operates, which tends to emphasize some directions for research and theory formation and to minimize the importance of others. One important and perhaps crucial selective factor is represented by the dominant general sociological perspectives. W. I. Thomas's influence on the point of view with which Shaw and McKay approached the problem of juvenile delinquency has been noted. Analogously, the most important theoretical influences upon subsequent work in delinquency theory appear to derive from the functionalist perspectives of Talcott Parsons and Robert Merton. According to Martindale (1960:465) this school is to be distinguished by its preference for relatively large-scale systems as the basic referents for theory, the central idea being that of "system": "Functionalism reaches its distinctive subject matter when it takes the organism-like *system* as its peculiar object of study and conceives of this as the primary subject matter of sociological analysis, studying all other items as system-determined and system-maintaining."

Within such a perspective one would expect functionalist interpretations to view delinquency in relation to the large-scale structures of the society. In fact, in this respect both Cohen and Cloward and Ohlin operated with similar conceptions (Cohen 1955; Cloward and Ohlin 1960). For both, the relevant large-scale structure was the class system in which all classes shared to a greater or lesser degree a common set of values. For Cohen these common values were criteria of achievement which were largely defined in middle-class terms and for which middle-class values provided a common measuring rod. For Cloward and Ohlin these common values were not so closely linked to the middle class. Rather they constituted overarching emphasis upon the goal of monetary success and the conventional institutional means which provided access to this goal. Both viewed gang delinquency as primarily concentrated among lower-class adolescent males and both construed it as a collective response of these boys to the system stresses to which they were exposed by virtue of their lower-class position. In each case the gang delinquent was viewed as a "frustrated social climber." Again, it may be seen how accurately the image of the delinquent tends to reflect the underlying sociological perspective. In Shaw and McKay's view the delinquent was "disaffiliated," one whose ties with traditional groups and institutions had been severed. In the view of Cohen and of Cloward and Ohlin, the delinquent as "frustrated social climber" was all too much a part of the society. He was one who took the moral mandate to "get ahead" too seriously. He was testimony not to the social disorganization of the community but to the powerful hold of its social organization upon even the least favored of its members.

Juvenile delinquency in the functionalist view is a product of integration of the delinquent into the total society and his internalization of its central values. But his behavior testifies to the hold upon him of such values, not directly by the manner in which he seeks to realize them, but indirectly by the faithful and meticulous manner in which his behavior expresses their anti-thesis. His ties to the society manifest a paradox. He is at once a creature of that society and at the same time its bitter enemy, an integral part of its social structure although committed to an attack upon some of its most important values. It is this apparent contradiction which the functionalist theories of delin-quency seek to explain. The question they deal with is this: What are the systematic properties of the society which produce the paradox of the delinquent?

Posed in such a manner the problem of delinquency lends itself to analysis in systematic terms. From the perspective of the social system the task becomes that of demonstrating the intimate interdependence between the delinquent and the rest of the society. More specifically, the theoretical task becomes that of tracing the chain of influences which lead from the relationship between the delinquent and the larger society to the expression of this relationship in specific types of delinquent acts. These theories first postulate that potential gang delinquents share some common problem of adjustment posed for them by virtue of their similar status in the system of social stratification of the larger society. Second, they postulate that under certain conditions such individuals may come to share their problems and contrive a collective solution to them, or a subculture.

The key concept in this theoretical formulation becomes the delinquent subculture. Without the emergence of a subculture it is doubtful whether many individuals would engage in delin-quency. It provides the social medium through which common status problems may be shared, given overt expression, and acted upon. In C. W. Mills's terms, subcultural formation provides a mediating mechanism through which the private troubles of lower-class adolescent boys become converted into a public issue. Subcultural development provides an interpersonal milieu in which norms prescribing delinquent behavior evolve. Such norms evolve out of intimate oppositional interaction between participants in the emergent delinquent subculture and the norms of the larger society. The delinquent norms are determined primarily by this process of opposition and social differentiation. Finally, once these norms evolve they become the major social bond between the participants in the subculture. Delinquent behavior becomes a direct expression of these norms.

The centrality of the concept *subculture* in the functionalist approach to delinquency is to be contrasted with that of the *group* in the Shaw and McKay formulation. The concept of subculture lends itself to systematic analysis in a way in which the group does not. The referent of the latter concept is primarily its members, the individuals who make up the group and the mutual relationships through which they may be conceived as some kind of social unit. The nature of this unity, of the bonds which relate members to one another and to the group, may be quite variable. In contrast, the concept of the subculture suggests a group whose major orientation is to some external encompassing society or organization. It presupposes, furthermore, that the key bonds among members and between members and the collectivity are provided by the shared norms and values which constitute the subculture. Consistently, usage refers to the individual in a group as a *member* of that group, and to the individual in a subculture as a *carrier* of its cultural values.

The main point of this exposition is that from the functionalist perspective the linkages which tie the gang delinquent to the society are just as tightly forged as are those which link society and the conventional person. Both delinquent and conventional persons are equally integrated into their society. The implications of this societal determination of gang delinquency for the image of the delinquent have been noted by Bordua (1970:159), who observes that "All in all ... it does not seem like much fun any more to be a gang delinquent.... Cohen's boys and Cloward and Ohlin's boys are driven by grim economic and psychic necessity into rebellion." The functionalist position provides a view of the delinquent as one who is trapped within the society by virtue of the difficulties of his status position and who adapts by resorting to delinquency as a collective solution.

## Functionalism and the Process of Becoming Delinquent

It was suggested that Shaw and McKay's focus upon the theoretical issue raised by the existence of the "delinquency tradition" led them to seek for its explanation in the larger social structures of society. The functionalist interpretation which resulted made it increasingly difficult to justify the search for sociological principles which identify the process through which the individual became delinquent. This implication of delinquency was clearly recognized by Cloward and Ohlin in their statement of the questions to be explored (1960:ix):

> Why do delinquent "norms," or rules of conduct develop? . . .
>
> [This] question involves a shift in emphasis from the traditional concern of the field—the analysis of delinquent acts or of the careers of individual delinquents. Detailed studies have been undertaken to explain why particular individuals are likely to become delinquent or why delinquent acts of various types are committed with varying frequencies in different social locations. Such studies take as their object of inquiry the careers of individuals or the delinquent act itself rather than the rules of conduct in delinquent gangs that require the commission of delinquent acts. Our emphasis on delinquent norms permits us to raise new questions and to offer new explanations which we believe may have both theoretical and practical significance.

Strictly speaking, functionalist theories of delinquency do not forgo an interest in accounting for the epidemiology of delinquency. This interest, however, is qualified, since it is recognized that not all delinquent acts can be regarded as expressions of subcultural norms. Nevertheless, Cloward and Ohlin (1960:28) in large part based their work upon the assumption that "the most costly and difficult problems in the area of delinquency control and prevention" were posed by the delinquent subcultures, which were concentrated and most highly organized in slum communities. In both their theoretical and practical import, then, subcultural theories of delinquency remained closely tied to epidemiological aspects of the problem.

## The Interactionist Approach

One of the aims of this discussion has been to suggest that each stage of the Shaw and McKay tradition has been deeply influenced by an encompassing sociological perspective. In each of the two instances so far dealt with, it was this larger perspective that determined what methodological approach was to be applied to the study of juvenile delinquency and, consequently, the relative emphasis upon the epidemiological aspects or the process through which the individual became delinquent. Furthermore, perspectives which incorporated both sociological and social psychological standpoints directed attention to both aspects of juvenile delinquency. Perspectives defined exclusively in sociological terms tended to view only the epidemiological aspects of delinquency as appropriate to sociological analysis.

In recent years the study of juvenile delinquency within this tradition appears to have been moving into a third stage. This division into stages is of course schematic and is not meant to imply that the functionalist approach is being completely superseded. It does mean, however, that a new approach, the "interactionist," has emerged, in large part as a reaction against some of the central assumptions of the functionalist approach and with many implications for a reformulation of the problems of juvenile delinquency.

The momentum shown by the interactionist approach has derived primarily from a reconceptualization of the sociology of deviant behavior. Its major contribution so far has been to reinstate as a central sociological issue the process through which the individual becomes deviant. Revival of the issue took the form of the notion that "labeling" provided a principle for analyzing the process of becoming delinquent.

"Labeling" refers to the process by which the individual comes to be defined as deviant by others. Labeling would have no particular independent theoretical implications if it were invariably associated with acts of rule violation, or if it were a random process in response to the commission of deviant acts. It may, however, be viewed as a process which is contingent upon the response of others to the rule violator in certain types of situations. Such regularities as the process exhibits then are viewed as the outcome of the interaction characteristic of certain recurrent types of situations. These regularities are viewed as being activated by influences which are to be distinguished from the act of rule violation itself. Moreover, it is because of this hiatus between rule violation and social response that the relationship between act and normative judgment becomes problematic.

Kitsuse (1972:238) has made this conception of deviance explicit and indicates that it is to be regarded as an alternative to functionalist formulations.

> When we examine the works of the interactionists concerned with deviance, we find a variety of conceptions of social norms that inform their research. The common element in these conceptions is that social norms are problematic as they are invoked by members of the community to identify, define, judge, and treat persons as deviant. . . . However it is expressed, the view that social norms are *problematic* has led them to examine the commonly held sociological assumptions that find expression in the literature in conceptions of "normative systems," "cultural prescriptions," "social roles," and so forth.

Comparing their respective conceptions of the relationship between society and the juvenile delinquent reveals both the continuity and the contrasts between Shaw and McKay's formulations and those of the interactionists. A key to each position is provided by their contrasting conceptions of social differentiation. The issue of social differentiation was forced upon the attention of Shaw and McKay by the conflicting value systems which they encountered in inner-city areas. They had tended to view such social complexity as a product of social disorganization, that is, as a product of the breakdown of consensus over norms and values. The interactionists, no longer holding to the assumption that society is characterized by such consensus, replace it with the assumption of pluralistic value systems. Deviance in one of its important aspects becomes both an intergroup and a political process, a product of the struggle of various groups to legitimize their norms through seeking to incorporate them into the legal order. The application of such norms must inevitably appear unjust to members of groups without the requisite power to endow their own norms with legal legitimacy. It is because the efforts of formal social control agencies are typically directed towards the acts of members of weaker groups in the community that the representative image of the deliquent in this perspective tends to become that of the "aggrieved citizen." For Shaw and McKay, delinquency is one of the consequences of the weakening of adherence to conventional norms that accompanies the processes of social change. Delinquency is an alien aspect of society which can be diminished through appropriate methods of social organization. For the interactionists, delinquency becomes an intrinisic aspect of a viable social order in a differentiated society. Ultimately, the perspective of Shaw and McKay and that of the interactionists do not clash so much as they focus upon different facets of social differentiation. Shaw and McKay were primarily concerned with determining the conditions under which the conflict between legitimate and delinquent values in society comes into existence. The interactionists accept the existence of such differentiation and investigate the issues it raises for social control and the maintenance of the social order.

## Convergence towards Interactionist Approach

The central premise of the interactionist perspective has been recognition of the problematic nature of the relationship between norms and behavior as these became linked in the actions of rule violators and the responses of others. Interestingly, the same interactionist premise became increasingly salient from another direction, the empirical study of gangs carried out by Short and Strodtbeck (1965) (see also Thrasher 1963:xlvii, xlviii; Short 1964:98–127). Both in research design and initial theoretical orientation, this work was deeply influenced by the subcultural theories of Cohen and of Cloward and Ohlin. The findings of Short and Strodtbeck, however, cast doubt upon the assumption of these theorists that gang delinquency could be explained in terms of conformity with subcultural norms (Short 1964:104).

> These boys do not seem as committed to delinquent norms as Cohen, and Cloward and Ohlin suggest. Indeed, their commitment to delinquent norms seems quite tenuous except in specific types of situations which involve the group, such as threat to the group from another gang, or, in some instances, threats to the status of boys individually.

In order to explain gang delinquency, Short was drawn toward a formulation of delinquent acts or episodes as occurring within a process of interaction, within which gang members responded to one another and to their common setting and in so doing built up collective acts (Short, 1964:124).

> What is lacking in most models of gang behavior is precisely this type of Meadian act, in which behavior is seen as a process of *continuous adjustment* of actors to one another, rather than as a sort of mechanical reaction to some one factor or

combination of factors in the situation, whether they be characteristics of actors, or sub-cultures, or other features. It is this conception, too, which is lacking in anomie theory.

The movement in Short and Strodtbeck's conceptual framework from a social structural towards an interactionist emphasis has a number of implications for the present argument. It suggests that a social structural approach to gangs that does not also encompass their members' interpersonal relationships cannot provide an adequate explanation of their delinquent behavior. It also suggests that the tradition initiated by Shaw and McKay has now come full circle. In their attempt to explain the group character of delinquency Shaw and McKay moved from a process to a functionalist perspective. In further pursuit of this line of inquiry into the group matrix of delinquency, Short and Strodtbeck were led by the implications of their data from a functionalist back towards a process perspective. Surely, the major inference to be drawn from this development within the Shaw and McKay tradition is that sociological theories should attempt to take account of both social structural and interpersonal aspects of gang delinquency.

Currently, then, there is evidence of a convergence within the Shaw and McKay tradition towards an interactionist perspective. As manifested in "labeling" or in Short and Strodtbeck's analysis of gang behavior, it has hitherto been strongly oriented towards the interpersonal or social psychological dimensions of the problem of delinquency. Will the applicability of the interactionist point of view be restricted to these areas and will it tend to ignore the role of larger social structures and the social context of delinquency? If it does so it will fail to illuminate the epidemiological aspects of the problem in our society. Conceivably, by restricting itself to the microsocial aspects of the problem it might come to share the field with a functionalism that would be directed towards the problem's macrosocial components. Such eclecticism has never proved to be particularly useful as a resolution of the theoretical or practical problems of juvenile delinquency. This issue has been explicitly recognized although not yet attacked. It appears that Short, for example, has regarded his emphasis upon the group-process approach to gang delinquency as supplementing and completing the social-structure and anomie paradigm rather than replacing it. Arriving at the interactionist position from a different route, that of labeling, Kitsuse (1972:235) has affirmed the necessity for broadening the interactionist approach beyond its social psychological applications in order to provide a sociological analysis of deviance.

## Conclusion: The Future of the Shaw and McKay Tradition

One cannot attempt to trace the development of a tradition of research such as that initiated by Shaw and McKay without raising a plethora of questions. Of the many issues which might be selected for discussion, two will be taken up in conclusion. I am concerned, first, with the lasting contributions of this tradition towards the understanding of juvenile delinquency in American society and, second, with the future of this tradition. In what direction is it heading? What are the salient issues which its continuing development poses for contemporary students of the problem of juvenile delinquency?

The contribution of each stage of the tradition is epitomized by its image of the delinquent. Each image of the delinquent, as "disaffiliated," "frustrated social climber," and "aggrieved citizen," offers an important insight into some aspect of juvenile delinquency in an urban industrial society. "Disaffiliated" appears to be a particularly appropriate notion to apply to adolescents of our era. The conflict of generations and the inability of traditional institutions to accomplish effectively their goal of socializing the young, appears to be even more marked today than at the time, two generations ago, when Shaw and McKay were writing. A condition which they viewed as confined to the youth of inner-city areas appears now to be diffused throughout the urban community. Theoretically, in terms of such trends one would expect the problem of delinquency to have become more widespread in the higher socioeconomic levels of the community. And thus it apparently has. The image of the delinquent as disaffiliated captures the insight that the urban industrial society has hitherto failed to integrate the young fully into its institutions.

In his classic article on urbanism, Wirth (1964:80) noted that the city had increased the contrasts in status among people: "While the city has broken down the rigid caste lines of pre-industrial society, it has sharpened and differentiated income and status groups." One of the consequences of this trend has been that it is in the cities that certain contradictions in the American social system have become most intensified and stressful.

> The American social system . . . is permeated with two conflicting social principles: The first says that all men are equal before God and man. . . . The second, contradictory to the first, more often found in act than in words . . . declares that men are of unequal worth, that a few are superior to the many, that a large residue of lowly ones are inferior to all others (Warner 1949:xiii).

> The two constitute the realities of American democracy. The democracy of the American Dream is true only because of the social gradation on the ladder where successful men are permitted to realize their ambitions. The social-class system is true only because the precepts of the Dream provide the moral code which enforces the rules of social mobility by insisting that all able men who obey the rules of the game have "the right" to climb (Warner 1949:297).

Functionalist theorists such as Cohen and Cloward and Ohlin applied this insight to the development of their theories. What is important in this context is not the detail of their theories but the fact that they were on firm ground in postulating that conflicts caused by inconsistency in the class system between egalitarianism, on the one hand, and the invidious distinctions of social status, on the other, should be experienced in most acute form by lower-class adolescents in society. Piaget's work on the cognitive functioning of adolescents is compatible with the notion that it is during this period that such issues should first become explicit and exercise their maximum impact upon behavior (cited in Flavell 1963:223–24).

> His (the adolescent's) conceptual world is full of informal theories about self and life, full of plans for his and society's future, in short, full of ideation which goes far beyond his immediate situation, current interpersonal dealings, and so on . . . (Flavell 1963:223).

> The adolescent's theory construction shows both that he has become capable of reflective thinking and that his thought makes it possible for him to escape the concrete present toward the realm of the abstract and the possible (cited in Flavell 1963:224).

The delinquent as "aggrieved citizen" is a third important insight into the condition of the delinquent in modern urban industrial society. Unlike the other two images, focus is upon delinquency as a legal status and upon the delinquent as a product of the legal order of the society. It is a notion which has been influenced by a consideration of the nature of the relationship between the delinquent and the agents of the system of juvenile justice and juvenile corrections. Theoretically, the interactionist point of view requires that attention be devoted equally to the standpoint of each of the actors involved in legal situations. Thus, as applied to juvenile delinquency it requires that inquiry be as concerned with the point of view of the official agents of social control as it is with that of the delinquent. It assumes that many important features of the problem of delinquency are emergent products of the interaction among these various perspectives.

Each of these three images of the delinquent—as "disaffiliated," as "frustrated social climber," and as "aggrieved citizen"—appears to have identified an important facet of the problem in urban industrial society. They are all partial insights, indicative of different aspects of the relationship between society and the delinquent. Not only has each contributed towards the understanding of delinquency but each has also been influential in suggesting programs of delinquency prevention and control. The substantial contribution which they have made both individually and collectively is indisputable. What is now at issue is the future evolution of this tradition of delinquency study. What are the most promising lines of future development that are suggested by the preceding analysis?

Ever since Cooley, sociologists have tended to pay lip service to the complementary nature of the relationship between the individual and the group.

> Life is an organic whole, presenting itself with equal reality in individual and general aspects (Cooley 1909:20).

> Without forgetting to see life as individuals, we must learn to see it also as types, processes, organization, the latter being just as real as the former. And especially, in order to see the matter truly, should we be able to interpret individuals by wholes and *vice-versa* (Cooley 1909:22).

However, as this discussion makes clear, it is difficult to maintain this dual perspective within specific areas of inquiry. The sociological point of view appears to resolve itself easily into two different levels of abstraction, those of social organization and social psychology, each of which may then be separately pursued. This tendency is clearly stated in the following citation from Olsen (1968:vi).

Social organization in all its various forms, always has an existence and properties that are not reducible to characteristics of its individual members. The whole is more than the sum of its component parts and can only be understood and explained as an entity in itself. . . . The study of social organization must, of course, take into account individuals' actions and interactions, for it is through these processes that organization arises. But interpersonal phenomena are not, in themselves, the primary focus of the sociologist concerned with social organization. They are, I would suggest, the proper objects of study for social psychologists.

This position, consistently applied to the problem of delinquency, results in the dichotomization of theoretical approaches, some being primarily social structural and others primarily social psychological. Perhaps the strongest argument against the adequacy of such a resolution is to be found in the work of Short and Strodtbeck. Their findings suggested that theories of gang delinquency formulated solely in terms of large-scale social structures are likely to prove empirically unsatisfactory. Important aspects of gang behavior cannot be understood if the theoretical level of abstraction ignores the interpersonal relations of gang members.

The argument of theoretical adequacy suggests that there is no escaping the conclusion that a theory of juvenile delinquency should attempt to include both sociological and social psychological aspects. The very statement of such a goal suggests a return to the intent of the work of Shaw and McKay. To the extent that the theme of social disorganization remained part of their point of view they were able to encompass both epidemiological and individual aspects of juvenile delinquency. This was possible because in social disorganization they had a transitive concept, that is, one which could be interpreted in both sociological and social psychological terms.

The present stage of theoretical development would appear to require such transitive or bridging concepts. Such a bridging idea may well be provided by the *gang*. Since this concept has remained of central importance at each stage of the Shaw and McKay tradition, it might understandably be questioned whether the gang possesses any new potential which has not already been developed. Closer inspection of its various usages suggests, however, how varied and mutually inconsistent these have been. In the work of Shaw and McKay, for example, it served two quite different conceptual purposes. In one usage, the gang was an informal indigenous society which arose spontaneously to meet the social needs of youth who had become detached from the conventional institutions. In a second quite distinctive usage, it became the medium through which the "delinquency tradition" was communicated from generation to generation of adolescents in inner-city areas. As we move to the functionalist theorists the gang has become a collectivity which, by virtue of its anticonventional norms, has become the medium through which delinquents are related to the larger social structures of the society. Finally, Short and Strodtbeck have directed attention to the gang as a drama of interpersonal relations in which boys struggle, scheme, and fight for a scarce supply of psychological gratifications and social status. As is readily apparent, some of these conceptions of the gang have been primarily sociological and others primarily social psychological.

We are here suggesting a conceptualization of the gang which would simultaneously embody the sociological and the social psychological points of view. It needs to be regarded both as a society in which some adolescents have their most meaningful personal and social experiences and as a social organization with very important relations with other institutions in the community. Again, this is a return to the explicit objective of Shaw and McKay to employ the concept of the gang as a means of interpreting the relationship between adolescents and traditional conventional institutions in inner-city communities. What is, indeed, being suggested is that this problem be revived in the light of the various contributions which have since been made by the development of this tradition. This paper has argued that three insights into the nature of juvenile delinquency in modern urban societies have been generated, and, furthermore, that such insights continue to be useful. If this be the case, future development of this tradition must seek to reformulate and consolidate these insights of the delinquent as "disaffiliated," "frustrated social climber," and "aggrieved citizen" into a single formulation. The challenge of such a synthesis is a task worthy of this generation of students of juvenile delinquency.

## References

Blumer, Herbert
1939        *An Appraisal of Thomas and Znaniecki's "The*

*Polish Peasant in Europe and America.* " New York: Social Science Research Council.

Bordua, David J.
1961        "A Critique of Sociological Interpretations of Gang Delinquency." *Annals* 338 (November):119–36. Reprinted in James E. Teele, ed., *Juvenile Delinquency: A Reader.* Itasca, Ill.: F.E. Peacock, 1970.

Cloward, Richard A., and Lloyd E. Ohlin
1960        *Delinquency and Opportunity: A Theory of Delinquent Gangs.* Glencoe, Ill.: Free Press.

Cohen, Albert K.
1955        *Delinquent Boys.* Glencoe, Ill.: Free Press.
1959        "The Study of Social Disorganization and Deviant Behavior." In Robert K. Merton et al., eds., *Sociology Today.* New York: Basic Books, pp. 461–84.

Cooley, Charles H.
1909        *Social Organization.* New York: Charles Scribner's Sons.

Cressey, Donald R.
1960        "Epidemiology and Individual Conduct." *Pacific Sociological Review* 3 (Fall):47–58.

Flavell, John H.
1963        *The Developmental Psychology of Jean Piaget.* Princeton, N.J.: D. Van Nostrand.

Kitsuse, John I.
1972        "Deviance, Deviant Behavior, and Deviants: Some Conceptual Issues." In William J. Filstead, ed., *An Introduction to Deviance.* Chicago: Markham, pp. 233–43.

Kobrin, Solomon
1971        "The Formal Logical Properties of the Shaw-McKay Delinquency Theory." In Harwin L. Voss and David M. Petersen, eds., *Ecology, Crime, and Delinquency.* New York: Appleton-Century-Crofts, pp. 101–31.

Martindale, Don
1960        *The Nature and Types of Sociological Theory.* Boston: Houghton Mifflin.

McKay, Henry D.
1959        "Juvenile Delinquency." Hearings before the Sub-committee to Investigate Juvenile Delinquency of

48     Finestone

the Committee on the Judiciary, United States
Senate, Eighty-Sixth Congress, First Session, May
28 and 29, 1959. Reprinted by State of Illinois,
Department of Public Welfare, n.d.

Olsen, Marvin E.
1968          *The Process of Social Organization.* New York:
              Holt, Rinehart and Winston.

Shaw, Clifford R.
1930          *The Jack Roller.* Chicago: University of Chicago
              Press.
1931          *The Natural History of a Delinquent Career.*
              Chicago: University of Chicago Press.

Shaw, Clifford R., and Henry D. McKay
1931          *Social Factors in Juvenile Delinquency*, Vol. 2,
              National Commission on Law Observance and
              Enforcement, Report on the Causes of Crime.
              Washington, D.C.: U.S. Government Printing
              Office.
1942          *Juvenile Delinquency and Urban Areas.* Chicago:
              University of Chicago Press.

Short, James F., Jr.
1964          "Gang Delinquency and Anomie." In Marshall B.
              Clinard, ed., *Anomie and Deviant Behavior.* New
              York: Free Press, pp. 98–127.

Short, James F., Jr., and Fred L. Strodtbeck
1965          *Group Process and Gang Delinquency.* Chicago:
              University of Chicago Press.

Sutherland, Edwin H.
1939          *Principles of Criminology*, 3d ed. Philadelphia:
              J.B. Lippincott.

Thomas, William I., and Florian Znaniecki
1927          *The Polish Peasant in Europe and America.* 2 vols.
              New York: Alfred A. Knopf; New York: Dover
              Publications, 1958.

Thrasher, Frederic M.
1963          *The Gang.* Chicago: University of Chicago Press.
              1927. Abridged and with a new introduction by
              James F. Short, Jr. Chicago: University of Chicago
              Press, 1963.

Warner, W. Lloyd
1949          *Democracy in Jonesville: A Study of Quality and
              Inequality.* New York: Harper.

Wirth, Louis
1964            "Urbanism as a Way of Life." In Albert J. Reiss,
               Jr., ed., *Louis Wirth On Cities and Social Life*.
               Chicago: University of Chicago Press, pp. 60–83.

# 2    Continuities
in Delinquency
Research

*William Simon*
*Joseph E. Puntil*
*Emil Peluso*

This paper compares the beginnings of sociological research on juvenile delinquency at the Institute for Juvenile Research—the work we most frequently associate with the names of Clifford Shaw and Henry McKay—with that presently underway at the Institute. The latter represents something of a renewal of research on juvenile delinquency initiated within the past five years. The opportunity to make such a comparison is as rare as the existence of a sociological research organization with a continuous, if uneven, history stretching over almost a half century. Moreover, it is an organization that has both described and reflected a half century of profound and continuing change in fundamental aspects of social life, as well as in the styles and contents of sociological practice.

The basic concerns of this paper include, of necessity, the sociology of sociology, even though only a relatively small part of sociology is involved. The question of continuities and discontinuities is clearly more than a simple issue of intellectual bookkeeping. Sociologists in considering their own past, including the relatively recent past, often adopt sociologically naive postures, viewing their own practice too exclusively as a self-correcting intellectual evolution wherein internal elements are highlighted, while those external factors that should serve to remind them of their lack of immunity to social gravity tend to be obscured. As a result intellectual continuities are often stressed almost as if lineage was translatable into legitimacy—something that does not happen except as a social process.

Of the two projected themes—continuity and discontinuity—the former is the most comfortable. The body of work we associate with the early IJR tradition is clearly the starting point, as well as the significant reference point, for virtually all

William Simon, Joseph E. Puntil, and Emil Peluso are staff members of the Institute for Juvenile Research, Chicago.

subsequent attempts at delineating sociological theories of juvenile delinquency. The attempt to relate occurrences of delinquency to the dynamics of community institutional response, placed in the context of a richly textured sense of the immediate social ex- perience, remains an ultimate paradigm for research design. The utilization of detached street workers and the current, relatively unexamined, commitment to "community based" programs for both prevention and treatment might well occasion a "What else is new?" response.

On a conceptual level, there is little need to belabor this point, as it is treated both thoughtfully and comprehensively in the appraisal of the legacy of the Shaw-McKay tradition prepared by Harold Finestone for this volume. The continuing relevance of Shaw and McKay for subsequent work, however, derives from something more than their general theoretical orientation. The essential naturalism of the Chicago school as an intellectual style (see Matza 1969; Short 1971) created so broad and permissive a range of imagery that elements of virtually all subsequent attempts at the formulation or modification of theory obviously have found, and can find, anticipation, if not partial support, in this remarkable body of work.

In the current research (to be described below) this sense of continuity has been even more self-consciously present. Aside from having the wise counsel of Henry McKay during the early design phase, the current program has sizable resources that derive in no small measure from the reputation that the present staff may have inherited more than earned.

The continuity between periods was heightened by a design that aimed at providing a data pool sufficiently comprehensive to sustain an examination of most current explanatory approaches. This included direct consideration of the early Institute for Juvenile Research tradition, as well as other viewpoints in- fluenced by that tradition. Moreover, there was an equally self- conscious attempt on the part of the current staff to emulate that same broadly cast "naturalism." Considerable priority was given to providing a picture of the adolescent experience that was as comprehensive and detailed as possible; the implicit goal was to provide the kinds of data that might be of use to those who did not share our own theoretical interests.

An additional note of continuity can be found in the fact that research in both periods was designed with the expectation that it would be referential to the formulation of public policy with respect to the treatment and prevention of delinquency. At the same time, however, there is a corresponding element of discontinuity on this level. While it is probable that research during both phases was conditioned by a not uncommon commitment to what has been called "underdog sociology," there is considerable discontinuity concerning the equally ideological question of views of legitimate forms of authority. Shaw and McKay tended to see the power structure of the larger community as being essentially benign and their own role essentially as that of facilitating brokers. In contrast, the implicit view of current elites held by the current staff tends to be ambivalently hostile, and their sense of mission, to the degree it has been coherently formulated, comes closer to that of the "double agent" with all the identity confusion typically attending that role.

Both periods of research share a double-pronged approach that seeks to work simultaneously with a data pool that contains both quantitative and qualitative elements. Common to both approaches is a concern for the kinds of "hard" data that lend themselves to quantitative analysis and consequently allow the researchers to examine relationships between select aspects of social life and fluctuations in the kinds and frequencies of adolescent violative behavior and "soft" data that afford a more textured and dynamic sense of the immediate social experience. Here, too, there are evident discontinuities. The hard data utilized by Shaw and McKay were largely derived from official statistics, while the current research draws upon an extensive program of sample surveys, utilizing self-reports to estimate involvement in delinquency. Both approaches, needless to say, produce biased estimates of delinquency rates. Where one stresses formal contact with law enforcement agencies, the other stresses the attributes and location of the individual offender. Where official statistics tend to underestimate the amount of violative behavior, including that involving serious offenses, the self-report style may in some sense tend to overestimate the amount of violative behavior. Not only does it critically require the respondent to match specific behavior with fairly broad category labels, it fails to discriminate between consequential and nonconsequential violations. The terms "delinquent" and "delinquency" obviously need not fully describe each other.

The qualitative data utilized by Shaw and McKay derived almost exclusively from individual life histories, which—not unlike many clinical studies—begin with outcomes and reason back to causes, creating the possibility of having the past significantly shape the present, or what has been called "the present of the past." The comparable data in the present research rely heavily upon direct ethnographic observations of adolescent group experiences and interviews that cast the respondent adolescent in the role of informant in an attempt to map the social ecology of adolescent worlds in twelve different community settings. Indeed, the simultaneous use of twelve different community sites represents an effort at comparative ethnography that might move the use of such materials beyond the exploratory to the more intrinsically analytic.

The discontinuities that have already been commented upon suggest that the later research stands as something of a mirror image of the earlier research. That is, the early "soft" data and current "hard" data focus upon the individual as the significant unit of analysis, while the earlier "hard" data (more often than not reported in terms of rates for given community areas or other local jurisdictions) and the current "soft" data represent attempts to characterize communities.

Whatever the differences, this shared double-pronged approach implies a common and commonly frustrated goal of many social scientists: to make their subjects both understandable and recognizable. A major defect of the earlier effort was a marked lack of effective integration of the two modalities. While work in both styles was unambiguously shaped by identical or nearly identical theoretical and ideological perspectives, one style rarely articulated sufficiently with the other in ways that might have provided additional complexity of vision. It is yet far too early in the experience of the current research to predict with confidence whether this later effort will meet with greater success. Given our initial awareness of this problem and the consequent effort of having the full staff (those whose primary assignment involved either work on the survey or the community ethnographies) share the experience of the design of the survey instruments and the field guide that organizes the comparative effort, failure would pose a number of intellectual problems.

The continuity posture is additionally comfortable because it describes the bulk of sociological writing on delinquency—at least that part of it that attends to matters of theory; indeed, more than by continuity, one can almost characterize the fairly large body of work on delinquency by its extensive inbreeding. Typical in this respect—and thus possibly revealing its only shortcoming—is the Finestone essay, as it moves in a remarkable performance from the work of Shaw and McKay to the group-process concerns of Short and Strodtbeck, the structural/strain approach of Cloward and Ohlin, and labeling theory. In the essay's vocabulary of closely related formulations, there is unfortunately little to suggest how the world may have changed during the interval, despite Finestone's valiant effort to distinguish varying images of delinquents which emerge from different theoretical perspectives. The essential words are largely constants—community, delinquent, gang, peer values, expectations, self-conception, etc.; an almost standardized vocabulary tends to homogenize a complicated and eventful social history. The gangs of Thrasher and the gangs of Short and Strodtbeck are different not only in terms of conceptual language and research strategies but also in their reflection of vastly changed social worlds—even when identical locations are used. *One of the major problems of continuity in sociological theory is that it tends to obscure discontinuities in social life.*

Even at this relatively early stage of our discussion, substantial discontinuities have appeared. A conventional strategy would be to acknowledge the traditional roots of the present research and then "excuse" the manifest departures from these earlier guidelines by making inarticulate references to the fact of "subsequent" advances in both theory and methods.

That profound changes in both theory and method have occurred during the intervening decades needs little specification. What may be questionable is the almost unself-conscious way in which one tends to adopt the term "advances," as if the sociological profession could clearly point to some process of continuous refinement of its basic contents rather than just change and evolution. This is not to suggest that what appear as "advances" cannot be pointed to. Methodological techniques and technologies may be such examples. However, on the level of concepts and organizing metaphors, the very notion of "progress" appears more questionable.

At any rate, for our present purposes, in considering discontinuities a nonjudgmental approach may be more productive. It is important to have in mind that, whatever the basis for judging the relative merits of different approaches, they, of necessity, raise the difficult question of meaning. Methodologies, insofar as they represent different ways of seeing, must also involve ways of not seeing. The critical question in the comparisons that follow should not be which tradition saw the world more accurately. Indeed, as part of this effort involves a comparison over fifty years, there may be no final resolution possible. The question to be considered might more properly be why there are differences in both what is seen and not seen. This is a question we might ask not only about our relationships with the history of our discipline but also about relationships among contemporaries.

An important aspect of such a concern must involve an examination of who we are and where we are coming from—and the latter in both a literal and a metaphorical sense. Another question must focus upon changes in both the character and social role of the sociological profession. Mostly, as was suggested above, we must consider the changes that may or may not have occurred in the surrounding social world. This last is something the profession at best attends to unevenly; something that is done most often within an area safely isolated unto itself. It is to the first of these concerns that we will now turn.

Though not fully meeting Mills's (1942) description of the backgrounds of the social pathologists of the 1930s, both Shaw and McKay approximate that collective profile. Both were white Anglo-Saxon Protestants journeying from nonurban backgrounds to careers as urban sociologists. For Shaw, who was clearly the more ideologically involved of the two men, a model of small-town social control became the solution to problems of inappropriate behavior, including delinquency. This view was facilitated by a Parkian view of the city as a natural organism whose constituent "natural areas" could be seen in many instances as bounded villages. Indeed, it was predominantly the areas of the city that contained heavy concentrations of recent immigrants and their children that required institutional reconstruction in order to achieve the mythologized small-town-like patterns of normative control. Other areas of the city either naturally evolved or did not require the constraining patterns of small-town life. In any event, such untroubled sections of the city were rarely studied, sparing the researchers the need to confront themselves.

In contrast, many of the current research staff members are the children and grandchildren of the immigrants who occupied so much of the attention of the Shaw-McKay research. Moreover, a larger number of the current research staff are urban-born and reared; they see urban life as a kind of constant that almost precludes seeing at all.

Lastly, where Shaw and McKay were interested in social reform within the context of the status quo—indeed utilizing what would currently be called "establishment" figures—the current staff predominantly represents a conventional range of political positions for sociologists—from lukewarm liberals to burned-out radicals. Where there is a curious optimism implicit in the early tradition, I think we would have to confess to a kind of fatigue that feeds the nonfires of cynicism. Though this difference in political tone may reflect surrounding conditions more than individual differences, it must be remembered that Shaw and McKay lived in a climate of relatively successful, though largely unexamined, reform, while we look back at a recent history of such attempts that not only failed but failed in remarkably noninstructive ways.

The second contrast involves the sociological context. The Shaw-McKay research begins, particularly in Chicago, with urban research and social-problems research occupying center stage; that clearly was where the sociological action was.

In contrast, few of the present research staff had any prior research commitment to juvenile delinquency. Indeed, few had had any prior academic work in the area, which over the past two decades occupied, at best, a minor, often isolated and unfashionable, position within the profession. For most sociologists, delinquency was a topic occasionally to be encountered on the way to a "grander" concern with deviant behavior. Curiously, most of us read the recent major works on delinquency, such as Cohen's (1955) parable, but this reading was rarely done in the context of a focus upon delinquency, or with any context of images provided by recent research. While delinquents were not as exotic to the present staff as the city must have initially appeared to Shaw and McKay, staff members have at times approximated that sense of the exotic, creating not only a fear of error but an equal fear of innocence.

The link of the current senior staff—lest this become an admission of unabashed opportunism—was a prior interest in adolescent and youth cultures. This, perhaps more than anything else, accounts for why the later approach begins with a focus upon delinquency in the context of the more general adolescent experience (where, in fact, most of it occurs) and not primarily at the interface between youth and law enforcement.

The changes, both substantive and methodological, that mark the distance between the two periods of research are too massive and complex even to begin to review in the present context. We should observe, however, that the very virtues of successive layers of development in available methodologies (as well as the extent of funding for such ventures) can only be termed something of a mixed blessing. All at once we see perhaps too much at one time; too many discriminations can be made, too many things held constant. It seems that only the naive or the irresponsible retain the capacity for the simple declarative sentence. In a sense we begin by trying to explain social life and end by accounting for variance— and rarely for much of that. Somehow, the more complex and necessarily condensed the strategies of data manipulation become, the more our discourse is emptied of human sounds (something that remains of little importance as long as the discourse is largely internal).

More telling than anything else may be the change in the very character of social life during this intervening period—including, possibly, changes in the very nature of the human. Of the many that could be alluded to , three changes appear to be most relevant to our present discussion. The first of these involves the very meaning—though not necessarily the character—of adolescence. Rarely did the Shaw-McKay research concern itself with nondelinquent youngsters. In a sense there was little need to; after all, there *appeared* little that was problematic about those who were not problems, were not delinquent. Even those who commanded the attention of the research were not problematic; they were youngsters in problematic situations, problematic environments. In contrast, for the last two decades adolescents as a category have been increasingly defined as problematic. As a category they have been cast alternately in the role of barbarians at the gate or potential recruits for some children's crusade. It is in this context that a concern for delinquency as part of the general adolescent experience became a necessity. Viewing adolescents as a suspect population capable of all manner of deviancies, one almost unself-conciously saw delinquency as a mere extension of modal behavior, rather than as an exceptional category.

Even more dramatic have been the changes in the character of the social structures that were so fundamental to the explanatory thrust of the Shaw-McKay research. Preeminent among these was the conception of the city as the master structure within which other elements of organized social life were ordered. The biological analogy of Park that led to a conception of the city as organic whole—unplanned but magically adaptive in its specialization of function and population—seems all at once remote from the contemporary experience. In a special sense, the major symbol of the passing of that kind of urban community may have been the very formulation of its natural origin and architecture; "natural" areas ceased being wholly natural as Park and his students made us conscious of the community's unconscious character. The growth of a fully national economy, the dominance of national political structures, and media systems that appear to be unable to stop this side of the global, provide the foundations of massive change, the character of which seems for the moment beyond our grasp. We now must ask: Who experiences in anything resembling its totality the metropolitan community? Indeed, who can even begin to describe it in terms translatable into a human scale? Communities and neighborhoods that had the property of small-scale social systems, in their seeming multigenerational permanence, have in increasing numbers proved to be fragile and ephemeral. Ironically, where the contemporaries of Shaw and McKay were deeply concerned about problems of assimilation, many of their present-day counterparts appear equally concerned about the necessity for maintaining an eroding pluralism, comprehended, unfortunately, in terms of traditional sources of pluralism.

This is not to suggest that either adolescents or adults live their lives in empty or unorganized social space but only that the shape, salience, and character of surrounding social space are less definable in terms of physical location than may previously have been the case; that social institutions impact upon individuals with less uniformity than may previously have been the case; and that social institutions are less likely to be generative of powerful correlations between individual or even group experience and dimensions of surrounding social structure. And while the lives of many, if not most, adolescents appear circumscribed by physical space—neighborhood and school district—the substance of structural input appears increasingly limited; it is limited not only by the heightened significance of cultural forces whose origins lie outside immediate territory but by a sense of the provisional. Such territories (the word "community" promises too much) have the most limited of capacities for history and a correspondingly shadowy relevance to the future.

Lastly, one must reflect upon the major macrosocial drift of a society. We still manage to protect ourselves from change by projecting terms like "postindustrial" into an adjacent but distant future, attached for the moment to the magical year 2000. Nonetheless, many of the aspects of this impending and largely unfinished—possibly still largely undetermined—transformation are critical elements of the present moment; we often fail to see these elements precisely because of the very continuities in sociological theory and research that we prize and celebrate. A great deal of our present stock-in-trade found its origins in giving names to emergent forms of social life associated with a developing urban-industrial society which may serve increasingly to obscure the changes associated with movement to a postindustrial society.

Though too many of us latently greet the present economic crisis as a return to a kind of normality, a return to the kind of social order our training and the predominant values of our society prepared us for, the preceding almost quarter-century of unanticipated affluence need not have been a digression from a "normal state of affairs." The "anomie of affluence," which changed even the character of those still describable in terms of the "anomie of deprivation," with its seeming capacity to call into question some of our most cherished assumptions about the nature of social life, human motivation, sex roles, life-cycle stages, etc., insofar as it linked to these broad macrosocial changes, should remain very much part of our agenda. Moreover, these changes may require language and concept development beyond those fashioned to describe the changes of an earlier epoch. Typically, much of the difficulty we experienced during the past decade in doing research on adolescents—both delinquent and nondelinquent—clearly involved the inappropriateness of much of our perceptual language, language we were too reluctant to abandon or consciously modify.

Many of these reflections derive from the experience of coping with our most recent data. Let us then share with you some of our recent findings, only small portions of which have as yet appeared in print. Our attempt at comparative ethnography does not lend itself to brief summary. However, one general observation might be attempted. These studies—averaging more than a year of fieldwork in each site—range from slums of Chicago (partly described in Horowitz and Schwartz 1974) to its affluent lakeside, from upper-income suburbs to blue-collar suburbs; they also range over most of the state, including relatively small communities in nonmetropolitan areas of southern Illinois. Obviously the design facilitates the possibility of dramatic contrasts and, indeed, many are observed. Far outweighing such contrasts, however, is a much larger pattern of essential similarities. While differing in the proportions or the quality of community response, with the exception of the extremes (such as the level of violence in the inner-city slum), most communities have much in common with one another. The language, costumes, activities, options that describe presentations of self have a striking uniformity. In a very profound sense, these communities, as experienced by their adolescents, are outposts of a national society. More concretely, as an example, the same drugs and the same drug ideologies are found in virtually all communities—except, possibly, in the case of heroin, which remains predominantly a problem of black communities.

This note is reinforced by the major survey—a household probability sample of three thousand adolescents that took us to over forty counties and involved screening in excess of nineteen thousand households and utilized a self-report instrument covering thirty-two violative acts—where with one major exception only negligible and inconsistent differences could be observed when the effects of community type and social class were examined. The categories of offense cover general misbehavior, car violations, alcohol, drugs, theft, and violence. The one exception finds significantly higher rates of violence and theft among inner-city nonwhites. Clearly, no one community type or social class milieu purchases immunity.

This general uniformity in levels of involvement in violative behavior, when compared to the marked differences observable in statistics generated by the law enforcement industry, reinforces other self-report studies and victim studies in the conclusion that the larger part of delinquency remains undetected. Indeed, except for the nonwhite and the poor, the interface between adolescents and law enforcement appears a massively inefficient, negative lottery that chooses its losers very selectively. The one group—identified because they frequently desert home—which was the most heavily involved in protocriminal behavior (85 to 95 percent of them being high on violence and theft) proved to be the lowest with respect to police contact of any kind.

Rates of violative behavior for males (with the exception of drugs) appear not to have changed in over two decades—at least to the degree that the self-report approach provides meaningful estimates. This finding has curious implications for all theories that assume that adolescents have reasonably sophisticated views of what surrounding social structure is all about. Rates of violative behavior on the part of females reveal levels of involvement higher than any reported in the previous literature, with cross-gender convergence being greatest at the most intense levels of involvement. (The convergence was also noted in patterns of sexual behavior as reported by Miller and Simon [1974], where a moderate elevation of female rates of nonvirginity is noted along with a surprising and substantial increase in male virginity.) This suggests, as do other aspects of the research, a pattern of heterosociality in the adolescent experience that may in fact represent a significant departure from older patterns and one with possible profound implications for the future of the issue of sex-role assignment and expectation.

We also note that most protocriminal acts are highly concentrated during the younger years of adolescence, in an age group rarely studied, indeed, one we are rarely given permission to study. However, these and other recent data suggest that the confused and almost totally neglected transition from childhood to adolescence may in fact have a higher pathogenic potential than any other point of transition in the life cycle.

Both peers and school experience were found to be significant, but not conclusively or exclusively. It should also be noted that little was seen reminiscent of the traditional literature on gangs. The drift of Matza (1964) and the "pick-up" game hypothesis of Gold (1970) seem more explanatory, though not at all comforting, as they raise the issue of the highly contingent nature of much of this behavior (see also Short [1974]). Similarly, perception of legitimate or illegitimate opportunities produced only marginal effects. The effects of the family, on the other hand, proved unsurprisingly to be relatively insignificant, being weakest at the level of most serious involvement in violative behavior. All our family variables—including such time-honored ones as family intactness or brokenness—accounted among white adolescents for about 5 percent of the variance. For nonwhite adolescents this was substantially higher.

Our major problem is that we have many findings in bits and pieces, but little that emerges even suggesting the promise of integrated explanation. We have an immense potential for generating articles, or for books that read like collections of articles, but a low potential for producing a coherent volume. We would like to think that more is involved than a failure of imagination or competence. We begin to understand why our profession so enthusiastically responded to "labeling theory," despite its terrible blandness. Though it only effectively describes a small portion of all offenders, its effects are wondrously demonstrable: a small token of keeping the promise of relating social structure to human lives.

In defense against our own data—defending those cherished beliefs reiterated in countless introductory texts—the one conclusion that we find ourselves repeating is that *there must be more reasons for being deviant than there are ways of being deviant*. This does not mean that we are about to abandon that which we most fundamentally share with the Shaw-McKay tradition: a commitment to the social determination of behavior, including—or especially—what appears as contranormative behavior.

The link between social structure and group life and individual destinies remains critical but hardly simple. Perhaps very much like the metropolitan complex that so thoroughly bewilders us, social life may be whole and coherent in its totality but may express neither quality in its specific elements. Perhaps this reflects the incoherence of a society in transition; increasingly, describing our technological core requires less coherence in more and more aspects of social life.

As has already been observed, one of the characteristics of a late urban-industrial society or postindustrial society may be a lack of master paradigms. The very unevenness of social change may require an indefinite period of eclecticism that will produce no master theory of delinquency. Thus, for example, the need to simultaneously deal with the anomies of deprivation and affluence points to the need for research that is self-conscious in delineating its potential scope of applicability. Perhaps what is indicated is at least a partial return to the "naturalism" typified by the early Chicago tradition; being concerned less with the questionable goal of "building science" and having a proportionately greater concern with a critical examination of social life.

To all of these problems we can offer no answer. We would,

however, offer an attitude. We think we might begin with a more careful scrutiny of what we are and do, and with an even more critical scrutiny of where we have been. Moreover, given the unevenness of all social life, while conscious of the continuities which are our heritage, we remain equally mindful of and unsentimental about its provisional character. We may have to prepare for a sociology as impermanent as the social world it studies and reports upon. If we do otherwise, we may leave to a later sociology the task of explaining why our sociology failed.

# References

Cohen, Albert K.
1955        *Delinquent Boys: The Culture of the Gang.* Glencoe, Ill.: The Free Press.

Gold, Martin
1970        *Delinquent Behavior in an American City.* Belmont, Cal.:Brooks/Cole.

Horowitz, Ruth, and Gary Schwartz
1974        "Honor, Normative Ambiguity and Gang Violence." *American Sociological Review* 39 (April): 238–51

Matza, David
1964        *Delinquency and Drift.* New York: John Wiley.
1969        *Becoming Deviant.* Englewood Cliffs, N.J.: Prentice-Hall.

Miller, Patricia Y., and William Simon
1974        "Adolescent Sexual Behavior: Context and Change." *Social Problems* 22 (October): 58–76.

Mills, C. Wright
1942        "The Professional Ideology of Social Pathologists." *American Journal of Sociology* 60 (September): 165–80.

Short, James F., Jr.
1974        "Collective Behavior, Crime, and Delinquency." In Daniel Glaser, ed., *Handbook of Criminology.* Chicago: Rand McNally.

Short, James F., Jr., ed.
1971        *The Social Fabric of the Metropolis: Contributions of the Chicago School of Urban Sociology.* Chicago: University of Chicago Press.

# 3    Settling the Frontiers of a Pioneer in American Criminology: Henry McKay

*Albert J. Reiss, Jr.*

There is scarcely a problem in modern criminology that has not been illuminated by the pioneering investigations of Henry D. McKay. He and his long-time collaborator, Clifford R. Shaw, have contributed to a more sophisticated sociological understanding of the causes and social control of delinquency and crime. The investigations of Henry McKay also demonstrate a willingness to utilize a broad range of methodological tools and approaches. One can point to sophisticated statistical analyses of aggregative data on crime and delinquency (Shaw and McKay 1931), pioneering work on the ecology of delinquency and crime (Shaw and McKay et al. 1929; Shaw and McKay 1942), case histories of criminal careers (Shaw, McKay, and McDonald 1938), and designs for delinquency prevention (McKay 1949). At the core of these investigations lies a genuine concern that explanations fit together to provide a sociological understanding of delinquency and crime. This chapter focuses on explanatory problems originally raised by these investigations but made equivocal by recent inquiries.

Let me summarize very briefly the work on delinquency to be examined. Shaw and McKay described the distribution of official delinquency in major American cities, showing that delinquency was endemic in some residential areas in that high official rates of delinquency persisted over long periods of time, periods during which there were substantial changes in the ethnic or race compositions of those areas (1931:383–93). As compared with areas with low rates of delinquency, high-rate areas were characterized by physical deterioration and declining populations, the economically less privileged, ethnic cultures, high adult crime rates, and a disintegration of traditional institutions and neigh-

Albert J. Reiss, Jr., is a member of the Department of Sociology at Yale University.

borhood organizations with the community failing to function as an agency of social control (1931:108). They observed considerable variation in the rate of delinquency within high delinquency rate areas, however, emphasizing local neighborhood as well as community variation in delinquency rates. Analytically, emphasis was given to the structures of delinquent groups, families, neighborhoods, and communities as factors producing delinquent and criminal behavior (Shaw and McKay 1931).

This line of research was subject to critical examination from several standpoints in recent decades. Whyte (1943:272-76) concluded that the slum is not a disorganized community, but rather that the problem of the slum lies in the failure of its social organization to mesh with that of the larger society. Methodologically, delinquency area research was criticized on the grounds that correlations for areas did not necessarily imply correlations for the individual units, thereby obscuring causal analysis (Robinson 1950:352). Subsequent work attacked the presumption that delinquency is disproportionally concentrated among lower socioeconomic status groups and race or ethnic groups. Several types of empirical investigation contributed to this line of criticism. The first were studies of self-reported delicts which show, Doleschal (1970) concludes, that there are few, if any, substantial differences in delinquency by social class and/or race. A second line of research, stemming from societal reaction, labeling, and organizational theory, held that official statistics of crime and delinquency were not an unbiased set. Official acts of detecting, defining, and labeling delinquents and criminals are viewed as biasing official statistics toward lower-income persons (Lemert 1951; Cicourel 1968).

Despite the fact that these theoretical, methodological, and empirical critiques have illuminated many of the questions investigated by Shaw and McKay, I contend they have not substantially refuted the basic conclusions of that work. The discussion focuses primarily on two major conclusions from Shaw and McKay: that delinquency is endemic in certain neighborhoods and that the probability of becoming delinquent is greater for persons in lower- than high-income status groups.

## Social Class Delinquency

Despite contradictory findings from a substantial number of studies of self-reported delinquency, it is commonly concluded

that official statistics on crime and delinquency not only underestimate the true rate of delinquency in a population but that
there are no significant differences by social class (Doleschal
1970). There is little reason to question the conclusion that
official statistics on delinquency underestimate both the prevalence of offenders and the incidence of offending in a population,
given the social organization of detection systems and discretionary decisions by agents of social control (Reiss 1974*a*:9–17).
At issue, however, is whether that underestimation occurs disproportionally for middle-class youth such that social-class differences commonly found in studies of official delinquency
disappear altogether when self-reported delinquency is taken into
account.

Two major lines of reasoning are advanced in support of my
contention that it is premature to conclude that there are no
significant differences in delinquency by social class. First,
contradictory findings on social class and delinquency could
result from differences in measurement techniques followed in
self-report studies. Second, the findings on self-reported delinquency are inconsistent with what is known about patterns of
delinquent and criminal offending, the relationship between
victim and offender, and the relationship of both victim and
offender with agents of social control. The findings from all of
these studies, if valid and reliable, should be empirically consistent and converge in a common theoretical explanation.

## Measurement of Self-reported Delinquency

Comparison of differences in delinquency among social classes
depends upon the selection of measures of delinquency and
appropriate tests of comparison. Examination of self-reported
studies of delinquency discloses many technical limitations in these
measures that call into question the comparisons of delinquency
by social class (Reiss 1974). We shall briefly review some of the
serious limitations for the effects they may have upon these
comparisons.

First, comparisons are usually made for an unstandardized
index of delinquency with no estimates for the reliability and
validity of items in the index. There is evidence, moreover, from
official statistics on delinquency that the older the boy the less
likely he is to be officially processed for offenses that apply to
juveniles only (Wolfgang et al. 1972:115). Yet self-report indexes
are usually disproportionally weighted with less serious criminal

offenses and those that pertain primarily to juveniles. Most indexes thus may obscure class differences in offense-specific delinquency. Comparison of social-class differences for the *same* offenses in official and self-reported delinquency would provide a basis for determining whether class differences attenuate in all, or only some, offenses when self-reports are the measure of delinquency.

Second, self-report studies often confuse measures of prevalence and incidence of delinquency. The prevalence of a phenomenon is the number of members of a population with a given condition over a period of time, while its incidence is the number of new conditions at some point in time. Most self-report surveys of delinquency estimate the prevalence of violators on the assumption that *any* event in the index of violating continues to characterize persons in a violator status, a form of sociological labeling. The list of violations, the length of time during which one could have violated, and the criteria for remaining in the violator status all lie with a particular investigator. Not atypically in such studies, one acquires the sociological label of delinquent by acknowledging that only once did one commit an offense for one of the violations in the index. This procedure also runs the risk that, if any single item with the highest frequency shows no class difference, there will be no class difference in the prevalence rate.

Prevalence statistics, of course, mask important differences in the incidence of offending. Indeed, since official statistics commonly ignore first offenses ever committed, they are in that sense biased toward persons with a higher incidence of offending. In any case, for any interval of time there may be important social-class differences in the incidence of offending for self-reported as well as for official delinquency.

Third, the statistics selected for comparison ignore both differences in onset and desistance from delinquent behavior. Typically, the prevalence statistic is defined so that there is no condition for exit from the prevalence state. Thus it is not possible to lose the condition of delinquent even though the incidence of delinquency for an offender may have been zero for a considerable period of time. On the basis of official statistics, one expects age of onset, the incidence of delinquency, and desistance probabilities to be greater for members of the lower social stratum.

Finally, the gross cross-section comparisons for self-report and official statistics mask important differences disclosed by a cohort analysis, particularly if the cohort is followed into adult years. A cohort design should also make it possible to test social-class theories of secondary deviation, since it would permit more precise examination of any effects of official processing of violations of the law.

## Consistency of Findings among Studies of Crime and Delinquency

Many different aspects of crime and delinquency have been investigated that affirm important social-class differences in offending and victimization by crime. Among these are studies of gang delinquency, offender selection of victims of crime, surveys of crime victims and the relationship between victims and offenders, and observations of the behavior of law enforcement agents toward victims and offenders. Some, but not all, of these studies are based on official statistics. Surveys of victimization by crime are based on self-reports of citizens. Those of gang delinquency are often based on field studies and observation and those of law enforcement agents on systematic social observation of citizen, offender, and agent transactions. The findings from self-report studies should be empirically and theoretically consistent with this body of findings, with logical explanations for any significant divergence among them. We turn, therefore, to examine the consistency of findings from these studies, explanations of their divergence, and their implications for conclusions from self-report studies.

## Access of Juveniles to Legal Processing

Societal reaction and labeling theorists argue that the police discriminate against lower socioeconomic status offenders in making arrests, thus biasing arrest statistics toward disproportionate numbers of low-status offenders. This argument is commonly used to explain why official statistics on crime and delinquency show disproportionate numbers of low-status offenders, whereas self-reported studies of delinquency fail to show significant social-class differences in delinquency. There are a number of reasons to doubt that discretionary decisions of police officers are per se discriminatory against low-status offenders.

The police ordinarily do not arrest juveniles who become known to them as committing an offense (Piliavin and Briar

1964:210; Black and Reiss 1970:68). Although in contacts with juveniles the police are more likely to arrest offenders who are known for past delinquencies, ordinarily they lack such information in making decisions to arrest juveniles (Piliavin and Briar 1964:209). Rather they rely upon criteria that are evident from the situation. The major criteria appear to be the seriousness of the offense, the deference and demeanor of the juvenile, and the preference of the citizen complainant.

The probability of arrest increases for juveniles with the *legal seriousness of the offense* as defined by the criminal law (Piliavin and Briar 1964: 209; Black and Reiss 1970:69); the same criteria hold for court referral (Goldman 1963:41–42). To the extent that the more serious offenses are committed more frequently by lower- rather than middle-class juveniles, they will be disproportionately represented in official statistics. The fact that the police release substantial proportions of middle-class offenders cannot be taken as evidence of police favoritism toward middle-class youth, since they also release substantial proportions of lower-class offenders; there is no evidence that social class itself is a factor in these discretionary decisions. The arrest policies of a community may be more important than the social class of offenders. Goldman found that the police in a middle-class community were more likely to arrest middle-class juveniles for minor offenses than were police in a large industrial city to arrest juveniles for minor offenses (1963:85).

There is strong evidence that the *deference and demeanor of juveniles* are highly determinative of the police decision to arrest. Despite the fact that blacks have a higher rate of arrest for juvenile offenses than whites, there is no evidence that race itself is related to arrest but rather that arrest is based on differences in deference and demeanor (Piliavin and Briar 1964:210; Black and Reiss 1970: 74–75). The same appears true with respect to arrests by social class. To the extent that deference and demeanor are class-linked, however, they should produce differential weighting in official statistics. The possibility that lower-status youth and blacks are less deferential to the police than high-status youth would result in their being disproportionately represented in official statistics of delinquency.

Most police encounters with juveniles arise in direct response to citizens who take the initiative to mobilize the police. Police sanctioning of juveniles by arrest is based primarily on the manifest preferences of these citizens for arrest (Black and Reiss 1970:76). The police are somewhat more likely to comply with white-collar than blue-collar complainants in making felony arrests but not in making misdemeanor arrests, where the status of the complainant appears to be irrelevant (Black 1970: 746). Police discretion to arrest, overall, rests with citizen preference. Unfortunately, it is not known whether citizen preference for arrest is substantially determined by the social status of the offender so that white-collar complainants are more likely to prefer the arrest of blue- than white-collar offenders, and vice versa. Given the importance of citizen mobilization of the police to arrest situations and of the power of their preferences in determining police behavior to arrest, any disproportionate representation of blue-collar offenders in arrest statistics may lie with white-collar citizens rather than the police.

Both the seriousness of the offense and the rate of offending of juveniles are factors in the decision to arrest. Both of these factors appear to be disproportionately distributed in the lower classes, a fact obscured by simple prevalence rates.

*Seriousness of Offenses*

Generally, official statistics on offenders disclose that the ratio of lower- to middle-status offenders is greater for felony or Part I offenses than it is for misdemeanors, though there is considerable variation by type of misdemeanor with social-class rates; motor vehicle violations, for example, show only small differences, while public drunkenness shows much larger differences. The class differences also appear to be greater for adult than juvenile offenders, owing perhaps in part to the fact that juveniles are often arrested for misdemeanors or offenses limited exclusively to juveniles (Wolfgang et al. 1972). Overall, however, information on the social status of victims, as discussed below, and official statistics on offenders disclose greater prevalence of lower-status offenders in serious offenses against the person. Information on recidivism of offenders and on multiple victimization likewise discloses a higher incidence among low-status persons for major crimes against the person.

Social-class differences for major crimes against the person should be reflected in self-reported studies of delinquency. Yet, while some studies disclose them, others do not. Just why results are contradictory is unclear, but it is possible that the answer lies in the measures used in self-report studies. Consider but one major crime against persons, that of assault. Self-report studies do not report rates separately for aggravated and simple assault, where an aggravated assault is considered one where there is serious bodily injury or when a dangerous weapon is used in the assault. Were they to do so, one would predict that self-report studies should show a higher rate of aggravated assault among lower- than middle-status offenders. Such a finding would also be consistent with those on gang delinquency. It also is possible that lower-status youth might show higher self-reported simple assault were the self-report measures carefully defined and validated. All too frequently the assault item in a self-report battery is of the sort: "Have you (ever) been in a fight?" or, "a fist fight?" Not only are such items subject to overreporting because they define masculine status, but not all fist fights are per se assaults, since questions of intent and culpability are at issue. It is well to remember that defenders against assaults are also "in fights."

Whether one should expect similar or less serious differences for major crimes against property is less apparent. This is owing in part to the difficulties in interpreting class differences in victimization for crimes against property, but also to the fact that less is known about class differences in offenses against property, using official statistics on crime and delinquency. What is apparent is that there can be enormous variation in self-reporting of larceny-theft depending upon the form of the item used in self-report studies and the seriousness of the larceny-theft (Belson 1968: table 2).

Perhaps it is worth noting that both the lack of operational standardization of measurement for social class and the definition of violations of law make comparison difficult and raise important questions about the reliability of classifications. It is no simple matter to operationalize either intent or culpability, whether in official or self-report studies. Even so quantitative an expression as the dollar value of goods is subject to high unreliability in classification, since any selection of a criterion for assessing value cannot be uniformly applied to property that is taken in theft; appraisal of the "market" value of used goods, for example, is a precarious standard.

## Delinquent Gangs

Shaw and McKay emphasized the importance of delinquency traditions in delinquency areas. They reasoned:

To a very great extent these traditions of delinquency are preserved and transmitted through the medium of social contact within the unsupervised play group and the more highly organized delinquent and criminal gangs. In the deteriorated areas, where there is little organized effort among the citizens for combatting lawlessness, these groups persist and tend to perpetuate delinquent and criminal forms of behavior (1931:222).

The prevalence of delinquent gangs in lower-class neighborhoods has been challenged by pointing to examples of middle-class gangs (Greeley and Carey 1963; Meyerhoff 1964). The recent work of Cartwright and Howard on gang areas in the city of Chicago concludes, however:

Gang neighborhoods were found to differ from the city as a whole in very many ways; younger population, lower income, working-class predominance, more family disorganization and others. However, although the gang neighborhoods were found in community areas with the highest delinquency rates (and therefore coextensive with high delinquency areas), and although there was an overall and significantly lower socio-economic status among the gang neighborhoods, nevertheless, these neighborhoods were by no means confined to the "poverty belt," as Thrasher had found some 40 years previously (1966:369).

Investigators of delinquent gangs similarly report that gangs are disproportionately located in lower-class neighborhoods (Klein 1971; Short and Strodtbeck 1965). Short reports that gang boys have higher rates of both official and self-reported delinquency than nongang boys. Comparing the rates of gang and nongang boys by their social status, he found that among whites, lower-class gang boys have the highest rates of official and self-reported delinquency, with those for lower-class boys next highest, and those for middle-class boys the lowest (Short 1965: table 5). Reiss and Rhodes found career-oriented delinquents— those who were members of groups that maintained contacts with adult criminals—almost exclusively among lower-class boys (1961:732).

It seems reasonable to conclude from these studies that delinquent gangs are disproportionately concentrated in lower-class neighborhoods and that their rates of both official and self-reported delinquency are above those of both lower- and middle-class boys. Unfortunately, we do not know whether white middle-class gangs have delinquency rates comparable to those of lower-class gang boys, but in any case, since the gang prevalence rate is much greater for the lower than middle classes, lower-class gang youth contribute disproportionately to the incidence of offending.

The prevalence and incidence of offending and, to a much lesser extent, of the incidence of events of delinquency are also determined by group as contrasted with individual participation in delinquent events. Since the early work of Breckenridge and Abbott (1912:35), there is strong evidence from official statistics and case studies of delinquents that not only are most delinquent offenses committed in groups but that most lone offenders are "influenced" by companions. Counting each individual delinquent as an offender for each offense in which he was known to the juvenile court to have been involved, Shaw and McKay (1931:194–99) found that only 18.2 percent of the offenders committed their offense alone; 19 percent of all individual delinquents known to the court always committed the offenses alone. There is considerable variation in group violation rates by type of offense, however, both for official statistics on delinquency (Shaw and McKay 1931:195) and for self-reported delinquency (Erickson 1971:120). Special tabulations available to the author from the victimization surveys in eight impact cities likewise show considerable variation in group violation rates by type of offense. For assaults against the person, 31 percent of all victims were victimized by a single offender, as compared with 21 percent of all robbery victims.

A recent report by Erickson on self-reported delinquency concludes that high group-violation offenses can be characterized as quite serious in nature, are less frequently committed than other offenses, but are accompanied by fairly high arrest rates; low group-violation offenses are less serious in nature, have a high frequency of occurrence, but have low arrest rates (1971: 124). Moreover, when Erickson calculates the group violation rate for the serious self-reported offenses, it approximates the group violation rate reported for official statistics of delinquency. The seriousness of an offense, its group character, and its arrest rate thus are relevant to any prevalence of incidence measure and affect any composite index in cross-class comparisons. Theoretically, group support should increase both the probability of committing more serious offenses and the risk of detection of offending, and, therefore, the probability of arrest. If lower-class youth have either a greater propensity to commit serious offenses or to membership in delinquent groups than middle-class youth, their rate of detection will be greater. Their higher probability of arrest does not mean, of course, that the police have determined it.

## Socioeconomic Status of Offenders and Their Victims

The relationship between the social status of victims and their offenders is not available, unfortunately, from official statistics on arrest, victimization surveys, or self-reported studies of delicts. Indeed, official statistics on arrest, and victimization surveys, cannot provide information on the status of the offender, since for a substantial proportion of such offenses the offender is never known to the victim or the police. Only self-report surveys provide an alternative for assessing the social status of offenders and their victims.

What information we have from official statistics shows that, while only one-fourth of the offenders for Part I crimes and one-third of those for Part II crimes reside in the same census tract as their victim (Reiss 1966:8), as the distance between census tracts increases the smaller becomes the flow of offenders (Smith 1972:80). On the whole, then, there is substantial propinquity in offender selection of victims. Though we have only ecological correlations with respect to the social status of victimization and offending, these correlations disclose that, in general, victims and offenders are of the same social status, though there is considerable variation by type of crime. This is more apparent for crimes against persons than against property. For crimes against persons, it is more the case where a prior relationship exists between victims and offenders, such as in assaults, than it is for robbery; and for property crime it is more apparent for burglary than larceny (Reiss 1966). Where offenders move some distance to commit an offense, income of the exporting area has a negative influence on the production of crime (Smith 1972:80–82). Thus the higher the income of an area, the less crime originated by offenders from that area. Offenders from low-income areas are more likely to move to high-income areas than vice versa (Reiss 1966; Smith 1972).

Unless self-reported studies of offending were to show either that middle-class offenders flow disproportionately to organizational victims or that there is a significant flow of middle-class offenders to lower-status victims, middle-class offenders should show much greater victimization of members of their own class than lower-status offenders.

All in all, research on official statistics of arrest leads to the conclusion that lower-class residents are victimized primarily by lower-class offenders and that middle-class victims are victimized by both middle- and lower-class offenders. Where higher victimization rates occur for middle- than lower-class residents, it will be unclear as to whether this is due to greater propensity of offending by middle-class offenders or simply to the flow of lower-class offenders to middle-class victims, while higher rates for lower-class residents would appear to result primarily from lower-class offending.

## Social Class and Victimization by Crime

There is no simple relationship between rates of victimization by crime and the social-class status of victims, since there is considerable variation by type of crime. The recent city surveys of the National Crime Survey Panel disclose an inverse correlation between social class and crimes against the person and a direct correlation between social class and crimes against households (USDJ 1974a,b,c). These gross correlations, however, mask important relationships by type of offense. The inverse correlation between crimes against the person and social class holds in general for rape, robbery with and without injury, aggravated assault, and personal larceny with contact (USDJ, 1974b). Generally, one can conclude that for the serious crimes against persons there is an inverse correlation with social class with lower-income persons and those who reside in low-income areas having a high rate of victimization. The relationship between social class and crimes against households is more complex. For burglary of households, low-income households have a higher rate of victimization by forcible entry, whereas income differences in victimization are small for unlawful entry and attempted burglary (USDJ, 1974c). Both petty and grand larceny show a direct relationship with income (USDJ, 1974c), and the results are inconsistent by city for auto theft (USDJ, 1974 a,b,c).

The social-class relationship between victims and offenders is not well understood, partly owing to the fact that offenders are never known for many crimes and partly because offender surveys do not gather information on the social-class status of their victims and victim surveys do not gather information on the social-class status of offenders. Victimization data, moreover, include offenses committed by offenders of any age and sex, and were the social-class patterns for juvenile offenders different from those for adults, any inferences we might make about the social-class status of victims and juvenile offenders would be subject to that error.

Information on the social-class status of offenders known to the police does not take into account the social-class status of their victims; as noted above, however, there is little evidence to suggest that middle-class offenders are mobile to lower-class areas while the reverse is not uncommon. If we assume that mobile offenders, at least in major metropolitan cities, are more likely to be lower- than middle-class, we have an additional link for interpreting victimization survey data. We tentatively advance two propositions on the social-class status of victims and offenders: (1) middle-class offenders are much more likely to choose victims of the same social status than are lower-class offenders; (2) mobile offenders are disproportionately lower-class offenders.

For crimes against the person, we would argue that since both the mobility rate of offending is lower for crimes against the person than against property and since lower-status persons are more likely to be victimized in crimes against the person, offenders in crimes against the person are disproportionately lower-class. If that is true, then self-reported surveys of delicts should show social-class differences in major crimes against the person, particularly if simple prevalence rates are discarded.

The situation is more complex for crimes against property, but given a greater propensity of lower-class offenders to be mobile and commit offenses against middle-class persons, offenders in property crimes *may* be disproportionately lower-class. Yet, what may be the case is that middle-class offenders are disproportionately concentrated in some, if not all, property offenses by selecting middle-class victims. The resolution of this matter lies in a convergence between findings from victimization surveys and findings on offending. Until self-report studies of delicts can provide information on the social-status differentials in victimization of both persons and their property, any reports of equal propensity to offending by middle- and lower-class offenders are open to question. Understanding this relationship will necessitate calculating social-class rates for the incidence of offending as well as for the prevalence of offenders. The derivation of such rates is no simple matter.

## Rates of Offending

Central questions in the relationship of social class to delinquency, then, are whether there are class differences in individual rates of offending and in the age of onset and desistance from delinquency or crime. Some specific questions requiring answers are these: For a given period of time, do lower-class offenders have higher average rates of offending than middle-class offenders? Do lower-class offenders desist from delinquency at an earlier age than middle-class offenders? Does a higher proportion of lower- than middle-class offenders have a longer average interval of offending? Prevalence rates obscure these differences and preclude examination of onset and desistance from delinquency. The practice of calculating incidence rates for long periods of time obscures short-term differences in rates of offending and without cohort and period rates, the examination of onset and desistance from delinquency and crime is also obscured. Indeed, unless one has a measure for removing an individual from a "prevalence" state, it is not possible to test theories that predict time changes in an individual's prevalence condition.

The age of onset of delinquency is related to socioeconomic status in official statistics of delinquency. First-offender rates have a sharply rising probability distribution for low-income boys, with a peak at age eighteen; although the distribution is similar for higher-income boys, it is much lower on the probability scale (Wolfgang et al. 1972:131). When race and socioeconomic status are jointly considered, white higher-status boys have the smallest probability of committing a first delinquent offense at every age of onset but age sixteen, while lower-status nonwhite boys are most likely to commit a first offense at all ages but seventeen (Wolfgang et al. 1972:131–34).

The younger the age of onset of delinquency, the higher the mean number of offenses committed per offender by age seventeen. At each age of onset, however, lower-status boys have greater mean arrest rates than do higher-status boys (Wolfgang et al. 1972:table 8:1). Thus, although arrest rates rise with the length of exposure to arrest, for equal exposure to arrest lower-status boys have a higher arrest rate. Lower-status boys thus contribute disproportionately to the incidence of offending at any point in time as measured by official statistics of delinquency.

Socioeconomic status is likewise related to desistance from delinquency. Examining delinquency in the birth cohort, Wolfgang and his collaborators show a sharp fall in desistance probabilities after the first and second offenses, with a leveling off after the third offense; there is a desistance probability of .2 to .3 after the third offense for each succeeding offense (1972:163). At each offense rank, the likelihood of desisting was greatest for high-status whites, followed by low-status whites, high-status nonwhites, and low-status nonwhites, in that order (Wolfgang et al. 1972:305). Further examination of desistance probabilities in this cohort by age eighteen shows that nonwhites were 5.4 times more likely to continue in delinquency to age eighteen than were whites, a matter that appears to be strongly influenced by their relative differences in socioeconomic status (Stone 1973:4).

Rates of individual offending by social class are ordinarily not calculated in self-reported studies of delinquency. Evidence from the few studies where they have been calculated is contradictory. The most carefully designed and validated of these studies, that of Belson on stealing by London schoolboys, shows that lower socioeconomic status groups report a greater variety and amount of stealing (1968:7). Unless valid and reliable data on individual rates of offending by social class replace simple prevalence rates, we cannot properly assess the effect of differences in social-class offending on victimization by crime.

We have observed that the incidence of individual offending varies by social class such that, on the average, lower-class persons have higher individual rates of offending. There is evidence that boys who get caught by the police are the ones most heavily involved in delinquency, both as to variety and amount (Belson 1968:9). The interesting question arises whether these relationships account for the higher proportion of lower-class offenders in official police statistics. Examining the relationship of getting caught by the police to the amount of stealing, Belson found that while high-status boys are less likely to be caught by the police than low-status boys, there were no significant differences in their probability of being caught when the amount of stealing was taken into account. Thus high-status boys with high incidence of stealing were about as likely to be caught by the police as low-status boys with high amounts of stealing, and vice versa. Were this finding to hold true more generally for delinquency, we would conclude that the chances of being caught by the police are closely associated with the amount of delinquency and that the disproportionate appearance of lower-status boys in police statistics is substantially due to their higher average rates of offending.

## Delinquency Areas and Social Class

The pioneering investigations of Shaw and McKay (1931; 1942) established that there is marked variation in delinquency rates for residential areas, that these rates vary inversely with socioeconomic status, and that the rate of delinquency in a residential area persists relative to that of other areas despite population mobility and changes in race and ethnic composition of the area.

The possibility that correlations for areas do not necessarily hold for the individual residents within them does not obviate the empirical observation that delinquents and delinquency violations are not uniformly distributed in residential space and that there is considerable variation in rates of delinquency both within and between residential areas. Recent work by Gordon affirms the earlier conclusions of Shaw and McKay by demonstrating that when appropriate multivariate procedures are used and appropriate cutting points are selected for socioeconomic status distributions, there is a marked association between the delinquency rate of an area and its socioeconomic status (1967: 943–44). Moreover, a review of intracity variation in delinquency levels disclosed a remarkably similar pattern of correlation between area delinquency rates and their socioeconomic status (Hodge 1965). Hodge concluded from a path analysis that the available evidence supports the proposition that the persistence of delinquency areas may be regarded as a simple causal chain (1965:19). Reanalyzing the Shaw and McKay data for Chicago for the periods 1900–1906, 1917–23, and 1927–33, he inferred that patterns of behavior over this span of time could exert no influence on current levels of delinquency, independent of the delinquent activity observed at the intervening period. At the ecological level then, when official statistics on delinquency are analyzed for residential areas, there is an inverse relationship between socioeconomic status and the rate of delinquency for such areas; these correlations persist over substantial periods of time.

Given the stability of these ecological correlations, some years ago Lewis Rhodes and I examined the relationship between an individual's social status and delinquency by the socioeconomic status composition and delinquency rate of residential areas. We found that, for both official juvenile court records of delinquency and self-reported delinquency, the probability of becoming a delinquent was greater for low- than high-status boys (1961:723, 732). We found, moreover, that both the occupational stratification of residential areas and their delinquency rate were independent sources of variation in the rate of delinquency for ascribed social-status groups (1961:726–28). The effect of the social structure of a residential community on an individual's life chances of official delinquency were such that the rate for any status group is at least twice that in the lowest-status residential community as the highest-status residential community. Moreover, in both high- and low-rate delinquency areas, the probability that a boy will be delinquent varied inversely with his status position. Examining the joint effect of the ascribed social status of an area and its delinquency rate, we observed that within each ascribed status group, the delinquency rate usually rises with the delinquency rate of the area, regardless of its social-status composition. In every ascribed-status residential area, the chances that a high-, middle-, or low-status boy would be delinquent was greater if he resided in a high- than a low-delinquency-rate area. Thus there is no simple relationship between ascribed social status and delinquency, since both the social-status structure of the residential community and its delinquency rate affect the delinquency life chances of a boy at each ascribed social-status level.

Like previous investigators, we were unable to account for these findings in any strict causal sense. We noted that lower-status boys in high-status areas seem hardly a random set of all lower-status youth, and vice versa. Recent work by Suttles (1968) on the normative order of slum communities suggests that the normative organization of territories explains delinquent behavior and responses to it in those areas, but we lack comparable information on the normative organization of other communities. The importance of normative organization and traditions in areas of the city is a central feature of the explanation offered by Shaw and

McKay and one that has been largely scanted in empirical investigation and explanation of social class and delinquency.

The work of Shaw and McKay on delinquency areas emphasized the persistence of high rates of delinquency and crime in some areas of the city over long periods of time. It did not address itself principally to the question of changes in rates of delinquency for areas of the city over time. Yet there is abundant evidence that there are changes in such rates over time, particularly in an increase of the number of areas that show high rates of delinquency. Moreover, there is growing evidence that official rates of delinquency and crime are rising in areas outside of central cities. These changes often are taken as evidence for an increase in crime and delinquency of the middle classes.

Changes in the rates of delinquency for central-city areas and suburbs are to be expected, however, as a simple consequence of the growth of a city, all other things being equal. Assume for the sake of exposition that rates of delinquency and crime may be higher among the lower than the middle or upper classes, and assume that as a metropolitan area grows the proportionate contribution of each social class to that growth remains constant. For purposes of simplification, assume also that, with growth, population succession occurs such that the lower classes generally expand into the more middle-class areas of lower housing densities and that there is a growing suburbanization of the white working class. From such assumptions, one would make several predictions. First, that as the city grows, a growing proportion of the central city will be occupied by lower-income groups. Given their movement to areas of lower housing density, even given their propensity to overcrowding, the lower classes will occupy proportionately more territorial area. With a constant delinquency rate for the lower class, an increasing proportion of the total area of the city will have high delinquency rates simply as a result of this movement. Second, to the extent that the lower and working classes shift to the suburbs, a movement that may be accelerated by shifts in residential segregation, more of the areas outside central cities which have not altered their boundaries should show a rise in delinquency rates. Basically, then, shifts in population succession with population growth should bring with them shifts in delinquency rates of areas, all other things being equal. And, indeed, if the assumptions of population-shifts to areas of lower housing densities are correct, a growing proportion of the central-city territory should have high rates of delinquency. Perhaps because of these shifts, perceptions about the changes in public safety in central cities (crime in the streets) are factually grounded.

Assuming, as previously noted, that victimization from crime is class related, we would similarly expect that there might be important variation in victimization from crime by types of residential areas. Unfortunately, data are not available on variation in rates of victimization by crime for small areas of central cities. Available data on area variation in rates of victimization are not altogether consistent, but the following general pattern emerges from the several published U.S. studies. First, rates of victimization by crime are higher in large than small cities and in urban than rural areas. Ennis (1967:30) reports that metropolitan areas had rates of violent crime five times greater than those of smaller cities and rural areas, and property crime rates twice as high. Second, in general, rates of victimization are greater for central-city than suburban areas, though the differences are attenuated for some crimes (Institute for Local Self-Government 1969; Reynolds 1973; USDJ 1974c). Third, rates of victimization are generally greater both for lower-income areas in central cities and for low-income persons, regardless of residential area, for crimes against the person (USDJ 1974a, b). Moreover, the rates of victimization for households in low-income areas for crimes against the person are estimated to be higher than those for low-income persons generally.

The relationship between personal and area income and victimization is different, however, for crimes against property. At the gross level for all major crimes against property, there is a positive relationship between income and victimization for all crimes against property (USDJ 1974a, b). The direct relationship for burglary, however, does not appear to hold for burglary by forcible entry, where the reverse relationship appears to hold (USDJ 1974c: tables 37, 38), a finding that is consistent with patterns of forcible entry in burglary reported in police statistics. It is also possible that the direct relationship between income and victimization by auto theft would disappear if the eligible victim population were automobile owners rather than households. When we examine victimization differences between households in low-income and all other areas of the city, low-income-area households show higher rates of victimization by burglary with forcible entry and for auto theft. Only larceny victimization shows a direct relationship with the income of areas and personal income.

Yet, what is particularly significant is that, for all crimes against property, the victimization rate for households in low-income areas is substantially greater than that for low-income persons generally in the central city, except for the crime of larceny. It is true for larceny also when metropolitan rather than central-city rates are examined (USDJ 1974c: tables 36, 38, 39).

Thus for both crimes against persons and property, a strong case can be made that the probability of victimization by crime is greater for low-income persons in low-income areas of central cities than for low-income persons in other residential areas within and without central cities. Perhaps the reason for such a greater probability of victimization lies in what we have suggested about the relationship between social class and offending—lower-status boys in lower-status high delinquency areas have the highest rates of offending, and the same should obtain for adult offenders. Such an explanation is consistent with the experience and reports of persons who reside in such areas. Moreover, it is consistent with Furstenberg's analysis of poll data, showing that fear of victimization by crime is directly related to the crime rate of an area, while concern about the crime problem is inversely related to the crime rate of an area (1971:605). Might one add that in choosing a place to live, amenities aside, many residents in high-crime-rate areas object to its high crime-rate as a condition of living? To be subject to victimization by both property and person crimes is quite different from being subject primarily to victimization by property crimes only. Unfortunately, data on multiple victimization are as yet largely unavailable.

## Epilogue

The foregoing didactic analysis of crime has been based on a consideration of some traditional common-law offenses of crimes against person and property. It is arguable that these offenses are class-biased and, were one to consider "white-collar" crimes such as fraud, conspiracy, and criminal violation of antitrust, the middle and upper classes would be proportionally more "criminal." The argument may have less force for juvenile than adult offenders, but, that apart, it is not clear that extending the range of "criminal" offenses necessarily produces a white-collar effect. Much depends upon the selection of offenses. Although some offenses, specifically defined, are generally limited to middle-class persons, others are equally limited to lower-class persons. Consider the matter of fraud, where certain forms such as embezzlement or corporate fraud may be exclusive to white-collar offenders, yet with the emergence of the "new property" (Reich 1964:733) fraudulent claims for welfare and other benefits are more exclusively lower-class forms of fraud.

There is no simple solution to a comparison of the "criminality" of the social classes since so much depends upon the mix of offenses that define criminality or delinquency. It perhaps is a mistake to construct indexes of criminality or delinquency on which social classes are compared, unless careful consideration is given to the effect of each type of offense on the index comparisons. We have tried to show that there may be substantial differences both within and between offenses against persons and property that have an effect on such comparisons. Moreover, the choice of an incidence or a prevalence rate will markedly affect comparisons among social classes. Simple prevalence rates over long periods of time, for example, readily mask important differences in rates of offending. Careful consideration of the complexities of index construction and choice of rates is the cautionary tale.

We have tried also to show that since crimes are socially defined events between victims and offenders in social and territorial space, our theoretical explanations and empirical verification must take account of these complex relationships. At the same time we have suggested that the social control of crime by agents of law enforcement may be more determined by these relationships between victims, offenders, and events than by the organization of discretion of official agents of social control.

## References

Belson, William A.
1968            "The Extent of Stealing by London Boys and Some of Its Origins." *Advancement of Science* (December): 1–15.

Black, Donald J.
1970            "Production of Crime Rates." *American Sociological Review* 35 (August): 733–48.

Black, Donald J., and Albert J. Reiss, Jr.
1970          "Police Control of Juveniles." *American Sociological Review* 23 (June): 1087–1111.

Breckenridge, Sophonisba P., and Edith Abbott
1912          *The Delinquent Child and the Home.* New York: Charities Publication Committee.

Cartwright, Desmond, and Kenneth L. Howard
1966          "Multivariate Analysis of Gang Delinquency I: Ecological Influences." *Multivariate Behavioral Research* 1 (July): 321–71.

Cicourel, Aaron
1968          *The Social Organization of Juvenile Justice.* New York: John Wiley.

Doleschal, Eugene
1970          "Hidden Delinquency." *Crime and Delinquency Literature* 2 (October): 546–72.

Ennis, Philip H.
1967          *Criminal Victimization in the United States: A Report of a National Survey, Field Surveys II.* The President's Commission on Law Enforcement and the Administration of Justice. Washington, D.C.

Erickson, Maynard L.
1971          "The Group Context of Delinquent Behavior." *Social Problems* 19 (Summer): 114–29.

Furstenberg, Frank F.
1971          "Public Reaction to Crime in the Streets." *American Scholar* 40 (Autumn): 601–10.

Goldman, Nathan
1963          *The Differential Selection of Juvenile Offenders for Court Appearance.* New York: National Council on Crime and Delinquency.

Gordon, Robert A.
1967          "Issues in the Ecological Study of Delinquency." *American Sociological Review* 32 (December): 927–44.

Greeley, Andrew, and James Carey
1963          "An Upper Middle Class Deviant Gang." *American Catholic Sociological Review* 24 (no. 1): 33–41.

Hodge, Robert W.
1965          "Ecological Studies of Juvenile Delinquency." Manuscript, National Opinion Research Center.

Institute for Local Self-Government
1969         *Criminal Victimization in Maricopa County.*
            Berkeley: Institute for Local Self-Government
            (June).

Klein, Malcolm W.
1971         *Street Gangs and Street Workers.* Englewood
            Cliffs, N.J.: Prentice-Hall.

Lemert, Edwin M.
1951         *Social Pathology.* New York: McGraw Hill.

McKay, Henry D.
1949         "The Neighborhood and Child Conduct." *The
            Annals* 261 (January): 32–41.

Meyerhoff, Howard L. and Barbara
1964         "Field Observations of Middle Class Gangs." *Social
            Forces* 42 (March): 328–36.

Piliavin, Irving, and Scott Briar
1964         "Police Encounters with Juveniles." *American
            Journal of Sociology* 70 (September): 206–14.

Reich, Charles A.
1964         "The New Property." *Yale Law Journal* 73
            (April): 7.

Reiss, Albert J., Jr.
1966         "Place of Residence of Arrested Persons Compared
            with Place Where the Offense in Arrest Occurred
            for Part I and Part II Offenses." Crime Statistics
            Series: Report No. 5 to the President's Commission
            on Law Enforcement and the Administration of
            Justice. Archives of the Commission.
1974         "Citizen Access to Criminal Justice." *British Jour-
            nal of Law and Society* 1 (June): 1–26.
1976         "Surveys of Self-Reported Delicts." In Albert Bider-
            man, ed., *Crime and The Public: A Symposium.*
            New York: Naiburg Publishing Co. (forthcoming).

Reiss, Albert J., Jr., and A. L. Rhodes
1961         "The Distribution of Juvenile Delinquency in the
            Social Class Structure." *American Sociological
            Review* 26 (October)): 720–32.

Reynolds, Paul Davidson
1973         *Victimization in a Metropolitan Region: Compari-
            son of a Central City Area and a Suburban Com-*

*munity*. Minneapolis: Minnesota Center for Sociological Research.

Robinson, W. S.
1950        "Ecological Correlations and the Behavior of Individuals." *American Sociological Review* 15 (June): 351–57.

Shaw, Clifford R., and Henry D. McKay
1931        *Social Factors in Juvenile Delinquency: A Study of the Community, the Family, and the Gang in Relation to Delinquent Behavior*. National Commission on Law Observance and Enforcement, Report on the Causes of Crime, vol. 2, no. 13. Washington, D.C.: U.S. Government Printing Office.
1942        *Juvenile Delinquency in Urban Areas: A Study of Delinquents in Relation to Differential Characteristics of Local Communities in American Cities*. Chicago: University of Chicago Press.

Shaw, Clifford R., Henry D. McKay and James F. McDonald
1938        *Brothers in Crime*. Chicago: University of Chicago Press.

Shaw, Clifford R. and Henry D. McKay,
Frederick Zorbaugh and Leonard S. Cottrell
1929        *Delinquency Areas*. Chicago: University of Chicago Press.

Short, James F., Jr.
1965        "Social Sructure and Group Processes in Explanation of Gang Delinquency." In Muzafer and Carolyn Sherif, eds., *Problems of Youth: Transition to Adulthood in a Changing World*. Chicago: Aldine.

Short, James F., Jr., and Fred L. Strodtbeck
1965        *Group Process and Gang Delinquency*. Chicago: University of Chicago Press.

Smith, Michael Wayland
1972        "An Economic Analysis of the Intracity Dispersion of Criminal Activity." Raleigh, N.C.: North Carolina State University. Ph.D dissertation.

Stone, Richard
1973        "Inverse Matrices in the Study of Delinquency." Cambridge, England (manuscript).

Suttles, Gerald D.
1968            *The Social Order of the Slum: Ethnicity and Terri-
               tory in the Inner City*. Chicago: University of Chi-
               cago Press.

United States Department of Justice (USDJ)
1965            *Crime in the United States: Uniform Crime
               Reports—1965*. Washington, D.C.: Government
               Printing Office.

1974*a*         *Preliminary Report of the Impact Cities, Crime
               Survey Results*. Washington, D.C.: Law Enforce-
               ment Assistance Administration (NCJISS).

1974*b*         *Crime in the Nation's Five Largest Cities: Advance
               Report*. Washington, D.C.: Law Enforcement
               Assistance Administration (NCJISS).

1974*c*         *Crimes and Victims: A Report on the Dayton-San
               Jose Pilot Survey of Victimization*. Washington,
               D.C.: Law Enforcement Assistance Administration
               (NCJISS).

Whyte, William F.
1943            *Street Corner Society: The Social Structure of an
               Italian Slum*. Chicago: University of Chicago Press.

Wolfgang, Marvin, Robert M. Figlio and Thorsten Sellin
1972            *Delinquency in a Birth Cohort*. Chicago: Univer-
               sity of Chicago Press.

**II**     **Delinquents and Gangs**

# 4 Youth Gangs in the Urban Crisis Era

*Walter B. Miller*

## Youth Gangs and the Work of Henry McKay

The work of Henry McKay spans almost five decades of American life. During this period substantial changes have affected many of the social circumstances and conditions that provide both the focus and the context of his major scholarly concerns, but it is evident as well that other conditions have shown very little change. A systematic consideration of these patterns—what has changed and what has remained stable, how the concepts of "change" and "stability" are defined, the analytic level at which these concepts are applied—involves an extremely complicated and critical sociological issue, that of change and stability. This issue constitutes a major theme in the work of Henry McKay, and it is a major concern of the present paper. McKay's analyses of change and stability involve a wide range of demographic variables, primarily as these affect the relation of different kinds of neighborhoods and different kinds of populations to different patterns of youth crime (Shaw and McKay 1942, 1969: 384). The present study addresses this issue with a much more limited and specific focus—American youth gangs.

Youth gangs as such do not constitute a major focus in the work of Henry McKay. But references to gangs do appear in his writings, primarily in connection with analyses of empirical findings and theoretical consideration of the nature and origins of delinquent behavior. Gangs are discussed in at least three contexts: (1) as a type of social institution (others of the type include organized and professional crime), they are part of a nonconventional or criminal tradition alternative to, and often conflicting with, the conventional tradition of law-abiding adults (Shaw and McKay 1942, McKay 1949); (2) gangs figure as a

Walter B. Miller is a member of the faculty of the Harvard Law School's Center for Criminal Justice.

major object of a treatment approach, the detached worker method, developed out of community-based service techniques of the kinds pioneered by the Chicago Area project (Shaw and McKay 1942, 1969): and (3) gangs are viewed as part of the educative milieu of the local neighborhood, as exemplified in "The Neighborhood and Child Conduct" (McKay 1949). The conception of gangs forwarded therein accords closely with that of the present study.

Much of the controversy currently surrounding the character and origins of gangs can be attributed to differences among the several schools in how they define their basic concepts. It is thus essential that any treatment of gangs specify as clearly as possible the sense in which the term "gang" is used. The present approach starts with a distinction among three major concepts: "gang," "delinquency," and "subculture." The term "gang" refers to a collectivity of humans comprising identifiable persons and is conceptually analogous to terms such as "group" or "organization." "Delinquency" refers to one particular category of behavior engaged in by identifiable persons ("delinquent" behavior) and is conceptually analogous to terms such as "morality" ("moral" behavior). "Subculture" refers to a set of conceptions of appropriate practice and is roughly analogous to concepts such as "cognitive map" and "definition of the situation." Thus, the term "gang" refers to people, "delinquency" to behavior, and "subculture" to conceptions (Miller, forthcoming).

All three concepts may vary independently of the others; there are no fixed linkages among them. Delinquency may exist independently of gangs, and gangs vary greatly in their involvement in delinquency. Subcultures apply to many associational forms and behaviors other than gangs and delinquency, and the notions of a "delinquency subculture" or "delinquent subcultures" have limited explanational utility. The definition of a "youth gang" used in the present study is as follows:

> A youth gang is a group of adolescents who congregate recurrently at one or more extra-residential locales, with continued affiliation based on self-defined inclusion criteria. Recruitment, customary assemblage locales and ranging areas are based upon location within a delimited territory, over some portion of which limited use and occupancy rights are claimed. Group boundaries and the composition of subgroups are

delineated on the basis of age. The group maintains a versatile repertoire of activities with hanging, mating, recreational and illegal activity of central importance, and is internally differentiated on the basis of authority, prestige, personality-roles and clique-formation (Miller, forthcoming).

On the basis of this definition it is possible to recast the terms of McKay's description of neighborhood youth groups in the 1930s and '40s for purposes of more direct comparison with present-day gangs. As part of his analysis of the informal educative process of the local community, McKay cites three kinds of youth groups—the play group, the social and athletic club, and the delinquent gang (McKay 1949). From the present perspective each of these represents a different facet or manifestation of the same basic associational unit—the youth gang. The term "play group" applies to gangs in at least two ways: the neighborhood play group frequently represents the preadolescent stage of what will become the adolescent gang: "play" in a variety of forms is one major component of the "versatile activity repertoire" of youth gangs (McKay 1949). The "social and athletic club" generally represents the "formal organizational" mode of operations of a street gang, involving features such as scheduled meetings, elected officers, dues, and so on which are still prevalent, although the actual term "social and athletic club" was more common during earlier periods (Miller 1956). The term "delinquent" in what McKay designates as "the delinquent gang" refers, under the present definition, not to a particular type of gang (the term implies the existence of a "nondelinquent" type), but to another component of a gang's "versatile activity repertoire"—the practice of illegal behavior.

Phrased in the terms of the present study, McKay represented youth gangs in the '30s and '40s as prevalent associational units in local communities, units whose customary activities included recreational, mating, and illegal activities, which often developed out of preadolescent play groups and which embodied and inculcated a set of subcultural traditions some of whose focal concerns and customary practices were at variance with conceptions of appropriate practice of the law-abiding adult community. Given this representation of youth gangs in the earlier twentieth century, one can ask, What is the youth gang situation today? With the issue of change and stability a major focus, following sections will examine the circumstances of youth gangs during the era of urban crisis, paying particular attention to the question of similarities to and differences from the gangs described by McKay.

## The Urban Crisis Era

During the decade of the 1960s a series of developments in the United States appeared to mark a kind of domestic watershed—a transition in national life from one phase to another. Among the precedents of these developments were a massive immigration during and after World War II of southern blacks to northern cities; the adoption of major new technologies, including automated industrial production and computerized information processing; and an extended period of military involvement in Southeast Asia. The effects of these developments on two categories of citizens were subject to particular attention—categories popularly designated during this period as "youth" and "blacks." For Americans of African background this period brought a marked acceleration of undertakings aimed at the achievement of full civil equality; an emergence of a new militancy in the pursuit of black interests and objectives; a wave of the most extensive and destructive civil disorders in the history of the country; drastic changes in the population composition of major cities and equally marked changes in the size and relation to the metropolis of the suburbs. The magnitude of these developments and the problems they posed—particularly as they affected the cities—prompted some to designate this period the era of "urban crisis."

For the youth of the United States a dominant feature of these times was the existence of armed conflict in Asia, which confronted males with the continuing prospect of active military service in a difficult war. This circumstance fueled an unparalleled measure of youth involvement with pacifism and associated ideological movements, particularly among college youth, but other developments also affected the youth subculture. Among these were a marked increase in the use and acceptability of drugs of various kinds, predominantly marijuana; an intensification of the degree of ideological content in popular music directed at youth; increased stress on sexual freedom and an expanded acceptance of sex relations before marriage; intensified concern with social justice as it affects blacks and other categories of Americans; a heightened emphasis on the value of "inner experience" and the value of warm interpersonal interaction, and a concomitant devaluation of the "Protestant ethic" emphasis on achievement, material success, and technological orientation associated with the "middle-class values" of the adult generation. To some, these and related developments were of sufficient magnitude and import to support a designation of "counter-culture," and some even talked of a radically new order of "consciousness" among youth of the urban crisis era (see also Short, Chapter 5 in this volume).

How did these developments affect the youth gangs of the United States? Gangs are represented in the present study as an associational form which maintains a high degree of formal continuity and is at the same time responsive to changing social circumstances. The perception by some that the urban crisis era brought a "new" culture to the country in general and to youth in particular engendered serious misconceptions concerning the status of youth gangs. This chapter explores the impact on gangs of selected events of the urban crisis era; it examines, first, patterns of media coverage and gang prevalence, then discusses gang involvement in civil disorders, political activism, and drugs, and concludes with an analysis of processes of change and stability as they affect gangs.

## Present-day Gangs: Prevalence and Publicity

Accurate information as to the current prevalence of gangs in the many communities of the United States is not available (Short 1968). It will be instructive, however, to examine briefly the pattern of media coverage of gangs during this period, both because of the clues furnished by such coverage as to actual gang prevalence and to better understand the bases of media coverage.

The media during the 1950s—newspapers, magazines, tele-vision—devoted a good deal of attention to youth gangs, with New York and its "fighting gangs" as a major focus. Although most research evidence indicates that gangs of this type were relatively rare both in New York and elsewhere, an impression was created that New York-type fighting gangs were prevalent throughout the nation. Starting in the early 1960s New York media attention to gangs began to wane and by the middle 1960s had ceased almost entirely—a trend that was paralleled in the national media. This period of low media attention was accom-panied by a belief in some quarters that gangs had died out entirely or at least experienced a major change in behavior.

In the early 1970s the New York media rediscovered the youth gang. Initial stirrings were confined to particular areas and types of gangs (August, 1970: "Wave of Youth Gang Wars in China-town"; November, 1971: "The Rat Pack of New York"), but by 1972 the rediscovery burst into full flower. A March 1972 story in the *New York Times*, reporting a killing in the course of fighting between the Savage Nomads and Galaxies gangs, stated that there were one hundred violent gangs in the South Bronx, and a few weeks later *New York* magazine, in a story heralded by the front-cover banner "Are You Ready for the New Violence?" officially announced the "Return of the New York Street Gang" (Bragonier 1972).

The use of the term "gang" by the *New York Times*, widely regarded as the nation's top daily, dramatically illustrated the influence of reporting fashions on perceptions of gangs. The *Times* maintained what was essentially a moratorium on the use of the term "gang" to refer to regularly congregating youth groups for a period of approximately six years between 1966 and 1972. A 1966 feature which asserted that "suddenly, after a decade of mounting violence, the era of the fighting gangs in New York came to an end" (Buckley 1966), seemed to serve as a kind of signal that the use of the term "gang" was no longer appropriate for *Times* reporters. During the moratorium period the *Times* used terms such as "a large group of youth," "bands of youths," "neighborhood boys banding together to commit crimes," and "predatory packs." A story of a gang fight during this period was headlined, "Rival Bands Battle 2 Hours" (*New York Times* July 24, 1968). The word "gang" was used very occasionally and selectively during this period to refer, for example, to "tong"-like youth gangs in Chinatown and to motorcycle gangs (also called "clubs").

Then, in late 1971, the moratorium was lifted as suddenly as the *Times* had claimed the gangs had vanished. Less than one week after a Sunday *Times* magazine story (Stevens 1971) echoed Buckley's 1966 feature in proclaiming that "The big days of the big fighting gangs are gone . . . gone are the . . . adolescent armies . . . each with its own (name) . . . turf . . . rules. . . dress . . . and reasons for fighting," a pioneering *Times* reporter, in a story headlined "Street Gang Chief is Slain in the Bronx," wrote that the incident was "the outgrowth of gang battles in the neighborhoods . . . between the Black Spades and the Savage Skulls" (*New York Times*, December 3, 1971). Following this break, the term "gang" began to appear repeatedly in the *Times*.

The contrast between pre- and post-moratorium usage was especially marked in the reporting of school-connected violence. Prior to the break, the term "gang" was never used in this connection (February 20, 1971: "Fighting . . . between Spanish-speaking students and black students"); afterwards it was used constantly (April 19, 1972: "Students are being 'mugged, harrassed, intimidated and stabbed' by other students who are members of South Bronx gangs").

A year prior to the *Times* report of one hundred gangs in the Bronx and many more in other boroughs, police and Youth Authority officials stated conclusively that the last gang had disappeared from the streets of the city and that there was *no* gang problem in New York.[1] Assuming it to be quite unlikely that the number of gangs in the Bronx had grown from zero to one hundred in a year's time, how can one explain the apparently sudden and mysterious "reemergence" of the gangs? The "disappearance" resulted from a combination of changes in gang and media behavior (see Miller 1969). City officials and media alike adopted a special and restricted definition of "gang." In the early 1960s the pattern of names, jackets, and large-scale fighting which had received so much publicity during the 1950s was essentially abandoned. Despite changes in these fashion-susceptible practices, gangs as defined here remained prevalent. By choosing to regard as gangs only those groups which exhibited characteristics of the outmoded 1950s pattern, officials with an interest in controlling gangs were able to claim their elimination. Messages were dispatched to New York patrolmen informing them that "disorderly groups of youths are in the streets fighting with knives."[2]

Media coverage in New York, then, has been characterized by a period of considerable attention to certain types of gangs, a period of virtually no attention, and a period of renewed attention.[What of the other major cities in the United States? The city with the most intensive media coverage has been Philadelphia, where headlines proclaimed, in 1965, "245 Teenage Gangs Roaming City; 49 Capable of Killing;" in 1969, "Teen Gang Carnage Reaches Peak; 47 Dead, 519 Injured in 17 Months," and 1972, "Is There No Way to Halt the Mad Violence of Gangs?" In Chicago, major press attention in the 1960s focused on a few well-publicized "politicized" gangs, but continuing coverage has also been directed to the activities of numerous local neighborhood gangs, with a 1972 story reporting over seven hundred identifiable gangs involved in "violent deaths, beatings, robberies and shakedowns." Los Angeles media have maintained fairly consistent coverage of gangs (1966: "Juvenile Gangs Accepted as Part of Life in City"), but in the early 1970s a series of highly publicized gang-connected killings sparked an upsurge in media attention resembling New York's, with a 1972 story stating that gangs "have been sweeping through south central Los Angeles and Watts, beating, robbing, raping and occasionally killing" (Jansen 1972). An upsurge of gang violence in Detroit has received considerable media coverage since 1973.

Youth gangs, then, are currently subject to media attention in five of the largest cities of the nation. No clear pattern is evident with respect to other major cities. Groups of youthful thieves or muggers ranging in size from three to six or more receive attention in a number of cities, notably Washington, D.C., but the media generally have not applied the term "gang" to such groups (Stevens 1971; Rae 1972). Why the media cover gangs in some cities but not in others, the basis for coverage when it occurs, the relation between the actual gang situation and what the press reports—all, regrettably are poorly understood. Clues may be found in the following considerations.

If one assumes that newspapers, television, and other media organs, perhaps not deliberately or consciously, devote some limited portion of scarce space and time to crime and violence, one can further assume that forms of violence which are more spectacular or novel will take precedence over those which are less so. During periods when highly violent events occur with some frequency, reports of these will consume available media space; during periods when such events do not occur or are less common, the media will move down the scale of severity and select from among the less serious forms for journalistic attention. Gang violence, while it may represent a very serious problem to citizens and police in particular localities and at particular times, must be ranked among "less serious" forms of domestic violence on a scale which includes insurrection and mass rioting (Miller 1966; Klein 1969).

During the 1950s the domestic scene in the United States was relatively peaceful, and against this backdrop gang fighting provided for the media one of the more newsworthy forms of domestic violence. In the 1960s, however, gangs and their activities were, in effect, driven from media coverage by the advent of far more serious and spectacular forms of domestic violence—massive urban riots, dramatic student demonstrations, armed conflict between police and black militants.

In the early 1970s these forms of violence, despite unequivocal predictions that each represented the start of a continuing or increasing national trend, had subsided sufficiently as to merit little media attention, and the media returned once again to publicize the activities of the ever-present youth gangs. While the absence of media coverage in a particular locality does not necessarily mean that gangs are absent, the presence of such coverage almost certainly indicates well-developed gangs. Recent survey evidence (Miller 1975) shows that gangs are numerous and active in five of the nation's ten largest cities—New York, Chicago, Los Angeles, Philadelphia and Detroit. In the remaining five, gangs pose problems in Baltimore, Washington and Cleveland, but not in Houston or Dallas.

## Gangs in Philadelphia

More direct evidence from two urban areas provides an opportunity to compare information available through public sources with research findings based on direct field reports. These cities are Philadelphia and Boston, where field data on gangs are available for both central city and suburban areas (see also Shaw and McKay 1942, 1969). In Philadelphia gangs are well publicized by the media; in Boston, virtually ignored. What do the field data show? Philadelphia gangs and their activities have received extensive press coverage; in August 1970 a major daily averaged one youth gang story every two days; several front-page headlines concerned gangs. And with good reason. The Philadelphia area in the late 1960s and early 1970s was swarming with youth gangs of every description—large and small, violent and peaceful, male and female, black and white. In 1969 a crime commission issued a report which contained a detailed summary of the gang situation to that date (Pennsylvania Crime Commission 1969). Estimates based on police reports concluded that there were in municipal Philadelphia about seventy-five gangs, mostly black, comprising about 3,500 members, which were sufficiently "active" (primarily in fighting) to be of continued concern to the police. Social agencies put the estimated number of gangs at about 200.

Between October 1962 and December 1968 gang members were reportedly involved in 257 shootings, 250 stabbings, and 205 "rumbles." In the period between January 1968 and June 1969, 54 homicides and over 250 injuries were attributed to armed conflict between gangs. Assailants ranged in age from thirteen to twenty, with 70 percent between sixteen and eighteen. Only a minority of these gangs were named, the majority being designated according to their major congregation corner (Twelfth and Poplar, 21W's [for 21st and Westmoreland]). In the year following the crime commission report, the number of "active" gangs approximated by the police increased from seventy-five to ninety, the number of gang members from 3,500 to 5,000. Moreover, the rate of gang-connected homicides established in 1968 and 1969, three per month, continued at a similar or higher level during the next four years.

It is important to note that the Philadelphia gangs responsible for so striking a record of violent assault do not conform to an image of the "fighting gang" developed out of some combination of sociological and journalistic reporting during the "West Side Story" era of the 1950s. Most gangs do not have gang names. There are no gang jackets. There is little evidence that gangs are specifically "organized for conflict," or even organized, in the sense of having formalized chain-of-command titles ("warlord," etc.), specialization of function and the like (Pennsylvania Crime Commission 1969). Instead, Philadelphia gangs in most significant respects approximate the classic urban corner groups of the 1910–60 period defined earlier: a territorial base (the term "turf" is common), strong ties to one's corner and gang-mates (one boy said, "the gang is your mother and father"), age-defined subgroups, related female groups, and a "versatile" repertoire of activities including the conventional forms of slum youth crime— theft, vandalism, drinking, and drugs—along with less violent kinds of assault. Intergang fighting appears as only one of a range of gang activities—an activity which may be pursued by different gangs with greater or lesser frequency, and with more or less serious consequences. Involvement in gang fighting thus is a matter of degree, with the intensity and seriousness of fighting by the more highly publicized gangs falling toward the more extreme end of the scale.

A particularly interesting aspect of the Philadelphia gang situation concerns its relation to the racial issues of the "urban crisis" era. The great majority of the more violent gangs in Philadelphia are black, during a period when issues involving race relations have been more of a national focus, and more highly charged, than at any time since the Civil War—a period which has seen the development and wide dissemination of an explicit and compelling philosophy based on the affirmation of black pride and racial solidarity. Given this ideological climate, one would expect some direct and obvious relationship between the impelling movement for black rights and the upsurge in gang violence. On the basis of black solidarity ideological emphasis, one might expect major conflicts between blacks and whites, particularly in a city where migration patterns and the spatial distribution of the races appear to create so fertile a climate for interracial conflict. Instead, the great bulk of gang clashes involves blacks versus blacks, and the great bulk of injuries and homicides is by blacks of blacks.

The reasons advanced for involvement in gang fighting have few ideological overtones; instead, they approximate the classic reasons described for traditional gangs—territorial defense, maintenance of personal and collective honor, achievement of stature and prestige through besting of one's peers. Similarly, the actual conduct of gang fighting generally follows the classic pattern of provocation, attack, and counterattack (Miller 1957, 1958, 1966; Klein 1969). Few engagements between gang members involve massed encounters with large numbers of participants. Instead, most take the more traditional form of gangster-style attacks by passing assailants (sometimes in cars) on single or paired members of rival gangs. One aspect of the Philadelphia situation does differ clearly from many past situations; firearms are widely used—the shotgun is a favored weapon. It is this fact, in all likelihood, rather than any special viciousness or blood lust on the part of Philadelphia youth, that accounts for the high incidence of gang-related homicides in Philadelphia. For the present, however, and in the absence of more extensive analysis, it would appear that traditional subcultural incentives involving adolescent status, masculinity concerns, social-class position, territorial competition, and the like are more influential in the genesis of Philadelphia gang violence than factors related in any clear fashion to new ideological currents of the urban crisis era.

It is important to note once again that the gangs involved in violent conflict, however well publicized locally, comprise only a minority of Philadelphia's youth gangs. Field research shows that scores of street corners, parks, and schoolyards throughout the city provide hangouts for a wide variety of less violent gangs whose activities, nonetheless, are regarded with dismay by local householders and businessmen. Moreover, youth gangs are prevalent in scores of outer suburbs as well, with gangs reported for many communities, large and small, in Chester, Montgomery, Bucks, and Delaware counties. Since these communities are predominantly white, the gangs are predominantly white, although black gangs are not uncommon in some of the larger ring cities such as Reading, Norristown, and Pottstown. No generalization about the national gang situation can ignore Philadelphia; gangs in the classic tradition flourish throughout the entire region. While the fighting gangs of the inner city whose violence is so marked constitute only a small minority of gangs in the total region, activities of many of the less violent gangs also pose serious problems for law enforcement officials and are regarded, justifiably, with deep concern and apprehension by local residents.

## Gangs in Boston

The most extensive current survey of gangs in a major urban region covers the area of metropolitan Boston.[3] This area contains ninety-four cities, towns, and urban districts, each with its own name and police headquarters. Fifteen of these are named districts of municipal Boston, ranging in size from about 20,000 to 100,000; thirty-seven are incorporated cities and towns also ranging in size from 20,000 to 100,000 and located for the most part within an "inner" metropolitan zone beyond municipal limits; forty-two are towns ranging in size from 2,500 to 20,000 and located in an "outer" metropolitan zone.[4] Between 1965 and 1972 information as to the presence of gangs was collected on a continuing basis for all ninety-four communities. Data were obtained through a variety of sources, with primary reliance on direct field observation and routine police reports (see Miller, forthcoming).[5]

What is the youth gang situation in the many communities of the metropolitan area? In municipal Boston itself, gangs are present in all fifteen districts. They are, in general, more numerous, active, and better developed in lower status areas. The district with the most persisting tradition of active gangs is not black but rather the predominantly Irish district of South Boston, the past homesite of the Kennedys, McCormicks, and other eminent political families. In fact, in contrast to Philadelphia, where gangs are clearly most numerous in black neighborhoods, gangs in Roxbury, Boston's best-known black district, are less in evidence than during the 1950s and considerably less active than in lower-status white districts such as East Boston, Charlestown, and South Boston.

The pattern of gang-connected youth offenses—those forms of gang activity which routinely evoke police action—shows a high degree of stability over a five-year study period. The most common form of offense is "creating a disturbance"—a variety of activities such as noisy rough-housing, obscene conversation, impeding public passage, and the like. Next most common are relatively mild forms of the "violent crimes"—assault and property damage—also in a variety of manifestations, such as stoning passing vehicles, small-scale set-to's, breaking school windows, and so on. Third and fourth are drinking and theft of various kinds, such as stripping autos and ransacking public buildings.

Gang fighting occurs according to what might be called the "traditional" pattern; that is, fighting between rival groups occurs with some frequency and regularity when viewed as a city-wide phenomenon (although rather rarely from the point of view of the life-history of particular gangs), but such fighting rarely results in serious injuries or commands much general notice, in sharp contrast with New York in the 1950s and '70s, or Philadelphia and Chicago in the 1960s and '70s. One major reason is that the use of firearms is rare; stones, sticks, clubs, and fists still are the major weapons of fighting gang members in Boston. It is of interest as well, during a period when the use of drugs by adolescents is increasingly prevalent, that use of or involvement with drugs only rarely provides a basis for police action with respect to gangs.

The gang situation in the thirty-seven cities and towns outside of municipal Boston is of particular interest, since most of the conclusions of the past fifty years of gang studies have been based on a few of the nation's largest cities, with little attention paid to the hundreds of medium-sized cities throughout the country. In the Boston area, many of the metropolitan-area communities ranging from 20,000 to 100,000 are substantial urban centers in their right, and some, such as Cambridge, Quincy, Lynn,

Somerville, and Medford, are major industrial cities with substantial working-class populations. Gangs are present in every one of these thirty-seven cities, and their general distribution and character reflect the situation of the major urban center itself; gangs are more prevalent, active, and better developed in cities with larger lower-status populations and, within these cities, in lower-status areas. In these neighborhoods youth gangs cluster on corners, in parks, parking lots, playgrounds, and commercial sections. The pattern of offenses dealt with by the police also resembles that of the main urban center, with group disturbances, vandalism, and drinking providing the most frequent reasons for police action and drug use seldom providing a basis for such action

The forty-two communities with populations of 2,500 to 20,000 vary widely, ranging from small residential villages with predominantly higher-status populations to industrial towns with sizable working-class populations. The gang situation presents a correspondingly mixed picture, with community size, density, social status, population composition, geography, and other factors all related to variations in numbers and kinds of gangs. Recurrently congregating groups of the kind being discussed here were noted for just about half of these forty-two suburban communities. Few present the picture of gang prevalence found in the larger ring cities. In the larger and more heavily working-class towns, however, local youth typically congregate in such locales as the town common, shopping plaza parking lots, pizza parlors, or ice cream stores. None of these gangs is black, since the population in this suburban zone is about 95 percent white, and children of local black residents are unlikely to form part of local adolescent "hanging" groups. The pattern of youth-group offenses dealt with by police resembles that already described with the less serious forms of "group disturbance" behavior constituting a relatively higher proportion of police-handled offenses, and action involving drugs, while still infrequent somewhat more common than in the more urbanized areas.

In many of these communities, as well as the "urban ring" cities and towns just discussed, the shopping plaza has become the new street corner for the youth gangs of the suburbs and has thus inherited many of the problems traditionally associated with the "kids on the corner" in the cities. The suburban supermarket or shopping mall youth gang has in fact become a highly prevalent phenomenon throughout the entire nation, deserving of more extensive treatment than it has yet received (King 1971).

## Gang Violence and Media Coverage

A comparison of the gang situation in Philadelphia and Boston suggests several important conclusions with respect to gangs and information about gangs in the United States today. The two metropolitan areas resemble each other in that youth gangs in large numbers and of a wide variety are present in both, with locality-based groups most common; patterns of gang activity in the scores of communities surrounding the major urban center resemble those of the center itself; gangs are more in evidence in lower-status communities; congregation patterns in the suburbs of the two areas are particularly similar; the racial and ethnic composition of the gangs reflect those of their local communities. The two metropolitan areas differ in that gangs in the municipal city are predominantly black in Philadelphia and predominantly white in Boston; also, a minority of the members of a relatively small proportion of Philadelphia gangs have been pursuing a pattern of violent intergang combat resulting in a high level of gang-related homicides, whereas the fighting activities of the Boston gangs have been far less lethal and have produced few widely publicized homicides in recent years. The primary differentiating factor, then, lies not in the presence, numbers, or distribution of gangs in the two urban areas but, rather, in the frequency and severity of gang-connected violence.

It is this factor, then, which accounts primarily for the striking difference between the two cities in the availability of information about gangs. Even a casual reader of the Philadelphia dailies is well aware that gangs are numerous and active in the city; even the most careful reader of the Boston dailies has no idea whatever, unless he has access to other sources, that literally hundreds of youth gangs are present both in the municipal city and in over fifty of the nearby suburban communities. Thus, while continuing media coverage of gangs is virtually always an accurate indication that gangs *are* present (and generally in larger numbers than indicated by the media), the absence of media coverage is by no means an accurate indication that gangs are *not* present.

In summary, available evidence as to gang prevalence and publicity during the present period indicates that, despite the widely held impression during the 1960s that youth gangs had vanished or altered radically, such gangs remain a common phenomenon in the United States.[6] Youth gangs in the nation's five largest cities have been pursuing a pattern of intergang conflict which has resulted in a level of gang-connected homicides sufficiently high as to bring about continuing media attention.[7] Moreover, outdoor congregation by youth groups in the "new" suburbs—now containing the largest proportion of the national population—appears to be widespread and growing, with many suburban gangs approximating the features of the classic inner-city gangs of past and present.

## Change and Continuity: Is There a "New Gang"?

American society, along with some others, is traditionally shortsighted about the relation of the present to the past. Americans tend to be profoundly impressed with the events of the immediate present and typically assign disproportionate weight to contemporary developments when attempting to explain social phenomena. Some in each generation have attributed the very existence of gangs to the specific happenings of their own historical period. Thus, youth gangs in the late 1800s were seen as a direct product of massive waves of foreign immigration; in the 1930s as a result of a grave national economic depression; in the 1940s and '50s as a consequence of basic changes in the character of the family unit.

The urban crisis era provides no exception to this predilection. There are those who feel that many of the numerous gangs of the present period represent a radical departure from past forms—that contemporary events have affected gangs so fundamentally that continuity with the past has been drastically attenuated or even lost (Yablonsky 1963; Gannon 1967; Poston 1971; Bragonier 1972). Of the major developments of the urban crisis period noted earlier, three in particular have been adduced to account for the emergence of the "new gang." Two are directly related to the massive civil rights movements of the period—an increased measure of militancy and readiness to employ force by urban blacks, and an increased involvement in political and/or ideological activism by residents of low-status communities. The third is the substantial growth in the acceptability and use of drugs among adolescents, accompanied in some instances by an ideological perspective characterized as "countercultural."

Since these developments directly involve population groups whose circumstances affect the existence and nature of gangs— youth, urbanites, and low-status populations—it is scarcely conceivable that they could fail to have an impact on present-day gangs. The issue, however, is whether that impact has been of sufficient magnitude as to justify speaking of a new gang, whose form, orientation, and customary pursuits represent a sharp break with the past rather than a contemporary version of traditional forms.

## Transformation through Protest: Youth Gangs and Civil Disorders

Of all the forms of domestic violence which marked the urban crisis era, the form which almost certainly had the most profound impact on public consciousness was a kind of collective social event designated, in more formal terms, as a "civil disturbance" or "civil disorder," and less formally as "rioting." Hundreds of such events occurred in the United States during this period. The basic pattern was set in 1963 and 1964; the rioting reached a peak in 1967–68, and diminished thereafter. These riots were subject to voluminous reports by many writers, several governmental commissions, and scores of social analysts (Lachman and Singer 1968; Report of the National Advisory Commission on Civil Disorders 1968; Wolfgang 1968; Hubbard 1969; *Civil Disorder Digest* 1969; Marx 1970; Baskin et al. 1972).

What part did youth gangs play in the disorders? Participation by youth gangs in urban rioting is nothing new; the activities of gangs during the "race riot" period of 1915–19 have, in particular, been well documented (see Thrasher, 1927, pp. 47, 53, 62, 138, 201–3, 373, 472; Rudwick 1966). But the nature of gang participation during this period differed significantly from that of the more recent period. The basic and most obvious fact about gangs and riots in the urban crisis era is that both the locale of the major riots (urban slum areas) and the social characteristics of the most active rioters (male youth and young adults) are coterminous with those of the classic urban youth gang. The riots occurred in their own home territory; the gangs were there, the riots were there, and hundreds of groups of black males were clearly in evidence, active and ubiquitous.

The character of gang participation in the rioting—what gang members did as well as what they did not do—deserves attention because of the light it throws both on the nature of the gangs and the nature of the rioting. It is important to note, in the first place, that in virtually no instance did the gangs start the rioting, either in the sense that they agitated actively for the advent of riot conditions or that incidents involving gangs served as major trigger events.[8] Once the riots were under way, however, gang members were among the most ardent and energetic participants.

The zeal of gang-member participation in the riots should come as no surprise. The vital concerns of gang members revolve around such matters as excitement, risk, daring, adventure, action, defiance of authority, freedom from constraint. Gangs are attracted to situations involving "trouble," and pursue their ends in a vigorous, activistic fashion (Miller 1958). It is hard to imagine a milieu more precisely calculated to promote the pursuit of these concerns. To the average member of the average black gang the riot represented an extraordinary convergence of desirable conditions, a situation of unparalleled opportunity: people milling in the streets, buildings in flames, police and fire vehicles rushing to and fro, the crash of breaking glass, the hubbub of police radios, the unstilled clangor of unattended burglar alarms. Observers of gang behavior during the rioting were struck by what appeared as a current of enormous excitement—an almost ecstatic perception that all things were possible, all delights within grasp. It was the sense conveyed in those kinds of ritualized events—the bacchanalia, the mardi gras, the corroboree—when ordinary rules of conduct are suspended and one is granted special license to pursue with fervor that which is denied in ordinary times. Even in those cases where the triggering incident was most unequivocally perceived as a racial affront, media observers of the 1965 Watts and 1967 Newark riots noted that the dominant emotions of most gang members appeared to be closer to elation than anger.

The pattern of participation by youth gangs in the classic civil disorders of the urban crisis era may be summarized by considering the relationship between gang behavior during the riots and during ordinary times. Analyses based primarily on a careful examination of the forms and frequencies of gang-member activity during the riots reveal a degree of regularity, rationality, and patterning which does not accord with a conception of youthful riot behavior as an irrational and uncontrolled outburst of long-suppressed emotions. The identity of targets of theft, assault, and property destruction reflects a process guided by orderly principles of selection. In particular, riot-period gang behavior does not support the thesis that racial hatred was the dominant motive for the rioting. Racial hostility was clearly a significant factor, but it was only one of a set of coexisting motives, many of which are common to American youth of all racial and ethnic backgrounds. Moreover, to those familiar with the behavior of urban low-status youth in ordinary times, the riot-period behavior of gang members appeared less a unique response to unique conditions than a logically continuous extension of customary motives and concerns. Riot conditions provided an extraordinary climate of opportunity for the actualization of these concerns, but the fact that gang members chose to pursue more avidly during the riots the same kinds of ends they ordinarily pursue attests to the enormous influence of motives derived from their subcultural status as males, as adolescents, city dwellers, and residents of low-status communities. The riot experience served to illuminate with great clarity the potency of those forces which engender gang behavior during ordinary times.

## Transformation through Commitment: Gangs and Political Activism

The notion of "transforming" gangs by diverting their energies from traditional forms of gang activity—particularly illegal forms—and channeling them into "constructive" activities is probably as old, in the United States, as gangs themselves. Thus, in the 1960s, when a series of social movements aimed at elevating the lot of the poor through ideologically oriented, citizen-executed political activism became widely current, it was perhaps inevitable that the idea be applied to gangs. The basic notion is simplicity itself. Once gang members can be brought to see that their energies should be devoted to a set of social reform and/or community betterment enterprises, great amounts of potentially productive energy can be harnessed to the achievement of needed social change, at the same time reducing the amount of energy available for criminal and other traditional forms of gang behavior. Two major models of activism were current: a more radical "militant" model, which saw gangs as a spearhead of a forceful attempt to undermine established sources of power (often white power), and a less radical "social betterment" model, which conceived gangs as the basis of a kind of indigenous community-services-delivery enterprise. The simplicity of this notion and the perceived desirability of social/

political activism by low-income citizens impelled many to predict, and some to assert the prevalence of, a "new" and politicized type of gang to replace the "conflict" gang of the past (see Geis 1965).

There were in fact enough developments along these lines in the middle and late 1960s to provide some substance to these predictions and perceptions. A small number of groups in some localities were the objects of sufficient publicity that an impression of a national trend was created. Prominent among the groups publicized were, on the "militant" model, the Black Panthers and the Young Lords and, on the "social betterment" model, the Blackstone Rangers and Devils Disciples of Chicago, and the Real Great Society of New York (Mouat 1966; Blank 1968; Webber 1969; McPherson 1969; Poston 1971). But the predicted transformation of American youth gangs never occurred. Even during the peak period of "politicization," the actual proportion of youth gangs involved was small, with the great majority of gang youth remaining essentially unaffected by political/social activism. Even for those most affected, there is little evidence that activism *replaced* illegal and/or violent pursuits in the repertoire of gangs; rather, traditional activities such as theft, assault, extortion, and various "hustles" were carried on in conjunction with, and frequently as an intrinsic part of, political and social-reform undertakings.

Moreover, even in those areas most affected, "politicization" appears as a relatively short-lived development. By the early 1970s, for example, in those areas of Philadelphia, Los Angeles and New York where hopes had been highest that political activism would replace gang fighting, levels of lethal intergang conflict were high or even increasing. Furthermore, even at its height, political activism and its associated ideologies had very little impact on the average "prime-age" gang member. This fact was widely misperceived. The prime age for male gang involvement in most localities runs from about thirteen to eighteen; all but a few of the publicized politicized gangs were composed largely of young men in their twenties or even thirties (see Miller 1966 and forthcoming; Klein 1970). Often the politicized gang was *not* the product of a direct progression by an established prime-age gang from traditional to political activities; instead, older males, generally with prime-age experience in other gangs, frequently assumed leadership in new groups after a period of separation from gang life as such. Thus, both men primarily responsible for the Real Great Society, an Hispanic activist gang, had been prime-age gang members in New York (Assassins, Dragons), but had severed ties with these gangs by the time the Real Great Society was started.

By far the greatest amount of publicity concerning political activism by gangs centered on Chicago, raising the possibility that this city may have represented an exception to the national picture (see Short 1974). In 1966 a reporter for the *Washington Post* wrote that "(Chicagoans) believe ... they are confronted with a new thing—a super gang, a gang with ideology, a gang larger and better organized than any previous juvenile gang" (Von Hoffman 1966). The gang he was referring to was called the "Blackstone Rangers," and it would appear that some substantial part of the general conception of the "politicized" gang in the 1960s was derived from the experience of a single gang in a single city—the Rangers of Chicago. There was more than a little substance to the *Post* writer's report. During the latter 1960s and early 1970s the "mighty Blackstone Ranger Nation"—in one or another of its changing designations ("Stones," "Black P. Stone," etc.)—remained a force to be reckoned with on Chicago's South Side. The Rangers claimed an extensive network of affiliates and/or subdivisions, bearing names such as the Maniac Rangers, the Conservative Rangers, the Imperial Pimps, the Viet Cong. They maintained an off-again-on-again state of "warfare" with a second "politicized" gang, the Disciples (e.g., Black, East Side, West Side), and achieved sufficient identity as an associational unit to apply for and receive a sizable grant under a federal anti-poverty program. Most press sources represented the number of Rangers and affiliates at their peak at somewhere around 3,000; the Rangers themselves claimed as many as 8,000; local youth workers reckoned the number of "dependable" members and affiliates at about 500.

There can be little doubt that various of the Chicago associational units included under the designation "Rangers" as well as a few other associational complexes going under general gang names both maintained some order of "lateral" or cross-neighborhood relations and devoted some part of their energies to activities which can be designated as "political" or "public service" oriented. Examples included youth employment and educational programs, day-care, security patrol, curriculum reform, and efforts to change union membership policies. More "militant" activities included participation in protest demonstrations and stockpiling arms and ammunition (see Short's discussion, 1974, and in the present volume). In addition, there were a few other nonblack associational units in Chicago and elsewhere whose activities importantly involved similar undertakings (e.g., the Young Lords, Spanish American, in Chicago, New York, and elsewhere; the Young Patriots, whites, in Chicago). The basic issue here, however, is just how prevalent were "politicized" gangs in the city where this phenomenon was best developed?

During the 1965–70 period the Chicago police estimated that there were approximately 900 "youth groups" in the city, of which about 200 were sufficiently troublesome to be designated "gangs" and about 20 difficult enough to be termed "hard core" (figures furnished by the Gang Intelligence Unit, 1966 and 1971). While reliable prevalence estimates in a loose and rapidly changing situation of this kind are extremely difficult to derive, a rough and generous estimate of the number of identifiable units and/or subdivisions affiliated in some manner with the major "politicized" gang names in Chicago (Rangers, Disciples, Vice Lords, a few others) would indicate something on the order of 80 units—less than 10 percent of the total number of youth gang units in the city. During the heyday of the "politicized" gang in the city with the highest number of such gangs, about 90 percent were *not* significantly involved in political activism. The politicization of the gang hardly represents a major national development. For the rest of the nation, including those Spanish-American units modelled in some degree after the adult Black Panthers the proportion of nonpoliticized gangs was probably closer to 95 percent.

Claims that the "politicized" gang had become the modern type of United States gang provide a classic instance of the principle whereby a small and atypical portion of the total population at issue becomes subject to extensive attention, and is then represented as a general and prevalent phenomenon (see Short, in this volume).

By the early 1970s it was apparent that one predicted product of the civil rights movement of the 1960s—a new, politicized gang, transformed by ideological commitment—simply had not developed. The media stopped heralding the politicized gang, headlining instead the rising rate of gang-connected homicide in major cities.

A more relevant question than "Did the civil-rights movement of the 1960s 'politicize' the gang?" would be "What *was* the impact of the movement on gangs in general and black gangs in particular?" A comprehensive analysis of this issue would have to entertain, among other results, the idea that one product of the movement was an important addition to the language used by some to characterize gang behavior. Many blacks and some Spanish-Americans—both gang members and others—added an important new kind of justificational vocabulary to the repertoire of traditional modes for explaining gang activity (see Sykes and Matza 1957; Matza 1964, chap. 10). This new vocabulary incorporated basic ideological tenets of the black rights movement and applied to customary forms of gang behavior concepts such as exploitation by the power structure, restitution for past injustices, brutalization by the system, and the like.[9] It is particularly important in this context to distinguish verbal behavior from actual practice. Black gang members continue, by and large, to do much the same kinds of things, but for some there have been changes in the ways they characterize and justify these practices. This must be seen as one effect on gangs of the civil rights movement, but it is not the kind of effect required to produce a new type of ideologically activistic gang.

## Transformation through Enhanced Experience: Gangs and Drug Use

During the urban crisis era a prime candidate for *the* paramount youth problem of the times (and as such subject to intensive attention and concern by the media, professionals, and the public) was the use of drugs. Given a widespread perception that "drug abuse" had become endemic among youth, it was perhaps inevitable that youth gangs be perceived in these terms. In fact, the prospect of increased drug use by gang members was suggested as early as the 1950s, on the basis of theoretical premises similar to those which produced predictions of the "politicized" gang and which served in part to motivate researchers to search for "drug-using" or "drug-addicted" gangs.[10] The predicted emergence of such gangs as a major new development, as was the case for predictions of politicized gangs, failed to materialize, although in both instances it has been possible to characterize a relatively small proportion of all gangs in these terms (Russell n.d.; Klein and Phillips 1968).

The issue of drug use by gangs provides a clear example of a process whereby a phenomenon perceived as a reigning social ill is granted great power to affect sundry other phenomena. During the urban crisis era drug use figured as a major element in a scheme used to explain both the death *and* rebirth of "the fighting gang." This formulation—which in some quarters, especially the New York area, became part of the conventional folklore of gangs—runs as follows. The fighting gangs of the 1950s were knocked out (sometimes snuffed out) by the advent of hard drugs, particularly heroin. Gang members took to heroin primarily out of frustration engendered by the exclusionism of a discriminatory society which afforded them only a few modes of response to their frustration, among which fighting and drug-use figured prominently. Thus, when gang fighting was made less practicable by police pressures, less untrammelled by social-work intervention, and less modish by an ascendancy of "cool" over "heart" as a valued quality, gang members were virtually forced into drug use as one of their few remaining outlets.

Then in the 1960s the intensification of civil rights activities provided a new outlet for their frustrated energies, and they abandoned heroin for political activism. Through the civil rights movement they came to realize that one *could* take action against the system instead of retreating into drugs, that the drug traffic was another means used by the power structure to exploit the poor, and that it served the interest of the establishment to cripple potential activists by pressing them into addiction. By the late 1960s the antidrug ethic of the gang members had become so powerful that they became increasingly frustrated by the apparently deliberate ineffectiveness of officialdom in coping with the problem and were thus impelled, again in line with the new activism, to *themselves* undertake the policing functions necessary to purge their communities of drugs. However, once having re-formed their gangs for these purposes, rather than devoting their aggressive energies to driving out the pushers and exposing the corrupt policemen, they began to direct them instead—for reasons not fully understood—toward their fellow gang members. Thus occurred a rebirth of a pattern of intergang violence much like the one that had been abandoned ten years before—with frustration-engendered violence intensified, if anything, by the failure of the recently attempted activism to effect any really significant changes in the social order.

The need for devising this rather imaginative scenario—fighting gang to narcoticized gang to politicized gang to fighting gang in ten years—was brought about, as shown earlier, by a prevalent impression that gangs had somehow flourished, been knocked out, and then revived—an impression not supported by available evidence. Note also that this explanation, while pivoting on drug use as its major dynamic, also works in the notion of politicization, just discussed. As is always the case for conventional-wisdom explanations of this kind, there are important elements of factual accuracy interwoven throughout its fabric. The problem of drug use in gangs can be more profitably addressed, however, through the question "What *was* the impact of increasing use and availability of drugs among American adolescents?" Analysis should encompass the situation not only of black gangs and/or the New York City area, and the use of hard drugs only, but the use of various types of drugs by the range of different kinds of gangs in all sections of the country.

The increased availability of certain drugs appears to have fitted quite readily into an established niche. The "versatile repertoire" of gang activities noted earlier traditionally involves the use of what might be called "experience enhancing" substances, a practice arising quite naturally from the "excitement" focal concern of the adolescent subculture which serves as a major influence on gang behavior (Miller, forthcoming). Such substances serve largely to enhance and facilitate participation in a range of activities such as mating and recreational activities. For the average gang member the use of such substances is governed by relatively simple criteria; he wants something which is easy to get and which will provide a quick but not too potent "high" at minimum cost. Traditionally these criteria have been met primarily by alcoholic substances, principally beer. However, use of drug and/or narcotic substances, particularly those involving easier-to-obtain substances (pills, glue, "bennies," cough medicine containing codeine) has been familiar to gang members in many locales for quite some time. Such gangs have often employed a pragmatic "mix" of alcohol and drugs. A major consequence of the increasing acceptability of drug use among adolescents (principally of marijuana) and the concomitant increased availability of certain drugs (again, primarily, marijuana) has been to increase the proportion of drugs to alcohol in the drug–alcohol mix of many gangs.

Increases in the extent of drug use by both gang and nongang adolescents have been accompanied by the development of serious misconceptions on the part of many adults. The fact that many gang members use drugs to greater or lesser degrees makes it possible to talk of "drug-using" gangs. This does not mean, however, that drug use is the central or defining activity of any significant proportion of gangs, any more than the almost universal use of alcohol justifies the term "the drinking gang" as a primary designation. Moreover, outside of some inevitable experimentation, the most common types of drugs used by gang members are the "soft" drugs, primarily marijuana and "pills." Heroin is rare and "psychedelic" drugs such as LSD even rarer.[11] Furthermore, as is the case for the adolescent population in general, alcohol remains far and away the most common form of experience-enhancing substance for gang members, with beer, the traditional staple, the most common form of alcohol.[12] Also, contrary to one prevalent notion, most gang members do not turn to drugs as a vehicle of withdrawal, passive escape, "dropping out," or "retreatism" but rather use them in much the same fashion and for much the same purposes as alcohol—to enhance or heighten the quality of active involvement with music, courtship, adventure-seeking, group conversation, eating and drinking, and other traditional gang pursuits.

An additional important point concerns the relationship of gang-member drug use to criminal behavior. The possession and/ or use of narcotic substances for nonmedical purposes is in itself illegal in many jurisdictions. It is not this kind of law violation which poses a major problem for law enforcement agencies, however, but those forms of traditional youth crime such as robbery, burglary, and violent offenses which may be related to drug use. In practice, as in the case of youthful drinking, police seldom take action on the basis of drug "use" or "possession" alone, if those using marijuana or other "soft" drugs do not at the same time engage in other more disruptive forms of behavior.[13]

What *is* the relationship of gang-member drug use to other forms of crime? Two apparently inconsistent positions are current. The first sees drug use as inhibiting crime, the second as enhancing it. The inhibition position argues that drug use serves as a surrogate for more serious forms of crime, in that drug users, unlike drinkers, are generally content with legally benign activities such as "digging" sounds or "rapping," whereas alcohol serves to spur more "aggressive" activities such as fighting, car theft, or dangerous driving. The enhancement position argues from a well-established "conventional wisdom" formulation which sees the use of relatively inexpensive "soft" drugs inevitably leading to costly "hard" drugs and the necessity for those thus addicted to engage in serious forms of non-"use" crimes in order to support their habits.

Neither the inhibition nor the enhancement positions, whatever their degree of validity, appear to have much application to gang-member crime. Although evidence in this area is fragmentary, it would appear quite tentatively that patterns of criminal activity (theft, assault, and so on) of contemporary gangs who may use drugs in greater or lesser measure do not differ significantly from those of analogous gangs in the predrug period.[14] A major factor here is that the pattern of drug use among typical gang members (mostly "soft" drugs) is not very costly and thus does not provide the incentive for intensified involvement in robbery or burglary postulated by the enhancement position as a major element in the behavior of hard-core addicts in communities such as Harlem or Berkeley. Certainly the contemporary gangs of Philadelphia, the Bronx, and Los Angeles are not abstaining from violence as a consequence of drug use (inhibition position), and there is little evidence which links rising rates of robbery and burglary with increases in the use of drugs by gang members (enhancement position.)[15]

It is significant that two of the inaccurately predicted or perceived bases of transformation of the American youth gang—politicization and narcoticization—accord with theoretical premises of the "counterculture" movement which enjoyed considerable currency among some proportion of college-level youth during the 1960s. Evidence from the present study indicating that neither the political/ideological nor the drug-use orientations represents significant developments among youth gangs recruited primarily from lower- and working-class populations constitutes one important kind of evidence that the influence of a "counterculture" was of a very low order among that portion of the population represented by youth gang members.

## Conclusion: Cyclical Elaboration and Perceptions of Newness

Conclusions drawn from this examination of American youth gangs in the urban crisis era afford an unusual opportunity to address the issue of change and stability in gangs, since major developments of this period would appear, on their face, to have harbored an unusual potential for altering established societal forms. Three developments in particular might have been expected to have had an especially significant impact on gangs. First, a marked increase in the acceptability and availability of drugs—because this exerted its most direct influence on persons in those age categories from which gangs most typically recruit. Second, a period of unusually intense activity involving race relations—since its most violent and dramatic events transpired in those locales where gangs are most typically found. Third, a vogue for an ideologically based rebellion against established forms—the "counterculture" movement—because it found its primary adherents among the young, depicted as "alienated" many persons whose behavior failed to conform to conventional middle-class ideals, and aimed to erode established forms, among which the gang must be counted.

This paper has concluded that, in common with others of this period, none of these developments, despite their potential for effecting change, had very much impact on American youth gangs. At the beginning of the period youth gangs, some quite violent, flourished throughout the nation, particularly in slum areas of the largest urban centers; at the end, youth gangs, some quite violent, flourished throughout the nation, particularly in slum areas of the largest cities. The basic forms and characteristic pursuits of these gangs, while certainly reflecting the changing fashions of the larger adolescent subculture, showed a high degree of continuity. If one grants validity to this conclusion, two additional questions at once present themselves. First, why do gangs persist, and why do their characteristic pursuits retain considerable stability in the face of changing circumstances? Second, how can one account for recurring representations that gangs have been substantially changed, radically transformed, or even extinguished entirely?

Answers to the first question can be presented here only in the most condensed form (see Miller 1971, and forthcoming). The youth gang remains as a persisting form because it is a product of a set of conditions that lie close to the basic building blocks of our social order. These include the necessary division of labor between the family and the peer group in the socialization of adolescents, the masculinity and collective-action emphases of the male subculture, the stress on excitement, congregation, and mating in the adolescent subculture, the importance of tough-ness, smartness, and trouble in the subcultures of lower-status populations, the density conditions and territoriality patterns which figure in the subcultures of urban and urbanized locales. It is these social conditions and their related subcultures which, taken in conjunction, generate the American youth gang, and, insofar as these conditions and subcultural concerns retain con-tinuity through time, so does the gang—their product—retain continuity.

How, then, to account for recurring perceptions that gangs come and go, and that current manifestations represent "new" forms? The average youth gang, as has been shown, is a "general-ized" rather than a specialized form, with a versatile rather than constricted repertoire of activities. Gangs, in common with other generalized and versatile societal forms, are sensitive to a wide variety of environmental developments, which are reflected in periodic modifications in gang characteristics (Miller 1959). These modifications, however, for the most part take the form of *stylistic elaborations* of existing forms and practices rather than "inventions"—genuinely original additions to or changes in tradi-tional features. Insofar as particular gangs devote significant portions of their energies to such elaborations, they move toward the "specialization" pole of a generalized-specialized continuum.

The fate of these elaborations varies. In some instances they remain localized; in others they spread to gangs in other areas through media publicization and other means. In the 1950s some gangs in other cities emulated, in varying degrees, the New York fighting-gang model; in the 1970s some New York gangs began to pursue the intensified patterns of homicide by firearms developed in Philadelphia some five years before. The bulk of the elabora-tions—especially those involving extreme manifestations of a form or practice—are relatively short-lived. Sometimes the more extreme manifestations leave a residue in the form of a more moderate version of the elaboration, as a vogue for intensive use of hard drugs in certain gangs was transmuted over time to a more moderate use of soft drugs as a continuing component of the gangs' repertoire of experience-enhancing substances. By and large gangs do not sustain for long those elaborations whose continued practice threatens to make substantially more difficult the conduct of other components of their customary patterns of activity.[16]

Once a type of elaboration achieves a sufficient degree of

development it begins to engage the attention of nongang societal agencies, which then undertake a characteristic set of responsive actions which in turn are reacted to by gangs as part of a complex process of mutual feedback and interactive influence. Among these agencies are those of control (police, probation agents), social service (social workers, youth workers), and government (elected officials, bureau personnel). Agencies whose responses bear most directly on the perception-of-newness phenomenon are the communications/information specialists, primarily media writers and social analysts. To professionals in these fields, "newness" is money in the bank, and "not-much-different-than-before" is of negligible value. Since the investment in newness as a salable commodity is generally coupled with a short time-perspective, periodic elaborations of gang behavior are seized upon and marketed not as recurrent stylistic variations in a continuing pattern but as the new, the spectacular, the sensational.

Throughout the progression of recurrent elaborations youth gangs continually scan, select from, modify, and absorb available subcultural materials and, as the new gang of today's writer becomes the old gang of tomorrow's historian, continue to thrive as a vital and adaptive form. Youth gangs in the urban crisis era show marked similarities to their predecessors in the earlier periods described by McKay.

## Notes

1. Interviews with officials of the New York City Police Department Planning Division, and of the Youth Services Agency of the Human Resources Administration, November, 1970. Police figures indicating a twentyfold increase in three and one-half years in the number of groups recognized by the police as "gangs," and a fiftyfold increase in the number designated as gang members (December 1969, 18 gangs, 380 members; July 1973, 348 gangs, 19,000 members), strongly suggest that what had changed was not so much the number of congregating youth groups as the willingness of the police to designate such groups as "gangs" on the basis of particular kinds of activities.

2. Direct field observation by the author.

3. As noted by Short (1968: 10) comprehensive studies of the numbers, sizes, and characteristic activity patterns of gangs in larger geographical areas (metropolitan areas, countries, states, regions) are virtually nonexistent. So far as is known, the present report on gangs in the Boston metropolitan area, while substantially falling short of the degree of depth and comprehensiveness necessary to an adequate study,

is the first published report based on a survey of all named communities in a standard metropolitan statistical area.

4. U.S. Bureau of the Census, 1960. Categorization of towns and cities is based on population counts of the federal censuses of 1960 and 1970 and the Massachusetts state census of 1965.

5. Sources of presently reported empirical findings include a ten-year study by the author of youth gangs in inner-city Boston, a five-year study of urban and suburban delinquency in the eastern Massachusetts metropolitan area, and a series of irregularly recurrent site visits of varying durations to approximately 220 American urban area communities in twenty-one states outside the areas just cited. These include six of the ten largest cities, and nine of the twenty largest.

6. Figures presented in Miller (1975) provide estimates that the number of police-identified gangs in the nation's five largest cities ranges between 740 and 2,700, and the number of gang members between 28,450 and 81,500 (table 15). These numbers would appear as an absolute floor for the current number of gangs and gang members in major cities.

7. For the three-year period between 1972 and 1974 Philadelphia led in the rate of gang-connected homicides (number of police-reported homicides per year per 10,000 male youth) with a rate of 7.4, followed by Los Angeles (6.0), Chicago (3.5), and New York (2.1) (Miller 1975, table 16).

8. This conclusion is based on an examination of accounts of "trigger events" sufficiently detailed as to yield evidence of gang participation in the case of approximately 130 civil disorders occurring between 1963 and 1968.

9. An example is furnished by a member of the Young Lords of Chicago: "You got to understand, man, that even *before* [our gang turned to activism] we were in some ways already revolutionary, dig? . . . what we were doing as a gang *had* to be against the capitalist institutions that are oppressing us" (Browning 1970).

10. Cloward and Ohlin (1960) provide the basis of two formulations; one, that the "bopping" gang would be replaced by the drug-centered gang (p. 183), and, two, that habitual use of hard narcotics and gang membership are incompatible (see also Wilmer, Rosenfeld et al. 1957). Neither of these formulations was borne out by the events of the next decade. Gangs appropriately characterizable as "drug-centered" appeared to be rare or nonexistent (Short and Strodtbeck 1965: 11–13), and the notion that drugs would replace gang fighting was badly weakened by the fact that gang violence remained prevalent in Philadelphia and Chicago during a period when drug use was increasing. An increase in drugs was accompanied by a decrease in gang violence in New York City during the 1960s, but in the 1970s gang violence again increased, with little commensurate decrease in drug use. A Spanish area of Los Angeles containing an active network of fighting gangs in the 1970s was "saturated with drugs."

11. Thrasher notes the "drug addict" as a type of gang member in the 1920s (Thrasher 1927: 340). Klein and Phillips report a peak of heroin

use and/or experimentation by members of white gangs in Queens County, N.Y., around 1953, with a subsequent decline in use of "hard" drugs (Klein and Phillips 1968). Varying use-patterns are reported in Wilmer, Rosenfeld et al. 1957; Klein and Phillips 1968; Chien 1956; Markham 1972.

12. A review of findings of a variety of local and national-level studies shows that approximately 85 percent of gang-age (ca. 12–18) youth reported no experience whatever with any form of narcotic drug and that "serious" or habitual use and/or any experience with "hard" drugs was reported by 5 percent or fewer. Reported use of alcohol was far higher; while 40 percent of one sample of older (15–18) adolescents reported some experience with drugs the previous year (only 3 percent claimed "habitual" use), 93 percent reported use of alcohol.

13. Despite claims that drug use has become an increasingly serious problem for suburban police, of 305 juvenile and youth violations reported by police in selected Boston suburbs during 325 evening hours in the late 1960s, 24 percent involved drinking, and only 1 (0.3 percent) drug use (Miller 1968). In one Massachusetts community, of forty-six high school students reported to have used drugs during the previous year, not one was booked on any drug charge (Gelineau et al. 1970).

14. Chien and his associates found little impact of drug use on involvement in traditional offenses (Wilmer, Rosenfeld et al. 1957). One recent study reports with respect to "acts of vandalism, shoplifting, stealing from institutions, stealing from individuals, fighting, being picked up and/or booked by the police [on nondrug charges] [involvement by drug users is] far higher than other young people" (Gelineau et al. 1970), suggesting a relationship of drug use to volume rather than character of crime.

15. Despite wide acceptance of the thesis that increasing rates of crime (particularly burglary and robbery) are attributable primarily or largely to addicts driven to constant theft to "support their habits" and the patent plausibility of the claimed relationship, little reliable evidence has been presented as to just *what* proportion of crime increases can be attributed to addict theft. One of the few careful studies of the crime-drugs relationship shows that of 441 adults arrested for "index-crimes" in 1971 by Chicago police, only about 12 percent were known to have any "narcotics involvement or background" (City of Chicago Department of Police 1971).

16. The relation between periodic elaborations by particular gangs, responses by external agencies, impact of these responses by external agencies, impact of these responses on gangs, impact of gang responses on further responses, and so on, is extremely complex. Elaborations in the area of illegal behavior, particularly violent forms, are most likely to engender strong responses, and their appearance brings into play actions by police, social agencies, government, and others aimed at their inhibition or extinction. Such actions appear under some circumstances to reinforce elaborations, under others to inhibit them, under others to produce an initial enhancement followed by a diminution, in complex combinations. Results of a limited number of alternative responses are discussed in Klein (1971).

## References

Baskin et al.
1972        *The Long, Hot Summer. An Analysis of Summer Disorders.* Lemberg Center, Report no. 2.

Blank, J.
1968        "Make Way for the Real Great Society." *National Civic Review*, December.

Blumberg, A., ed.
1974        *Current Perspectives on Criminal Behavior.* New York, Knopf.

Bragonier, R.
1972        "The 'Pres' of the Reapers: A New Style City Street Gang." *Life*, August 25.

Breasted, M.
1973        "Youth Gangs and Their Crimes Growing Steadily." *New York Times*, July 2.

Browning, F.
1970        "From Rumble to Revolution: The Young Lords." *Ramparts*, September.

Buckley, T.
1966        "Fighting Gangs Vanish from the City's Ghettos." *New York Times*, June 26.

Chien, I.
1956        "Narcotics Use among Juveniles." *Social Work* 7 (April).

City of Chicago Department of Police
1971        "Index Crime-Narcotic Involvement or Background." Criminal Investigations Division.

*Civil Disorder Digest*
1969        Vol. 1, no. 1 (September). Cambridge, Mass: Civil Disorder Research Institute.

Cloward, R., and Ohlin, L.
1960        *Delinquency and Opportunity: A Theory of Delinquent Gangs.* Glencoe, Ill., Free Press.

*Detroit Free Press*
1973        Detroit, Michigan, November 30.

Gannon, T.
1967        "Dimensions of Current Gang Delinquency." *Journal of Research in Crime and Delinquency* 4:2 (January).

Geis, G.
1965          *Juvenile Gangs*. President's Committee on Juvenile
              Delinquency and Youth Crime.

Gelineau, V., et al.
1970          "Portrait of a Suburban Community." Mass. Divi-
              sion of Drug Rehabilitation.

Hoenig, G.
1973          "Turf: Where the Reapers are Supreme." *New
              York Times Magazine*, November 4.

Hubbard
1969          "Five Long, Hot Summers and How They Grew."
              *Public Interest*.

Jansen, D.
1972          "Violence by Youth Gangs Found Rising in Three
              Cities." *New York Times*, April 15.

King, S. L.
1971          "Supermarkets Hub of Suburbs." *New York Times*,
              February 7.

Klein, J., and Phillips, D.
1968          "From Hard to Soft Drugs: Temporal and Substan-
              tive Changes in Drug Usage among Gangs in a
              Working-Class Community." *Journal of Health
              and Social Behavior* 9 (June).

Klein, M., ed.
1967          *Juvenile Gangs in Context: Theory, Research and
              Action*. Englewood Cliffs, N.J. Prentice-Hall.
1969          "Violence in American Juvenile Gangs." In Mulvi-
              hill and Tumin, *Crimes of Violence*. National
              Commission on Causes and Prevention of Violence,
              13: 1428.
1971          *Street Gangs and Street Workers*. Englewood
              Cliffs, N.J., Prentice-Hall.

Kneeland, D.
1971          "Youth Rebellion of Sixties Waning." *New York
              Times*, October 23.

Kunen, J.
1973          "The Rebels of '70." *New York Times Magazine*,
              October 28.

Lachman, S., and Singer, B.
1968          *The Detroit Riot of July 1966*. Detroit: Behavior
              Research Institute.

Laing, J.
1969        "A Chicago Gang Strives for Potency but Clings to
            Violence." *Wall Street Journal*, September 15.

Markham
1972        "Youth Turning from Use of Heroin to Other
            Drugs." *New York Times*, December 24.

Marx
1970        "Issueless Riots." *Annals* 391.

Matza, D.
1964        *Delinquency and Drift*. New York, John Wiley.

McKay, H.
1949        "The Neighborhood and Child Conduct." *The
            Annals of the American Academy of Political and
            Social Science* 26, 32–41.

McPherson, J.
1969        "Chicago's Blackstone Rangers." *Atlantic Monthly*,
            May.

Miller, W.
1956        "The Place of the Organized Club in Corner-
            Group-Work Method." Roxbury Youth Project,
            unpublished report.
1957        "The Impact of a Community Group Work Pro-
            gram on Delinquent Corner Groups. *Social Service
            Review* 31 (December).
1958        "Lower Class Culture as a Generating Milieu of
            Gang Delinquency." *Journal of Social Issues* 14.
1959        "Preliminary Theroetical Orientations, to the Study
            of Gang Delinquency." *International Newsletter of
            Mental Health* 1 (October).
1966        "Violent Crimes in City Gangs." *Annals of the
            American Academy of Political and Social Science*
            364 (March).
1968        "A Preliminary Report on Urban and Suburban
            Delinquency." MIT-Harvard Center for Urban
            Studies, unpublished report.
1969        "White Gangs." *Trans-action* 6 (September 11–26).
1971        "Subculture, Social Reform and the 'Culture of
            Poverty." *Human Organization*, Summer.
1975        "Violence by Youth Gangs and Youth Groups as a
            Crime Problem in Major American Cities." U.S.
            Department of Justice Law Enforcement Assis-
            tance Administration. August 1975.
Forthcoming *City Gangs*. New York, John Wiley.

Mouat, L.
1966          "Teen Gangs Vie for Reputations." *Christian Science Monitor*, November 12.

New York City Police Department
1969          Annual Report, Youth Aid Division.

*New York Times*
1968          "Rival Park Slope Bands Battle Two Hours." July 24.
1971          "5 Hurt in Fights Inside Washington High." February 20.
1971          "Street Gang Chief is Slain in the Bronx." December 3.
1972          "Stabbing of Washington High School Student Points Up a Resurgence of Youth-Gang Violence in City." April 19.
1972          "Lindsay Terms the Gang Situation Well Under Control." May 10.

Pennsylvania Crime Commission
1969          *Gang Violence in Philadelphia*. Harrisburg, Penna.: Department of Justice, July 31.

*Philadelphia Bulletin*
1970          Frank Rizzo's Testimony to the U.S. House of Representatives Select Committee on Crime, July 16.

Poston, R. W.
1971          *The Gang and the Establishment*. New York, Harper and Row.

Rae, G.
1972          "Rat Packs." *Man Magazine*, Spring.

Report of the National Advisory Commission on Civil Disorders
1968

Rudwick, E. M.
1966          *Race Riot at East St. Louis, July 2, 1917*. Cleveland, Meridian Books.

Russell
n.d.          "'The Mob'; A 'Participant Observation' Study of a Drug-oriented, Non-addicted Peer Group." Special Projects Section, National Institute of Mental Health, Adelphi, Md.

Segerberg, O.
1972          "Watch Out for the Mini-Muggers." *New York*.

Shaw, C. and McKay, H.
1942        *Juvenile Delinquency and Urban Areas*. Revised
1969        edition, ed. James F. Short, Jr. University of Chi-
            cago Press.

Short, J. F., Jr., ed.
1968        *Gang Delinquency and Delinquent Subcultures*.
            Harper and Row.
1974        "Gangs, Politics, and the Social Order." Chap. 5 in
            present volume.

Short, J., and Strodtbeck, F.
1965        *Group Process and Gang Delinquency*. University
            of Chicago Press.

Stevens, S.
1971        "The Rat Packs of New York." *New York Times
            Magazine*, November 28.

Sykes, G., and Matza, D.
1957        "Techniques of Neutralization: A Theory of Delin-
            quency." *American Sociological Review* 22 (De-
            cember).

Thrasher
1927        *The Gang: A Study of 1,313 Gangs in Chicago*.
            University of Chicago Press.

Tolchin, M.
1973        "Gangs Spread Terror in the South Bronx." *New
            York Times*, January 16.

United States Bureau of the Census
1960        *Census of Population and Housing: PHC (1)–18,
            Census Tracts*, Boston, Mass.

Von Hoffman, N.
1966        "Mighty Blackstone: A 'Nation' in Chicago." *Wash-
            ington Post*, December 23.

Webber, T.
1969        "The Real Great Society and the Reformers' 'War
            on Poverty.'" Honors Thesis, Harvard College.

Weingartern, G.
1972        "East Bronx Story—Return of the Street Gangs."
            *New York*, March 27.

Wilmer, Rosenfeld et al.
1957        "Heroin Use and Street Gangs." *Journal of Crimi-
            nal Law, Criminology and Police Science* 48, no. 4.

Wolfgang, Marvin E.
1968        "Violence, U.S.A.! Riots and Crime." *Crime and Delinquency* 14, no. 4 (October).

Wright, R.
1972        "Rise in Youth Gang Killings Alarms Police in Three Cities." *New York Times*, November 27.

Yablonsky, L.
1963        *The Violent Gang*. New York, Macmillan.

# 5     Gangs, Politics,
and the Social Order

*James F. Short, Jr.*

"The importance of the gang as a social factor
which the politician manipulates has never been fully appre-
ciated except by the politician." So wrote Robert A. Woods in
1898. Despite the vintage of this statement (which I found in
sociology's "old green Bible," Park and Burgess's *Introduction to
the Science of Sociology*, first published in 1921) the subject of
gangs and politics has received remarkably little scholarly attention. Asbury (1927) and Thrasher (1927, 1963) remarked the
historical relationship, and the fact that gangs of the day often
developed the "ability to trade some advantage in the way of
votes, influence, money, or what not, with the politicans in
return for subsidies, immunities and so on"; but by the late 1930s
election reform and the decline of at least some political machines
had weakened the relationship. New interest has emerged in
recent years, but systematic study has lagged behind popular
concern, as evidenced by congressional hearings and press coverage. Recent social trends compel renewed and systematic attention to this topic and to the relation of gangs to the social order.
This chapter concerns these trends and their relation to the
nature of gangs, political realities, and problems associated with
relating the two.

Five recent trends seem especially important in understanding
many "social problems," including the very definition of what is
considered problematic. These five are : the civil rights movement; the youth movement; the revitalization of pluralism and of
participatory democracy; the increasingly political nature of
social issues and what we have traditionally thought of as "social
problems;" and the overriding importance of rapid social change.
While these are likely to be familiar to most socially aware

people, their relevance in the context of this paper probably is less familiar.

1. *The civil rights movement* of post–World War II, has many phases and variations; in the present context I refer to the surge of militancy which extends not only to blacks and women, Chicanos, American Indians, Puerto Ricans and native Hawaiians but also to persons on welfare and so-called "deviant" groups, such as homosexuals and marijuana users. And I include a variety of countermovements.

The civil rights movement was influential during the 1950s and '60s in exposing young people to a major domestic social problem on an unprecedented scale. Young people were thrust into the front lines—at times literally—in the struggle of black people for housing, education, and jobs, and for integration of public facilities. Those in militant opposition to this struggle often were young, as well. Black and white youths fought countless battles in countless neighborhoods undergoing racial transition. Field observations from our Chicago research during the late 1950s and early 1960s and reports from other cities suggest that these encounters often had a game-like quality, as though the combatants were playing out a script handed them by their elders, but with distinct youth culture features. Except for situational details, these encounters were the results of forces beyond the control of either adults or young people on the scene—urban congestion and segregation, economic and political forces extending beyond city boundaries. On the scene, however, the issues were immediate and the behavior of young and old alike was ennobled by appeal to common sentiments. Whites defended their neighborhoods, schools and churches, public beaches and swimming pools, and white womanhood.

While white gangs occasionally were active in opposing organized civil rights demonstrations (as was the case when civil rights groups sought to integrate previously all-white beaches on Chicago's South Side in summer, 1961; see Short and Strodtbeck, 1965, pp. 193–94), their opposition most often took the form of spontaneous incidents in the course of normal play activity. An incident which occurred on Chicago's South Side in the fall of 1959 is illustrative:

> At approximately 12:30 at night, the worker was loitering with a group of teenage white kids at the corner of the park

which is immediately across the street from the church. The group was a mixed one of boys and girls ranging in age from 16 to 20. There were approximately 15–20 teenagers and, for the most part, they were sitting or reclining in the park, talking, drinking beer, boys wrestling playfully with girls. I had parked my car adjacent to where the group was gathered and was leaning on the fender of my auto talking to two youths about the remainder of the softball season. The group consisted of members of the Amboys, Bengals, Sharks, and a few Mafia. They were not unusually loud or boisterous this particular hot and humid evening because a policeman on a three-wheeler had been by a half-hour earlier and had warned them of the lateness of the hour.

I noticed a solitary teenage figure ambling along on the sidewalk, heading toward the avenue. I paid no particular heed, thinking it was just another teenager walking over to join the park group. However, as the figure neared the group, he made no effort to swerve over and join the group but continued by with no sign of recognition. This was an oddity, so I watched the youth as he passed the gathered teenagers and neared the curb where I was sitting on my car fender. At this point, I suddenly realized that the teenager was black and in danger if detected. I did not dare do or say anything for fear of alerting the teenagers sitting in the park, and for a few moments I thought the youth could pass by without detection. However, a Bengal who had been drinking beer spotted the youth and immediately asked some of the other teenagers, "Am I drunk or is that a Nigger on the corner?" The attention of the entire group was then focused on the black youth, who by this time had stepped off the curb and was walking in the center of the street toward the opposite curb. The youth was oblivious to everything and was just strolling along as if without a care in the world. Behind him, however, consternation and anger arose spontaneously. Muttered threats of "Let's kill the bastard," "Get the mother-fucker," "Come on, let's get going," were heard. Even the girls in the crowd readily and verbally agreed.

Within seconds, approximately a dozen youths arose and began running in the direction of the black youngster. I realized that I was unable to stem the tide of enraged teenagers, so I yelled out to the youth something to the effect of "Hey man, look alive!" The boy heard as he paused in mid-stride, but did not turn around. Again I shouted a warning as the white teenagers were rapidly overtaking him. At my second outcry, the black youth turned and saw the white teenagers closing in on him. Without hesitation, he took off at full speed with the white mob at his heels yelling shouts of "Kill the black bastard—don't let him get away!"

I remained standing by my car and was joined by three Amboys who did not participate in the chase. The president of the Amboys sadly shook his head, stating that his guys reacted like a bunch of kids whenever they saw a colored guy and openly expressed his wish that the boy would get away. Another, in an alibi tone of voice excused his non-participation in the chase by explaining that he couldn't run fast enough to catch anybody. He merely stated that the black youth didn't bother him, so why should he be tossed in jail for the assault of a stranger.

As we stood by the car, we could hear the actual progress of the chase from the next block. There were shouts and outcries as the pursued ran, his whereabouts echoed by the bedlam created by his pursuers. Finally, there was silence and in approximately fifteen minutes the guys began to straggle back from the chase. As they returned to my car and to the girls sitting nearby, each recited his share of the chase. Barney laughingly related that Guy had hurdled a parked car in an effort to tackle the black, who had swerved out into the street. He said that he himself had entered a coal yard, looking around in an effort to find where the boy had hidden, when an adult from a second floor back porch warned that he had better get out of there as the coal yard was protected by a large and vicious Great Dane.

The black youth apparently had decided that he couldn't outrun his tormentors and had begun to go in and out of back yards until he was able to find a hiding place, at which point he disappeared. His pursuers then began to make a systematic search of the alleys, garages, back yards, corridors, etc. The boys were spurred on to greater efforts by the adults of the area who offered advice and encouragement. One youth laughingly related that a woman, from her bedroom window, kept pointing out probable hiding places in her back yard so that the youth below would not overlook any sanctuary. This advice included looking behind tall shrubbery by the fence, on top of a tool crib by the alley and underneath the back porch. Other youths related similar experiences as the adults along the avenue entered gleefully in the "hide and seek." Glen related that, as the youths turned onto the avenue, he began to shout to the people ahead in the block that "a Nigger was coming" so that someone ahead might catch or at least head off the black youth. The other pursuers also took up the hue and cry (John LaMotte, field report).

Such incidents had little impact on black gangs whose turf was deep in the ghetto and who in any case were little affected by the momentous civil rights developments of this era. The contrast between black and white gang boys in this respect was striking. For both, gangs represented essentially a street world, a transitional stage to adulthood. Some of the white boys were beginning to associate with the "social and athletic clubs" which have become traditional in their communities, often serving as an important link to the political structure. A few would drift away from such associations altogether, moving on to college, business, or professions. For black gang boys, however, prospects for stable jobs and connections with the political and economic power structure were bleak, indeed. They perceived legitimate educational and occupational opportunities as much less open than did the white gang boys (and still less than nongang boys and middle-class boys of both races; see Short, Rivera, and Tennyson 1965). They regarded local adults in business, education, and politics as less interested in teenagers and less helpful than did the other boys (Short, Rivera, and Marshall 1966). Yet they were more firmly embedded in the local cultural milieu, and the adults with whom they had the most contact were both less successful occupationally and less interested in youth problems (Rivera and Short 1967a, b).

Throughout the period of our most intensive observation of Chicago's youth gangs system (from June 1959 through August 1962), we had been impressed with the lack of political and social awareness and involvement displayed by the black gang boys, despite feverish political and civil rights activities during the Kennedy–Nixon campaign of 1960 and the emergence in Chicago during this period of such activist organizations as the Nation of Islam and The Woodlawn Organization. The boys were neither informed nor concerned with these matters, judging from many hours of informal observation by our research team, and they expressed only the vaguest comments when directly questioned. Unlike several other problem areas in their lives—such as jobs, education, relations with girls, marriage, keeping out of trouble— they never spontaneously asked detached workers or our graduate student observers about matters related either to politics or civil rights.[1]

The lack of interest in political matters puzzled us, and we sought means to determine how the boys would react to communication of a particularly shocking political message. Rita James Simon suggested we take members of a gang to see a Swedish motion picture of Hitler's *Mein Kampf*, which was playing at a local theater, and that observers accompany them to the movie and afterwards to our University of Chicago offices where we occasionally brought the boys for entertainment, food, and a variety of research tasks. The outcome of this "experiment" can be summarized as follows:

> A dozen members of the Senior Rattlers went to the movie and afterwards willingly returned to "the research" for the inevitable soft drinks and hot dogs. Very little conversation took place in the cars following the movie. We wondered if the starkly racist view of der Fuehrer had shocked the boys. Soon, however, they were shuckin' and jivin' about the usual street matters. Over refreshments the question was put, "What did you think of Hitler?" The response at first was one of silence—a perhaps too abrupt change of pace from concerns of the moment. Finally, one of the boys said, "Man, anybody crossed *that* cat got burned." Everyone laughed in agreement and the conversation continued in terms of the street fighting about which they talked so often—a more familiar and immediate context for burning.

Other scholarly observers agree that civil rights and other political and social movements of the late 1950s and early '60s had little direct impact on most black gangs (Miller, in this volume; Suttles 1972, Kalberg and Suttles 1974; Spergel 1969, 1973). But the impact on others, including their perceptions of gangs, was considerable. That impact was enhanced by another "movement" of the times, the youth movement (as distinguished from any of its many variants).

2. *The youth movement*. Members of this younger generation, like their predecessors and contemporaries virtually the world over, have their detractors among their elders and the not so old, for shortcomings both real and imagined. But the generation game these days is played with a profound ambivalence. Even the shrillest voices among the disenchanted with the young recognize, and scholarly research confirms, the continuity of generations—the debt for both vices and virtues owed to parental generations by those of their children. While many youths may

be in "revolt"—individually and/or collectively—the overall picture clearly is colored more strongly by continuity than by radical departure, except perhaps among the most revolting (no pun intended).

Perhaps even more important, we are, as a society, so obsessed with "thinking young," and with attempting to *be* young, that the cutting edge of youth criticism has been blunted; and the opening of the society to fuller participation by youth continues apace. The eighteen-year-old vote was an important wedge, politically, but it was preceded by increased political activity and influence even without the franchise and by extended freedoms and institutional influence in other sectors as well.

Coupled with the civil rights movement, the youth movement has tremendous power and special significance for the ghetto. For while the civil rights movement of the '50s was dominated by middle-class and, particularly, by white college students, in black communities during the '60s an important thrust came from high school youth. While scholarly attention has been scant, news reports demonstrate considerable activity of this kind (see Skolnick 1969). Other evidence comes from national polls, which invariably indicate greater militance among young blacks than among their elders, and from sources such as the report of the National Advisory Committee on Civil Disorders, which emphasized the youth of riot participants. The impact of these developments on gangs is not clear. Some have suggested that gangs and gang leaders have played important roles in many of the confrontations both in and outside schools over the past half-dozen years. A 1967 rally around Forrestville High School on Chicago's South Side, to protest police brutality, resulted in fifty-four arrests and twelve injuries. According to the *Chicago Tribune*, "A local gang leader was credited with clearing the street when the police were ready to use force" (*Chicago Tribune*, September 15, 1967; the quotation is from Skolnick 1969, p. 123). Earlier that summer, when a major riot erupted on the West Side, detached workers from the YMCA of Metropolitan Chicago and other agencies, and gang leaders with whom they worked, were able to persuade West Side gangs to stay away from the riot areas, thus averting even greater destruction of both life and property. In the spring of 1968, following the assassination of Martin Luther King, the Blackstone Rangers helped to "cool" the South Side. In the words of a white minister with a long-time association with the Rangers,

"This was their way of saying, 'You have to reckon with us because, if we cannot stop one riot, well, you know the alternative.' This was a naked display of power" (Rev. John Fry, quoted in Skolnick, p. 125).

Incidents such as these appear to be exceptional, however. Miller's survey of "Youth Gangs in the Urban Crisis Era," reported in Chapter 5 of this volume, seems persuasive. While gangs were not involved in agitation or incidents triggering rioting, once rioting began gang members typically "were among the most ardent and energetic participants." He notes also, however, that on-the-scene media observers of riots found "the dominant emotion of nongang members . . . to be closer to elation than anger," suggesting that ideological fervor was not a prominent motive for gang participation in rioting.

3. *The revitalization of cultural pluralism and a new spirit of participatory democracy*. While these are certainly separable, and honest persons may argue the vitality of the one and the viability of the other, their roughly parallel development in the public consciousness in recent years has important consequences. Despite perceived threats by some, the new stress on social and cultural identity of racial and ethnic minorities strikes a responsive chord in this culturally polyglot society. We remember the trials and tribulations of Irish forebears who fled the great potato famine, of Swedes, Germans, and others who sought relief from religious persecution or military conscription. "Black power"—or brown or red—is but a few generations removed from the struggles of Italians and Poles, of Jews and Catholics, for a toehold on the political and economic ladder, achieved through the labor movement or by way of organized crime or city hall. These new struggles, and the determination of the young to explore "alternative life styles" fascinate and titillate even as they shock and threaten cherished values. The fact that such challenges arise from the children of middle-class guardians of those values, as well as from those of lower class or ethnic status, makes it easier to examine—or at least to be entertained by—alternative life styles from other segments of the society. A Sam Cook can emerge from a Chicago slum to sell millions of records (his brother was a member of one of the gangs we studied in Chicago) and a singing group from that same setting, calling themselves the Blackstone Rangers, after the gang of the same name, can make an appearance over national television on the Ed Sullivan

Show. In and around college towns, and in many other locations throughout the land, rural and urban communes develop, their members committed to such values as craftsmanship and love of the land, the "simple life" and environmental protection. They and their neighbors often discover that they have many of the same problems and can live with one another, at first suspiciously and often with hostility, but generally in harmony and at times with profit to both parties.

This heightened appreciation of alternative life styles comes at a time when the virtues of participatory democracy are asserted on almost every hand. Many of the young may now be disenchanted with the ideals set forth in the Port Huron statement, but institutions throughout the land have gotten the message, thus contributing to the relative quietude of our campuses and political campaigns. Whether as a result of the persistent prodding and confrontation tactics of students (Morgan 1972) or of administrators and faculty who were willing to share power in any case, student power on the campus is a far greater reality than it was a decade ago. Ralph Nader has become a culture hero for his consumer advocacy, but even more importantly, for his success in challenging establishment institutions in and outside of government. Both major parties have undertaken major efforts to reform nomination procedures, aimed at bringing in "grass roots" participation.

Among the new leaders are street workers of the 1950s and '60s. A program to prevent and control delinquency—Mobilization for Youth—became the first "Great Society" agency and the spearhead for the National Welfare Rights Organization (see Piven and Cloward 1971). The turbulent emergence of the poor as a political force is documented in the history of the Southern Christian Leadership Conference, and the transformation of CORE, SNCC, and other militant civil rights organizations (see Meier and Rudwick 1973).

But the political viability of the poor remains problematic, for a variety of reasons, and these reasons are compounded for members of street gangs. The chief impact of these trends on gangs has been indirect, by changing the public image of gangs and making possible new opportunities for gang members, individually and collectively. Many of these new opportunities developed as a result of political decisions.

4. *Social issues and "social problems" have become increas-*

*ingly politicized.* If we do not understand this trend we wil seriously misjudge the significance of what is today different from the past. Surely much is the same, and recurring cycles of publi awareness and concern over crime and delinquency, wars and poverty, and relations among subgroups in this country and throughout the world tempt the observation that nothing is new under the sun. But there are differences—important differences—which if ignored will compound the violence and disorder of th 1960s, for that decade is the backdrop of the 1970s (and *that* is a *important* difference), and may lead to higher peaks of violenc and lower depths of despair in the future.

Historian Hugh Davis Graham, co-director of the History an Comparative Studies Task Force of the Violence Commission notes that our capitalistic, federal structure has historically pitte our racial, ethnic, and economic groups against one anothe rather than against the state and its vital institutions. Expansio of the power of the federal government during the depression o the 1930s and following World War II appears to have altere this process fundamentally, however, as groups have com increasingly to look to government in search of redress fo grievances, of whatever kind. As a result, social conflicts hav come to be identified with the political process through whic government, and particularly the federal government, operates

Among these social conflicts are many which concern behavio defined by custom or law as *deviant*. The social roots an implications of *labeling* as deviant groups and behavior whic are *different* from those approved by a majority (or a powerfu minority) of citizens have increasingly come under scrutiny Groups so labeled have in turn come to view their problems i and with the larger society in more political terms and hav sought redress through the political process. Examples includ attempts by homosexuals to gain civil rights protection, th efforts of many groups to change repressive laws relating t marijuana usage (see Becker and Horowitz 1970), and the mo radical view that traditional criminals are victims of a repressiv system of criminal law (Quinney 1974). In these terms grouf that have not been accorded social equality view their problem fundamentally in terms of power relations with other groups, an government is looked to, not only for relief, but for positiv action in redress of grievances.[2]

## Societal versus Gang Impact

These developments converge powerfully in their impact on societies undergoing rapid social change, in modern as well as in "developing" countries. Tradition loses its hold on increasing numbers of citizens, institutions find their authority undermined, "rights" of property and control over the lives of employees and constituents are challenged. Conversely, many among those who feel most threatened by such changes react negatively, sometimes harshly and repressively, thus enhancing the challenge of those who protest and thereby further undermining the legitimacy of institutionalized authority in many contexts. The impact of these forces is especially great, in our highly nationalistic society, on *political* authority. In this process, collective representations of what is considered "right" and "proper," and of what is politically sanctioned in law and its enforcement, become changed, and new conceptions develop. We know far too little about the extent and specific location of such disaffection. Certainly it is more characteristic of some groups than others but simplistic notions about "generation gaps," black (or red or brown) power, or "alienation," do not do justice to the phenomenon. Political and economic implications may not be entirely clear, but the fact that this disaffection is both political and economic in nature can hardly be doubted.

Others might interpret these trends differently, or choose other developments of greater significance to the topic at hand. The major point I wish to make is that each of these trends has served to change the *image* of gangs and the *behavior* toward gangs of important elements of the larger society. The direct impact of these trends on most members of most youth gangs apparently was small. Indirectly, by means of the intervening and direct actions of a variety of social and governmental agencies, they altered the course of change which is a constant feature of gang life. The very character of gang organization was in some cases changed, as indicated by the following developments.

1. A large number of gangs have "gone conservative," that is, they have attempted to change from delinquent and disruptive behavior—with the public images which accompany such behavior—to law-abiding and socially constructive activities.

2. Some gangs have become involved in large-scale illegitimate

activities. While this is hardly new among white gang members, its development among black gangs is more recent.

3. A few gangs—very few, apparently—have become politicized to some degree.

The nature and the extent of these changes, as they are related to the trends and intervening actions of specific groups, is the subject of the remainder of this paper.

### "Gong Conservative" versus "Making It" in the Rackets

"Making it" is the name of the game in either case (Cloward and Ohlin 1960). Or, to invoke a more enlightened model, in terms of the trends discussed above, the goal for either legitimate or illegitimate pursuits may be helping one's people, or "the movement" (any one of several—that is, a movement that helps a community, an ethnic group, or others "in the life," whatever life-style may be at issue). For gangs, going conservative or illegitimate are alternative ways of "making it," in terms of either individual or collective goals.

In the late 1960s, aided by grants from private foundations, and later from federal agencies, efforts were made to promote and institutionalize efforts already begun by a few street gangs to better themselves and their communities. One such effort on a national scale, Youth Organization United (YOU), has been described by its president, a forty-year-old ex-Vice Lord from Chicago (Blackman 1971; see also Dawley 1973). At that time YOU was reported to consist of 381 chapters in 95 cities, with a total membership "between 3,500 and 4,000." These chapters included approximately 350 street gangs which have "gone conservative." Organized to promote and coordinate self-help programs among minority youth, YOU received a large grant from the United States Department of Health, Education and Welfare, plus smaller grants from private foundations. A variety of programs in Chicago, New Orleans, Philadelphia, and San Francisco were cited as examples of YOU efforts.

National organization was less important, for our purposes, than was the rise of "supergangs" in individual cities. We will focus our discussion on Chicago, where supergangs perhaps reached their most sophisticated development, and on two such gangs, the Conservative Vice Lords (also known as the Vice Lord Nation) and the Black P. Stone Nation (an outgrowth of the Blackstone Ranger gang).

Observers have often noted the tendency of gang members to inflate their numbers when assessing gang strength (Yablonsky 1962; Jansyn 1966). Smaller numbers typically relate to specific tasks and organized events, such as an athletic team, a dance, or other social events, while larger (and probably more fanciful) numbers are associated with defense against attack by rival gangs or other perceived threats and are often intended to impress outsiders. We suspect that numbers associated with the rise of the supergangs and their activities are similarly fanciful. The fact that the Conservative Vice Lords, "claiming 8,000 members in 26 divisions," were incorporated by the state of Illinois in 1967, "as a non-profit organization" (Sherman 1970, p. 29) tells us little about the nature of the organization, save that it had acquired a new legal status. The existence of these 8,000 members, the nature of their obligations to the organization, the viability of the organization and its assets were, and are, problematic.

The "rise" of supergangs, symbolized by their more formal status, was associated with two dramatic changes, however: (1) the launching of new economic and social activities, with substantial external funding, and (2) changed perceptions by and relationships with the outside world. Concerning the first of these, Sherman notes that in April 1968 the Conservative Vice Lords "received $30,000 in grants from the Rockefeller Foundation and Operation Bootstrap, a 'grassroots ghetto group.' The money went to support a restaurant, an African Heritage Shop, two recreation centers, a tenants' rights group, and a summer beautification project" (p. 22). An Office of Economic Opportunity grant in excess of $900,000 for a job-training program was made to the Blackstone Rangers and the Disciples, South Side gangs in Chicago, under the sponsorship of The Woodlawn Organization. None of these enterprises has been notably successful, however, and there have been spectacular failures. As of this writing, for example, the Vice Lords still have a headquarters and limited business interests, but profits have been slim and there have been suggestions of racket influence. Even the most sympathetic journalistic accounts of supergang activity have been unable to ignore the severe personal and group problems of gang youngsters seeking to "change their image" by such collective enterprise (Weingarten 1972; Bragonier 1972).

The public hue and cry related to the OEO-funded job-training and placement program operated by the Stones and Disciples is perhaps the most dramatic case in point. The official view is presented in Hearings of the McClellan Committee, as reported in the 1968 annual report of the Chicago Crime Commission (Peterson 1969):

> The principal beneficiaries of the $927,341 Federal grant were members of the Blackstone Rangers gang and its principal rival, the Disciples. Administrating the program was The Woodlawn Organization (T.W.O.) which is made up of 102 community groups on the South Side.

> As assistant project director of the T.W.O. program, Eugene (Bull) Hairston, leader of the Blackstone Rangers, received a salary of $6,500 a year. Jeff Fort was on the payroll at a salary of $6,000 a year. David Barksdale, president of the East Side Disciples gang, was paid $6,000 a year as an assistant basic education supervisor. Nicholas Dorenzo, vice-president of the Disciples, was listed as an assistant project director at an annual salary of $6,500.

> The Federally funded anti-poverty training program began on June 1, 1967, and ended in May, 1968. Public hearings held in Washington, D.C., conducted by the U.S. Senate Permanent Subcommittee on Investigations, headed by Senator John L. McClellan, exposed the prevalence of widespread abuses. A high percentage of signatures on attendance rosters were forged. Some of the students who received $45 a week to attend classes as well as some of the instructors were required to make kick-backs to the gang leaders. Some of the instruction programs were in the hands of persons with low I.Q.'s and of doubtful capacity to train.

There is much disagreement concerning precisely what did happen in the Stones' attempt to achieve respectability, ranging from Fry's (1973) staunch defense of the gang and his charge that official opposition was responsible for failure of the program, to the official view of gang violence and fraud. In any case, there is general agreement that the program failed in its objectives. Failure is hardly surprising. Small businesses fail by the thousands each year in this country even when run by knowledgeable adults who are dedicated to their success. There is little reason to believe that young men such as the Stones and Vice Lords possessed the required skills and know-how for successful operation of enterprises such as have been mentioned, and it seems clear that they were given little support by the loosely organized administrative structure created by The Woodlawn Organization. A manpower training program presents extremely complex problems, even when not dealing with gang youngsters with low basic skills (and administered by experienced personnel rather than by young men with many of these same problems). To gang boys' lack of technical skills must be added the compounding effects of the general lack of social skills noted among black gangs (Short and Strodtbeck 1965; Klein and Crawford 1967; Gordon 1967; cf. Horowitz and Schwartz 1974, for a contrasting report concerning gangs in a Mexican-American community in Chicago).

Large-scale organization, if it is to be successful, requires stability, which in turn requires legitimacy. Gang leaders, streetwise and skilled in relations within and between gangs, are not necessarily possessed of large-scale organizational skills—indeed, the transferability of leadership skills in the two situations seems most unlikely. Caplan's (1974) study of the failure of two youth development and job training programs is instructive. He concludes that "skills learned in the ghetto have little survival value in the conventional world of work," that in fact, "the skills which may make a man an 'executive' on the street—hustling, rapping, signifying, gang leadership, psyching out people, fighting, athletics, and so forth—may also serve to make him a failure as a dish washer, mechanic, or maintenance man" (p.5). Incorporation or other more formal organization is unlikely to overcome the social disabilities of gang youngsters (or the handicap of their social abilities, in Caplan's terms), or to remove the frequent challenges to leadership, and even membership, so frequently found in gangs. Hence, legitimacy is likely to be problematic. One of the clearest messages of recent gang literature is the fact that gangs are a volatile, if recurrent and continuing, form of association and organization (see Miller, this volume; Short and Strodtbeck 1965, 1974; Gordon 1966; Klein and Crawford, 1967). Status threats are played out on a day-to-day basis, on the street and in other contexts. The trappings of formal organization, even when combined with incentive to rally around business enterprise or improvement of the lot of one's fellows is unlikely to compensate for these problems.

Ironically, one of the chief advantages enjoyed by gangs in their search for legitimate identity and achievement—the active participation of influential business leaders in such programs—appears to have backfired. There was a good deal of romanticism among business leaders and many social agency personnel concerning their relationships with the gangs. Detached workers and occasionally an especially articulate gang boy found it easy to regale businessmen and middle- to upper-class groups with "war stories" from the street. Both workers and their audiences were reinforced in their hopes and beliefs that they were "doing good" by means of such programs, and the gang boys felt good about them, too. Many gang boys saw in street work new career possibilities which would allow them to utilize their street know-how and "help other kids."

Most of the romanticism was harmless, but at least one "spin-off" was not. As Russell Hogrefe commented, when this paper was presented at the McKay symposium, some elements of the business community, convinced that the gangs represented truly indigenous organization with potential for community leadership, in addition to their participation in agency-sponsored programs, began dealing directly with the gangs, putting money into their enterprises. In effect, businesses attempted to buy favors and influence among gangs in return for what they thought would be community peace and stability. But gangs are *products* of their communities. They do not control them, and especially they do not control entrenched criminal elements in these communities. Even their control of other groups of young people is subject to constant threat, particularly when these groups perceive an opportunity for getting a piece of the action.

When the gangs were unable to stop crime in their communities (whether or not, or how seriously, they actually attempted to do so), the flow of funds from businessmen was cut off. Gang members became disillusioned and bitter over what they interpreted to be inaction and unfulfilled promises (Dawley 1973). Some of the gangs reacted with violence. The criminal threat to businesses and their personnel was more serious than ever. Hogrefe remarked that the agencies were hit hard, all as a result of a chain of events which started out innocently enough with "respectable" people trying to help the "disreputable."

One further note concerning gang failures to achieve legitimate economic goals seems appropriate. It has been pointed out to me by a former detached worker with the Vice Lords that many local adults are resentful over the public attention received by the gangs, and particularly so of funds granted in support of businesses. "How is a guy going to feel who has run a business when he sees a bunch of young gang boys without experience getting money to run a competing business? Or if he has had to quit that business because he didn't get that sort of help?" (Interview by James F. Short, August 1971). Regrettably, we know little about the extent of local community support of or opposition to gang efforts to launch legitimate economic enterprise. Even the most ardent defenders of the Stones and Vice Lords concede that the gangs were feared and resented in their earlier manifestations (Fry 1969, 1973; Dawley 1973). Convincing evidence of widespread and sustained community support of the supergangs, such as Ianni (1974) finds for illegal enterprises (numbers, fencing, loan sharking), is lacking. In the eyes of many, the supergangs remain tainted by their former violent and predatory activities which victimized local citizens.

## Expansion of Illegitimate Enterprise

The historical relationship between juvenile gangs and organized crime is well documented (Thrasher 1927; Ianni 1974). In their classic *Black Metropolis*, Drake and Cayton (1945) documented the importance of the policy racket—socially as well as economically—in Chicago's black ghetto even during the depression 30s. Two decades later, when we were studying Chicago gangs, policy and other generally less lucrative hustles continued to flourish, and drugs had been added to the scene. One of the groups we were studying, the Egyptian Cobras, had a profitable relationship with some of the prostitutes in the Maxwell Street area. The boys knew the prostitutes well, and they regularly avoided "rolling" potential tricks until after the girls had first crack at them. One of the boys graduated into running policy numbers and many were involved in minor hustles of various kinds. As drugs became a big thing in the ghetto some gang members became involved in another aspect of organized crime—again at a very low level—as pushers on ghetto streets. Except for drugs and policy, our initial study of Chicago gangs failed to discover systematic links between members of black gangs and adults engaged in organized crime, though adult strong-arm men, burglars, prostitutes, and pimps were common. Only among members of a criminally oriented clique within a larger white gang was systematic theft for sale through adult fences discovered. Ianni (1974) has documented the involvement in a neighborhood network of criminal activities of men who first came together as children in a street gang. This appears also to have happened among some of the Vice Lords who are now involved in an extensive illegal drug operation in the old Vice Lord territory, but we have not documented the full extent of the network or of its illegal operations (see Short and Moland 1974). This network clearly involves several of the former Vice Lords, however, and is quite consistent with Ianni's observations in New York of ethnic succession in organized crime. What is new, and unique to the 1960s, is large-scale fraud with public monies, made possible, paradoxically, by sincerely meant efforts of well-wishers both in and outside of government and by political imperatives which changed urban and minority policies of the federal government.

## Gang Politicization and the Politics of Delinquency Control

With the close of the Eisenhower years and the beginning of the Kennedy-Johnson period, the politics of delinquency control shifted dramatically. Piven and Cloward (1971) argue that delinquency prevention became a high national priority after 1960, when the newly elected Kennedy administration realized that the margin of its victory was provided by the solidarity of the black vote in large northern cities. The need, therefore, was to consolidate this vote while not threatening the Democratic party's traditional white, ethnic-based organization. Delinquency prevention seemed ideal for this purpose. It was a "law and order" issue, focusing on rising fear of "crime in the streets," and it promised to "do something" about the problem in ghetto communities instead of further threatening embattled white neighborhoods by moving blacks into them. Much of the money poured into ghetto neighborhoods bypassed local political machinery, however; it financed activities of groups highly critical of entrenched political power and so inevitably jeopardized the tenuous alliance between that machinery, ghetto communities, and the federal bureaucracy. In Chicago conflict soon erupted between political authorities and a combination of social agencies and local community groups working with gangs. The gangs, always vulnerable because of their challenge to police authority and their predatory and violent activities, were caught in the middle of this conflict, and a few became active participants in it.

During the late 1950s and early 1960s the principal focus of street work was the relationship between individual workers and their boys, individually and collectively. Other resources were limited, though there was experimentation with employment, educational, and other programs. Resources were greatly expanded in 1965, with approval by the Office of Economic Opportunity of a grant of nearly $700,000 to STREETS (Socialization, Training, Recreation, Education and Employment Technical Services). STREETS involved the cooperative efforts of four Chicago youth-serving agencies: the YMCA, Chicago Youth Centers, the Chicago Youth Development Program (a Boys Club of America program), and Hull House, all with street-oriented outreach programs.

With expansion, street work became more visible to more people—particularly to police, many of whom already were resentful of the presence of workers on the street. As Sherman (1970) notes, police:

> usually first met the the worker on the street, often during a crisis situation. The presence of the workers implied that the police were not adequately dealing with the gang problem. This was aggravated by the police perception of a public which lacked respect for the force. When they had dealt with each other for a while, stereotypes developed of each role ... as Mary Blake of the Children's Bureau ... described:
>
>> The street worker (seen by the policeman) is soft; he lets youth go too far; he overprotects them; he has teamed up with them in opposition to law and order. The policeman (seen by the street worker) is tough; he has no regard for civil rights; he is more interested in punishing people than he is in protecting them (p. 18).

Over a decade, the goals and programs of street work changed in ways which greatly exacerbated these normal police-youth-worker tensions; notably those goals changed "from reduction of crime to advancing the status of minority groups" (Sherman 1970, p. 21).[3]

I have noted elsewhere that:

> Even before the civil rights movement became "radicalized" and black militancy became popular, detached workers were being compared to the old "ward heelers" of urban politics. Among the host of services performed for the youngsters with whom they worked, detached workers mediated relations with adults and institutions in local communities and in seats of power outside those communities. They also performed

services for adults, similar in many respects to those of the old ward heelers. Most of the young blacks and whites who worked the streets were motivated by the same commitments to egalitarian values which spurred the Civil Rights Movement. As that movement became more militant, it was inevitable that the detached workers and others associated with delinquency prevention programs would be affected (Short 1974, p. 10).

It was within this highly charged political context that the supergangs emerged. There is much disagreement concerning the reality of and the reasons for the "rise of the supergangs." Sherman (1970, p. 22) summarizes:

The city government asserts that the money given to gangs made it profitable to be a gang leader, so intensive recruitment on the basis of threats built up the gangs. University of Chicago [now University of Illinois, Chicago Circle] criminologist Hans Mattick feels that the police pressure on gangs created a self-fulfilling prophecy, forcing the gangs to band together for protection, though he questions the reputed size of the super-gangs. The youth welfare agencies maintain that gangs saw that it was in their own self-interest and in the interest of the community to band together. A corollary theory is that inter-gang warfare produced a series of alliances found to be useful for purposes other than combat.

In any case, as part of this process a variety of churches and other community organizations actively supported the "conservative" overture of gangs, and they, too, became caught up in a "war" between the Gang Intelligence Unit (GIU) of the Chicago Police Department and the gangs. Formed in 1961, the GIU served at first as an integral part of the official Youth Division policy of cooperation between police and street workers with gangs. In the spring of 1967, increasing tensions between city government, youth-serving agencies, and gangs resulted in the transfer of the GIU to the police department's Internal Investigation Division and appointment of a new director who was unsympathetic to gangs and street-work programs. It was then that the "war" began in earnest. Gang members were frequently stopped on the street for questioning, often picked up and dropped deep within "enemy" territory, thus endangering the individuals involved and contributing to the tensions already existing between rival gangs. Some agency program centers were raided by police (one halfway house sponsored by a theological seminary for ex-convict gang members was raided sixteen times, according to Sherman), resulting in extensive damage. Such an atmosphere of suspicion and hostility developed between police and many of the eminently respectable businessmen and social agency personnel who were involved with street gang programs, that executives of Youth Action (the successor to STREETS)[4] met with a volunteer group of lawyers (Lawyers for Civil Rights Under Law) to provide around-the-clock legal services.

> In case of a police incident, a lawyer would go to the scene to gather immediately the relevant information. Staff members were instructed to note such items as badge numbers and squad car numbers (Sherman, p. 23).

Sherman (1970), Fry (1973), and Dawley (1973) concur that the GIU war on gangs politicized the supergangs. Both supporters of the gangs and their detractors (Government Operations Committee 1969) agree that previous appeals for gangs to support them by civil rights organizations such as the Southern Christian Leadership Conference and by the militantly political Black Panther party had failed to attract that support. The political interpretation favored by these sources holds that "the civil rights movement had not clearly been in [the gangs'] self-interest" (Sherman 1970, p. 23) and that the Stones at least were "too well-entrenched in the community. They ... probably ... [feel] that the Black Panther Party can offer them nothing" (Government Operations Committee 1969, p. 4446). It may also be the case, as I suspect, that the gangs simply lacked political interests, as we had found in the early 60s. This view is supported by former detached worker and Chicago alderman Fred Hubbard. Shortly after he was first elected to the latter post, Hubbard received a telephone call from one of the Stones' leaders, inquiring as to "what this politics was all about and how could they [the Stones] get into it." Asked about the level of political sophistication of the Stones and other gangs, Hubbard replied in a 1972 interview, "They didn't have it; they don't have it now," referring specifically to knowledge of how the system works and how to make it work. "Gangs can play a part but they can't do it on their own." The extent and degree of political sophistication even among the Stones, therefore, seems questionable at this time. Hubbard also noted, however, and other observers agree, that the most prominent of the Stones' leadership was a genius at organization. Jacobs's (1974) report of highly politicized and successful gang organization within Illinois prisons (including the Stones, Vice Lords, Disciples, and Roman Saints) suggests ironically that the imprisonment of much of the Stones' leadership may have had the effect of creating a political force which previously had been weak, and perhaps illusory. Whether that force will prove viable outside the prison context is problematic and may well be of fateful consequence.

## Discussion

It is axiomatic that every group is shaped by its external environment, but the dependence of gangs in this respect seems especially great. This has been an important theme running through much of the recent literature on juvenile gangs, as researchers have attempted to account for differences between gang and nongang youngsters (Rivera and Short 1967*a*, 1967*b*), for public (and therefore private, in both an individual and a collective sense) identities of gang boys (Brymmer 1967), for gang cohesiveness (Klein and Crawford 1967), and for the quality of interpersonal relations among gang boys (Short and Strodtbeck 1965; Gordon 1967). It seems equally important in relation to the politicization of some gangs and to the political potential of gangs in general. The community context of street gangs, with ethnic and economic nuances, and the degree of integration of conventional and criminal elements, has long been recognized as crucial to the nature of these groups (Shaw and McKay 1929; Whyte 1943; Miller 1958; Cohen and Short 1958; Cloward and Ohlin 1960; Short and Strodtbeck 1965; Kobrin, Puntil, and Peluso 1967; Klein 1971). Analyses of these influences, however, generally have not been fine-grained enough to detect subtle differences of great importance. In most of our studies, for example, my colleagues and I lumped together black gang members in Chicago and compared them with similarly lumped white gang members and with nongang boys of each racial group. While this procedure was useful because of the small number of gang studies, it obscured important differences between groups and the possibility of relating community differences to differences among these groups.[5]

Henry McKay's study of delinquency *trends* in Chicago from 1934 through 1961 sets the stage for such study (McKay 1969).

McKay found that the three Chicago communities with the most pronounced *increases* in official delinquency rates and the three communities with the most pronounced *decreases* in these rates all were predominantly black communities. A crucial difference between these two sets of communities is that the three communities with the largest increases in delinquency (Lawndale on the West Side and Woodlawn and Englewood on the South) are areas of *recent* black settlement, while those with the most pronounced downward slopes in trend (Douglas, Grand Boulevard, and Washington Park) are areas in which blacks have been concentrated for several decades. McKay compares these communities with the experience of the several ethnic groups which have moved through Chicago's inner-city areas on their way to assimilation and lower delinquency rates. His discussion of the underlying processes is appropriate:

> Disorganization accompanying rapid change may be virtually complete. If the institutions and social roles of the newcomers do not meet the needs of the new situation, and if the population is not able or is not given opportunities to perform the roles in their traditional institutions, the disruption in the incoming group is serious. The evidence, however, is that these problems tend to get solved except in a few areas where rapid change is a permanent characteristic. Given time, some groups make adjustment and move out, and others make their adjustment without moving out. Projection of the downward trends, discussed above, suggests that a new equilibrium of social control has been achieved, or is in the process of being achieved, in these communities.

Kobrin makes the point that the linkage of gangs and politics has varied historically.[6] In some immigrant communities it was strong, in others weak or nonexistent *depending on the extent to which communities were politically strong.* Some groups coming to the country found politics a way of "making it"—for jobs, power, influence—some did not. Some groups assimilated without politics as a specific focus. Here, again, the dependency of the gang on external forces seems clear. Yet little attention has been given to systematic study of these matters (see also Spergel 1969).

My own failure to consider sufficiently these community differences has been impressed upon me in the course of our present research. We have recently contacted most of the former detached workers with whom we worked and a few former gang members for especially detailed interviews and as interviewers of others. These included a former gang leader from a West Side gang who had been picked out for special treatment in a number of ways because of his prominence in the street world. He was one of the first gang leaders to be paid as a "consultant" by the YMCA program in the early 1960s. Arrangements had been made for him to complete high school and to go to college. It was even arranged for him to attend a prestigious eastern college, which he did for most of two years. But the streets of the small town in which the college was located were not the streets of Chicago, and weekends were particularly difficult for him. When he returned to Chicago, in the summer of 1971, we hired him to help with our research, locating former gang members, telling us about others, and acting as an important historical resource. It soon became clear that his return to college was problematic, so we encouraged him to do so as much as we could. He was invaluable to the research effort during that summer, and he continued to work sporadically for several months after. But he did not return to college. In the spring of 1972, his work on the research project stopped. We attempted to retain contact, but during the summer he dropped from sight, reappearing only late in the fall. His disappearance apparently was related to the fact that his involvement in drugs (as both user and pusher) was creating serious personal problems. The point to the story is best made in contrast with the South Side man.

As we talked about our research interests, the young man from the South Side objected to our classifying his former gang with those on the West Side. His gang, the Nobles, no longer exists and, he continued, "The Nobles never was a gang in the Vice Lord sense. We were a baseball team that got united for self-protection. There was a unity sort of thing, you know. We help each other out." He has agreed to talk with us more about what it meant to be a member of the Nobles, and why the gang ceased to exist, and why the Blackstone Rangers rather than the Nobles developed into a "supergang" with political overtones. This young man participated in survey research for the YMCA, and for more than a year he was employed by the Kenwood Oakland Community Organization, an OEO-funded program which developed considerable political sophistication in that area. He objected to our interview instrument as "too elementary" for former gang members in Kenwood. Discussion revealed that he had participated in interviews of former gang members and others a few years earlier, and he did not wish to go back to them again with similar questions. "I can't come back on them again. What good did it ever do them?" It developed that he felt we wanted to find out "Why people who don't have anything don't have anything." And so it must have seemed as we proposed to survey, among other things, educational and occupational experiences of our former gang members. I explained that we wanted such information as a link between what we had studied in the past and social and political awareness and activity today. It was with this understanding that he agreed to work with us.

The contrast in these two cases is, of course, at best suggestive. The individual histories of these young men differ in many details, and they are in any case incomplete and still very much in process. But it is important also that the forces that shaped the West and South Side gangs differed significantly. The Vice Lords' territory centered on the local community with the most rapidly rising delinquency rates (Lawndale, in recent years). The Nobles' community, though it was known as "Dopeville" during the late 1950s and early '60s, was on the stabilizing South Side (Douglas). On the West Side, despite considerable effort and publicity to the effect that they had "gone conservative," the Vice Lords, as Suttles remarks, seems to have "found it impossible to shake its reputation as a criminal gang and get itself authenticated as a bunch of subversive radicals" (Suttles 1972, p. 10). Efforts of the Vice Lords to "go conservative" were partially successful, aided by federal grants, but the transition to respectability was marred by intra- and inter-gang status threats and by the lack of skills and capital necessary to sustain the variety of enterprises launched (see Keiser 1969).

While it may be the case, as Sherman suggests (1972), that "the gangs were finally on the threshold of significant redirection of their energies from violence to constructive activity" when police attacks "prevented them from making real progress," it would be naive to assume that this was the only deterrent to realization of such goals. Historically, a variety of strategies has been employed to improve the ability of poor communities to manage their problems, and some success has been achieved. Success has been most notable when the focus of such efforts has been specific as, for example, protesting a particular governmental decision, or demanding some specific action on the part of private or governmental agencies. Little impact has been made with respect to the basic systemic forces which create the conditions faced by poor people. Difficulties stem not only from the intractability of those forces, that is, from the "profit motive" in a capitalist economy and, more generally, the nature of industrialized societies, but from basic problems among the poor. The nature of these problems is commented on by Weissman (1969*d*), assessing the Mobilization of Youth Experience in New York City.

Community action, the attempt to organize low-income communities to protest and demand change, was extremely important as a spur to social reform. Its basic strategy was to bring small resources to bear at key leverage points in society in order that larger resources would be made available. It was hoped that through community-action efforts the political power of the poor would be organized and would force social institutions and ultimately political parties to accommodate to th demands of the poor.

It has become clear that this strategy has certain limitations. First, *the poor comprise many different groups, whose needs are not altogether congruent; political organization is therefore difficult.* Welfare-client groups including many Puerto Ricans were booed by other Puerto Ricans when they marched in a Puerto Rican Day parade. In New York, Negroes and Puerto Ricans are constantly battling for jobs and control of the poverty program. Second, *outside resources of money and organization skill are needed if the poor are to be organized.* It is clear at this point that these resources are not forthcoming from public funds in the amounts needed. Third, community action has tended to focus first on gaining power for the poor—power to control local schools, to influence the policies of the Welfare Department, and then ultimately sufficient power to have their economic demands met. The strategy assumes that the poor themselves desire power and will enlist in efforts to gain it. *In fact, the poor man is much more concerned about money and purchasing power than he is wielding power over malfunctioning social institutions.* His interest in community action is therefore episodic, related to the short-run prospects of immediate gain, and unsuited to a long-range strategy of developing a political power base. (Emphasis added.)

In a footnote to these paragraphs, Weissman notes that "After five years of MFY's efforts in community action, relatively few leaders emerged from the local population." The experience of the

Chicago Area Project and the Industrial Areas Foundation suggests that effective indigenous leadership can be developed in inner-city communities. Sustained accomplishment is slow and difficult, however, and requires continuous technical and financial support beyond locally available resources (Kobrin 1959; Sorrentino 1959; McKay 1969; Short 1969; Helfgot 1974).

It should be added, then, that "experiments" such as Mobilization for Youth, The Woodlawn Organization, the Kenwood Oakland Community Organization, the Conservative Vice Lords, or the Black P. Stone Nation have had neither the time nor the continuity of resources to prove themselves in this respect. But the record is not encouraging. The cultural and structural conditions associated with these processes continue to be debated, but the outlines surely are clear. Blacks as a constituency remain fragmented and conflicted, and economically weak, despite political and economic gains in recent years. Little progress has been made by the black poor. The mobility channels through which previous (white) minority groups climbed to political and social recognition and power, and relative economic affluence—politics, the labor movement, and organized crime—have been largely preempted and slow to admit blacks. Change can be more readily forced in organized crime because of its illicit character, and there is evidence of black (and Spanish American) power emerging in this area (Ianni 1974). In an earlier paper (Short 1974), I quoted an assessment of a black political figure with whom I have talked on several occasions over the past few years concerning these matters:

> Black people ain't never going to make it until they can get it all
> together.... Blacks have a chance right here (in Chicago)....
> The jails are full of blacks, and here they have a black warden, a
> black deputy warden and blacks in other top jobs.... Blacks
> will make it only when these guys get out of jails and take
> over organized crime. I think politics will put it all together—
> business, jobs, crime, power. Some people think it will be
> economic, but that ain't all going to happen until we get it
> all together, and that will be through politics.

In later interviews this man elaborated on the necessity for politics to "get it all together" for blacks.

> There is money in the ghetto—thousands of dollars lying
> around or stashed away in mattresses and closets by people in all
> sorts of hustles. But they don't know what to do with the money

[politically], or they don't care. It ain't like other ethnic groups in the past. They came to this country with businesses to put money in, and politics for them was always ready to take money and put it to work for business and politics. What is needed is organization—so that money can be put in the right places (Interview, April 1974).

Commenting on the changing political scene in Chicago in late summer, 1974, my friend again addressed the problem:

Now is the time for black politicians to get together—before [Mayor] Daley drops out and the struggle for power heats up. But they won't do it. They're too busy doing their own things. If I was in a position to do it, I would move now to get all the black politicians together. Then we would be ready when the bargaining for black support begins (Interview, August 1974).

Thompson (1974) attributes the powerlessness of the black ghetto to ineffective organizations, noting that "social organization is the most versatile instrument in getting things done" (p. 121). This insight, which was shared by Henry McKay and Clifford Shaw and buttressed by dozens of empirical studies, remains as valid today as in the past. Its implications continue to be debated and to be the object of countless "experiments" in social action. The political role of gangs in these efforts has been largely inarticulate and ineffective (Kalberg and Suttles 1974). Whether it can be otherwise will depend primarily upon forces outside the gang—both outside and within the black community.

## Notes

The National Institute of Mental Health (Research Grant MH 2072) and the Social Research Center of Washington State University have provided much of the stimulation and the support for this paper. I am grateful for this support and for the critical comments and suggestions of numerous colleagues who have contributed to my understanding and interpretation of the matters discussed in this paper. Special thanks go to Gerald Suttles, Solomon Kobrin, Albert J. Riess, Jr., Hans Mattick, Russell Hogrefe, Lois B. DeFleur, Howard Becker, Trutz von Trotha, Irving Spergel, and Fred D. Hubbard.

1. In his weekly research interview, a detached worker once reported that Black Muslim representatives had made overtures to members of the West Side gang with whom he was working. He reported an incident which is particularly revealing of the type of reception accorded this approach. The man spoke to Eddie, a member of the gang, asking him if he was "coming to the meeting tonight." Eddie, playing Keiser's (1969 pp. 42–44) "street man" role to the hilt, asked the man for a dime,

indicating he would have to call his mother about the matter. The man produced a dime and Eddie promptly took off, returning only after the man had departed. The rest of the boys laughed at Eddie's deception but appeared uninterested in the Muslim movement. When the worker inquired as to what the Black Muslim meeting was about, one of the boys commented, "Aw, they tell you a lot of bullshit about there being more than one God"—suggesting that such communication as may have occurred between the boys and the Black Muslims was none too effective.

2. The most important of these political constituencies are the poor, for they constitute the most important challenge to any social system. The young are too transient in that status and too much the product of their elders. Women and ethnic groups can be accommodated today even as the latter were yesterday (though the economic situation is quite different and resistance to racial integration remains high). Most deviant groups are too small to be very important, and when they become large enough their "deviance" is likely to be legally embraced. But the poor we have always with us. Whether it can be otherwise, one suspects, depends chiefly upon the political power of the poor—power to force economic reforms substantial enough to effect drastically the distribution of wealth and to abolish the status of "poor person."

3. Sherman (1970) whose major purpose is to describe the history of police-youth-worker relationships in Chicago, beginning with recent street-work programs, divides this history into three phrases: "Years of Trial: 1956-60," "an era of corruption and brutality in the police force, a submissive attitude on the part of the young blacks and the first tentative steps of the welfare agencies to reach out to gang youths with street-oriented ... (rather than) building-centered programs"; "Years of Support: 1961-66," "at time of police professionalism under [Superintendent of Police] O. W. Wilson with City Hall and community support for the idea of middle class street workers co-opting gang leaders"; and "Politics and Hostility: 1966-70," which brought about "the demise of street work and youth gangs in the eyes of City Hall, the community and the police, coupled with the rise of the super gangs and their war with the Gang Intelligence Unit" (p. 18).

4. STREETS lost OEO support as a result of its alleged political activities. Sherman (1970, p. 20) notes that, while the extent of STREETS workers' involvement in political activities was unclear, the 1966 congressional primary election candidacy of a former director of the YMCA Program for Detached Workers (against the incumbent, a long-entrenched regular party man) "produced enough appearance of involvement to result in termination of STREETS funding by the Chicago Committee on Urban Opportunity, the local poverty agency." My own research into the matter (interviewing several of the former detached workers and the candidate) suggests that the workers were very much involved in that (unsuccessful) campaign as well as in later (successful) aldermanic campaigns.

5. Desmond S. Cartwright, Kenneth I. Howard, and Nicholas J. Reuterman have continued analysis of the psychological data from our research program, taking individual gangs as their basic unit of analysis. Their monograph, *The Psychology of Gang Delinquency* is in prepara-

tion.

6. In discussion of this paper at the McKay symposium.

## References

Asbury, Herbert
1927         *The Gangs of New York*. New York: Knopf.

Becker, Howard and Irving L. Horowitz
1970         "The Culture of Civility." *Transaction* 7 (April): 12-20.

Blackman, Anne
1971         "Street gangs go conservative." *Spokane Daily Chronicle* (November 22): 35.

Bragonier, K.
1972         "The 'Prez' of the Reapers: A New Style City Street Gang." *Life* (August 25).

Brymmer, R. A.
1967         "Toward a Definition and Theory of Conflict Gangs." Paper delivered at annual meeting of Society for the Study of Social Problems (August 26), mimeographed.

Caplan, Nathan
1973         "Street Skills of Many Hard-to-Employ Youths May Hinder Success in Job Training Programs." *ISR Newsletter* (Autumn): 5.

*Chicago Tribune*
1967         September 15, as quoted in Jerome Skolnick, *The Politics of Protest*. Report of the Task Force on Demonstrations, Protests, and Group Violence, National Commission on the Causes and Prevention of Violence. Washington, D.C.: U.S. Government Printing Office.

Cloward, Richard, and Lloyd E. Ohlin
1960         *Delinquency and Opportunity*. New York: The Free Press.

Cohen, A. K., and James F. Short, Jr.
1958         "Research in Delinquent Subcultures." *Journal of Sociological Issues* 14: 20-27.

Dawley, David
1973         *A Nation of Lords*. Garden City, New York: Anchor Books.

Drake, St. Clair, and Horace R. Cayton

1945          *Black Metropolis: A Study of Negro Life in a Northern City*. New York: Harcourt Brace.

Fry, John
1969          *Fire and Blackstone*. Philadelphia. J. B. Lippincott.
1973          *Locked-Out Americans*. New York: Harper and Row.

Gordon, R. A.
1966          "Social Level, Disability, and Gang Interaction." *American Journal of Sociology* 73 (July): 42–62.

Government Operations Committee, Senate
1969          *Riots, Civil and Criminal Disorders, 1969*. Hearings before the Permanent Subcommittee on Investigations of the Committee on Government Operations, United States Senate, part 20. Washington, D.C.: U.S. Government Printing Office.

Helfgot, Joseph
1974          "Professional Reform Organizations and the Symbolic Representation of the Poor." *American Sociological Review* 39 (August): 475–91.

Horowitz, Ruth, and Gary A. Schwartz
1974          "Honor, Normative Ambiguity and Gang Violence." *American Sociological Review* 39 (April): 238–51.

Ianni, Francis, A. J.
1974          *Black Mafia: Ethnic Succession in Organized Crime*. New York: Simon and Shuster.

Jacobs, James B.
1974          "Street Gangs behind Bars." *Social Problems* 21: 395–409.

Jansyn, L.
1966          "Solidarity and Delinquency in a Street Corner Group." *American Sociological Review* 32 (October): 600–614.

Kalberg, Stephen, and Gerald D. Suttles
1974          "Gangs, the Police and Politicians in Chicago During 1964–1970." Paper prepared for the E. W. Burgess Memorial Symposium, University of Chicago.

Keiser, R. Lincoln
1969          *The Vice Lords: Warriors of the Streets*. New York: Holt, Rinehart and Winston.

Klein, Malcolm
1971          *Street Gangs and Street Workers*. Englewood
              Cliffs, N.J.: Prentice-Hall.

Klein, M., and L. Y. Crawford
1967          "Groups, Gangs, and Cohesiveness." *Journal of
              Research in Crime and Delinquency* 4 (January):
              63–75.

Kobrin, Solomon
1959          "The Chicago Area Project: A Twenty-five Year
              Assessment." *The Annals of the American Academy
              of Political and Social Science* (March): 19–29.

Kobrin, S., J. Puntil, and E. Peluso
1967          "Criteria of Status among Street Gangs." *Journal
              of Research in Crime and Delinquency* (January):
              98–118.

McKay, Henry D.
1969          "Recent Rates of Delinquents and Commitments in
              Chicago: Distribution and Trends," pp. 329–58,
              and "Rates of Delinquents and Commitments:
              Discussion and Conclusion," pp. 374–89 in Clifford
              R. Shaw and Henry D. McKay, *Juvenile Delin-
              quency and Urban Areas*. Chicago: University of
              Chicago Press. Rev. ed.

Meier, August, and Elliott Rudwick
1973          *Core: A Study in the Civil Rights Movement, 1942–
              1968*. New York: Oxford University Press.

Miller, W. B.
1958          "Lower Class Culture as a Generating Milieu of
              Gang Delinquency." *Journal of Social Issues* 14
              (Summer): 5–19.

Morgan, William
1972          "Campus Conflict as Formative Influence." Chap-
              ter 21 in James F. Short, Jr., and Marvin E. Wolf-
              gang, eds., *Collective Violence*. Chicago: Aldine-
              Atherton.

National Advisory Commission on Civil Disorders.
1968          *Report*. Washington, D.C.: U.S. Government
              Printing Office.

Park, Robert E., and Ernest W. Burgess
1924          *The Science of Sociology*. Chicago: University of
              Chicago Press.

Peterson, Virgil W.
1969            *A Report on Chicago Crime for 1968*. Chicago: Chicago Crime Commission.

Piven, Frances Fox, and Richard A. Cloward
1971            *Regulating the Poor*. New York: Pantheon.

Quinney, Richard
1974            *Critique of Legal Order: Crime Control in Capitalist Society*. Boston: Little, Brown.

Rivera, Ramon J., and James F. Short, Jr.
1967a           "Significant Adults, Caretakers, and Structures of Opportunity, an Exploratory Study." *Journal of Research in Crime and Delinquency* 4 (January): 76–97.
1967b           "Occupational Goals: A Comparative Analysis," pp. 70–90 in Malcolm W. Klein, ed., *Juvenile Gangs in Context: Theory, Research, and Action*. Englewood Cliffs, N.J.: Prentice-Hall.

Shaw, Clifford R., and Henry D. McKay
1929            *Delinquency Areas*. Chicago: University of Chicago Press.

Sherman, Lawrence W.
1970            "Youth Workers, Police and the Gangs: Chicago, 1956–1970." Master's thesis, University of Chicago.

Short, James F., Jr.
1969            "The Chicago Area Project as a Social Movement." Addendum to Introduction to the revised edition of Clifford K. Shaw and Henry D. McKay, *Juvenile Delinquency and Urban Areas*. Chicago: University of Chicago Press.
1974            "Youth, Gangs, and Society: Micro- and Macro-sociological Processes." *The Sociological Quarterly* 15 (Winter): 3–19.

Short, James F., Jr., and John Moland
1974            "Political Consequences of Street Work with Gangs." Paper presented at the 69th Annual Meeting of the American Sociological Association, August 26–29.

Short, James F., Jr., Ramon Rivera, and Harvey Marshall
1966            "Adult-Adolescent Relations and Gang Delinquency." *Pacific Sociological Review* 7, no. 2 (Fall): 59–65.

Short, James F., Jr., Ramon Rivera, and Ray A. Tennyson
1965          "Perceived Opportunities, Gang Membership, and
             Delinquency." *American Sociological Review* 30,
             no. 1 (February): 56–67.

Short James F., Jr., and Fred L. Strodtbeck
1965          *Group Process and Gang Delinquency*. Chicago:
1974          University of Chicago Press.

Skolnick, Jerome
1969          *The Politics of Protest*. Report of the Task Force on
             Demonstrations, Protests, and Group Violence,
             National Commission on the Causes and Preven-
             tion of Violence. Washington, D.C.: U.S. Govern-
             ment Printing Office.

Sorrentino, Anthony
1959          "The Chicago Area Project After 25 Years." *Federal
             Probation* (June): 40–45.

Spergel, Irving
1969          "Politics, Policies and the Youth Gang." University
             of Chicago, School of Social Service Administra-
             tion (mimeographed).
1973          "Community-based Delinquency-Prevention Pro-
             grams: An Overview." *Social Service Review*
             (March) 16–31.

Suttles, Gerald
1972          "Recent Social Movements and the Politicization of
             Juvenile Corner Groups in Chicago." Lecture
             given at the CUNY Graduate Center.

Thompson, Daniel C.
1974          *Sociology of the Black Experience*. Westport,
             Connecticut: Greenwood Press.

Thrasher, Frederick M.
1927          *The Gang: A Study of 1313 Gangs in Chicago*.
1963          Chicago: University of Chicago Press.

Weingarten, Gene
1972          "East Bronx Story—Return of the Street Gangs."
             *New York* 5 (March 27): 31–37.

Weissman, Harold H., ed.
1969*a*        *Individual and Group Services in the Mobilization
             for Youth Experience*. New York: Association Press.
1969*b*        *Community Development in the Mobilization for
             Youth Experience*. New York: Association Press.

1969c        *Employment and Educational Services in the Mobilization for Youth Experience*. New York: Association Press.

1969d        *Justice and the Law in the Mobilization for Youth Experience*. New York: Association Press.

Whyte, W. F.
1943         *Street Corner Society: The Social Structure of an Italian Slum*. Chicago: University of Chicago Press.

Woods, Robert A.
1898         "The Roots of Political Power," pp. 114–23 in Robert A. Woods, ed., *The City Wilderness, a Settlement Study*. Boston: Houghton, Mifflin.

Yablonsky, Lewis
1962         *The Violent Gang*. New York: Macmillan.

**III**     **Cross-Cultural Observations**

# 6     Shaw-McKay
        Theories of Delinquency
        in Cross-Cultural
        Context

*S. Kirson Weinberg*

This chapter compares the forms of delinquency in American society as analyzed by Shaw and McKay during the nineteens, twenties, and early thirties with those in contemporary American society and in Accra, Ghana, of West Africa (Shaw 1930, 1931; Shaw and McKay 1929, 1931, 1969; Shaw et al. 1938). The comparison involves three types of societies: (1) Western laissez-faire, (2) Western welfare-oriented, and (3) Western with tribal features, with all three having common social denominators of urbanism and somewhat similar legal codes (Weinberg 1964, 1965*a*, 1965*b*, 1973; Glueck 1950; Short and Strodtbeck 1965; Cohen 1955; Spergel 1964; Miller 1958; Cloward and Ohlin 1960). My aim is to determine the extent to which the Shaw-McKay findings are transcultural in terms of the following criteria: (1) the zonal and area models of the distribution of juvenile delinquents in the urban community; (2) the relationship between ecological succession of ethnic groups and the transmission of delinquent orientations in the recruitment and acculturation of delinquents; (3) the group experiences and deviant subcultures among delinquents; and (4) the function and influence of the family.

American cities as metropolitan centers have been the loci of most studies of delinquency and are somewhat similar to Accra, Ghana, which is a cosmopolitan metropolis. Ione Acquah (1958) notes these relevant facts:

> Accra is linked with all parts of the country and the world by modern means of communication. It is affected by world events, ideas and policies. Forty-eight per cent of the population are non-Gas (the Gas are the aboriginal tribe) and are drawn from every tribal division in the country and from many parts of the world. It is inevitable that this heterogeneity

S. Kirson Weinberg is a member of the Department of Sociology at Loyola University, Chicago.

coupled with extremely rapid population growth has posed
social problems common to Western urban societies. Delinquency in old and young alike ... has emerged.

Accra combines indigenous non-Western and Western charac
teristics. Urbanization in Africa preceded Western influence
Industrialization is not widespread, but commerce is widely
developed and a vast administrative bureaucracy exists. The
urbanization of Accra depends less upon industrialization than
upon its vast governing bureaucracy and its commerce and retai
trade. Its Western counterpart would be Washington, D.C.
rather than Chicago.

At the time of the Shaw-McKay studies, Chicago was differen
in important respects from the same city today. During the 1920s
Chicago was a relatively laissez-faire socioeconomic community
with minimal social planning and government intervention in
local communities and meager institutionalized efforts to aid
persons in distress. Delinquents concentrated in the zone of firs
settlement adjacent to the center of the city and in a few othe:
disorganized areas (Burgess 1925; Shaw and McKay 1929). Thi
period was prior to mass unionization of industries. The ten-hou
work day was common and, since the technology of that time wa
not extensively automated, industry accommodated many un
skilled workers. The majority of delinquents were children o
Eastern Europeans who had migrated to the large urban center
for jobs (Shaw and McKay 1969).

Contemporary American urban communities such as Chicago
despite historic continuity with the past, differ in several ways
We are a more affluent society. Commissions and agencies ar
concerned with planning urban change. The patterns of growth
in urban and suburban communities have diffused the distribu
tion of delinquents. Advanced technology has reduced the need
for unskilled labor. Changing social values and the spread of dru;
abuse have complicated the very nature of juvenile delinquency
My object in this discussion is to compare the findings from
Shaw-McKay studies with those of several studies of contem
porary delinquency and with those of Ghanaian delinquency.

### Ecological Aspects of Delinquency Distribution:
### Zonal and Area Models

The Shaw-McKay ecological analyses of delinquents extend i

time from the turn of the century through the early sixties. Zonal and area models aid in the interpretation of these findings as manifestations of social disorganization in the radial expansion of the city from the center outward. This pattern of urban growth was observed to occur as a result of competition for favorable location by trade and industrial sectors of the ecological order (Burgess 1925).

This zonal model is to some extent culture-bound and historical. It applies only with considerable modifications to contemporary urban communities, which are in part rationally planned, where first settlement of urban immigrants may occur in areas away from the central zones, and where, for historical reasons, disorganized areas reach to the perimeter of the city (Chilton 1964). The centrifugal flow of middle-class people to the suburbs and the planned renewal of areas near the central urban community have diminished the concentration of juvenile offenders in areas in the second zone.

Delinquency distribution in Accra displays some features consistent with the zonal model. Originally a fishing village, Accra has developed as a trade center and its growth has been shaped by unhampered competition. Some disorganized areas are adjacent to the business district with high concentrations of delinquencies. But this is as far as this zonal model obtains (see Acquah 1958).

The theory of radial growth by ethnic succession depends in turn upon the successive occupancy of used housing. In Accra, however, shanty towns such as New Town arise *de novo*, without used housing, on the outskirts of the city. Along the highways are villages, consisting of mud huts with thatched roofs, where transplanted migrants live. When the inhabitants leave the village, their homes are abandoned. Thus no ethnic or tribal succession exists in these villages. Because city housing also is sometimes abandoned, the neighborhood concept of the American city is limited in its application to Ghana.

The delinquency-area hypothesis seems more appropriate for this cross-cultural comparison. The processes that characterize deteriorated and disorganized American communities with high rates of delinquency—physical deterioration, decline of social control, high rates of adult crimes, alcoholism, poverty, lack of education, and unskilled labor—obtain with some qualifications in all three cultures.

These traits of disorganized areas in laissez-faire and contem
porary welfare-oriented, planned urban communities are similar
but with notable differences (see Weinberg 1970a). In some
contemporary urban slums, high-rise apartments have deterio
rated and have become skyscraper tenements. In these area
neighborly relationships seem virtually nonexistent. Older youth
may coerce younger boys to "join" their gangs and demand or
extort "dues." Often these children attended the same schools
where the older ones find younger victims accessible. The
transmission of delinquent attitudes and practices apparently wa
not disrupted by the high-hise apartment dwellings which re
placed the old two- and three-story apartments whose occupant
saw and knew each other and whose children influenced each
other.

In Accra, where homes were built as compounds rather than a
open dwellings, children also knew each other by attending a
common school, and families knew one another particularly
because many were from the same tribe. A deteriorated sector o
Jamestown, a neighborhood in Accra, had similar indices o
disorganization to those of a disorganized American urban
community. New Town in Accra, a shantyville of makeshif
shacks, also had the traits of a disorganized American slum area
But the nonfamily areas, such as the central business district where
homeless delinquents—"veranda boys"—usually slept, were no
disorganized except for lack of informal social controls.

Application of the urban-area model to the transplanted
villages near Accra is difficult. Externally these villages have th
features of a folk society with few technical facilities, population
homogeneity, emphasis on kinship ties, sacred and animisti
beliefs including witchcraft and magic, and retention of some
effective primary family and village controls. But the foll
character has diminished as urban influences changed the village
into an urban neighborhood and transformed the resident triba
group into an ethnic group. Most male villagers were part-time
farmers, but some also worked in and about the city. When
employed, the adults left the village during the day, many
women as petty traders in the city. Many youths did not perceiv
their fathers as role models but were influenced by person
outside the family. This type of family and community organiza
tion is relevant to the emergence of delinquency. The village wa
close to a road leading to the central business district, th

marketplace, and the homes of "wealthy" European residents. Youths would wander regularly to the central business districts and to places where they were not known in order to steal. Within some villages, groups of criminals were mainly concerned with stealing from Europeans and from stores (Weinberg 1965a). Secret societies existed within these villages and sometimes included groups of thieves. Groups of older offenders influenced the younger delinquents. Women also were involved in thefts, often "casing" homes where people were moving in or out. Points of arrival and departure for Europeans were especially vulnerable to thievery.

## Delinquency and Ethnic Groups

As in an earlier era in Chicago, described by Shaw and McKay, there was evidence in Accra of the transmission of delinquent norms from youths of one tribe to those of another. This process occurred chiefly in hangouts away from local areas of residence, however. Veranda boys introduced new vagrants into the ways of thievery. In addition, an infrequent but distinct mode of recruitment of delinquents also occurred. Some gangs roved into villages near the city where they induced restless juveniles to steal from their parents or neighbors, after which the novices joined the gang to roam and steal (see also Busia 1950).

A question unanswered in the Shaw-McKay studies concerns the varied extent, forms, and duration of delinquency among diverse ethnic groups. The early studies emphasized the equal susceptibility to delinquency of youths in diverse ethnic groups located in disorganized areas. They found that rates of delinquency declined among ethnic groups as they moved into middle-class, socially organized areas:

> One European ethnic group after another moved into the areas of first settlement, which were for the most part inner-city areas, where their children became delinquent in large numbers. As these groups became assimilated and moved out of the inner-city areas their descendants disappeared from the Juvenile Court and their place was taken by offenders from the groups which took over the areas which had been vacated.

> From these data it was possible to make several generalizations relevant to delinquent behavior. The first is that most of the delinquents in Chicago have been produced in turn by the newest large immigrant or migrant groups in the city. During

the first decades of this century a large proportion of the delinquents were the children of German or Irish immigrants. Thirty years later a large proportion of the offenders were the children of Polish and Italian immigrants who replaced the German and Irish in the inner-city areas (Shaw and McKay 1969, p. 374).

Ethnic uniformity and susceptibility to delinquency have been severely criticized on methodological grounds (Jonassen 1949). Shaw and McKay concede some of these limitations, but their interpretation of high rates of delinquency among blacks defended the view (Shaw and McKay 1949). Later work by McKay established the fact that black areas experiencing rapid invasion of lower socioeconomic groups had the highest rates of delinquency, and that black areas that became residentially stabilized experienced declining rates of delinquency (Shaw and McKay 1969). The important consideration in these discussions is that the crucial community factor as related to delinquency was the rapidity of ethnic and/or class turnover and the ensuing decline in social controls within the community.

Some ethnic groups remain longer than others in high delinquency areas and vary in their capacity to resist delinquency. Ethnic groups differ in modes of family organization (as in the extent of intact families), in their emphasis upon family responsibility, traditions of achievement, and in community organization and socioeconomic autonomy. Ethnic groups that emphasize achievement, that respond to educational influences, that have a developed sense of community and active, indigenous institutions to guide youths, are apt to resist sustained high rates of delinquency. For example, Japanese in Seattle had low rates of delinquents (Hayner 1933); the high rates of Jewish groups during their sojourn in slum areas declined in a relatively short period because of mobility to middle-class areas and agency intercession with problem youths (Robison 1960). Shaw and McKay doubtless desired to avoid stigmatizing any ethnic group and to demonstrate that delinquency affects all youths who reside in disorganized urban areas. Delinquency varies in frequency, form, and duration for diverse ethnic groups. Southern white delinquents differ from Puerto Rican and black delinquents, as do Irish and Polish delinquents. Despite differences, however, the processes associated with delinquency are similar. The urbanization process did in fact level many ethnic differences. To demonstrate their ecological-cultural transmission hypotheses, Shaw and McKay emphasized similarities rather than variations among ethnic groups (Shaw 1931; Shaw and McKay 1938, 1969).

Among the varied tribal or ethnic groups in Accra, the Gas had the highest percentage of delinquents. They were the first settlers in the area and comprised almost half the population. The Fantis, who came from the west coast, had fewer delinquents because of their tradition for pursuing education. Many youthful delinquents were in families that had migrated from the northern rural areas and had settled in slum areas. Thus, somewhat similar processes of susceptibility to delinquency occurred among youths in Accra and in Chicago.

## Delinquency as a Group Process

One crucial Shaw-McKay finding emphasized that delinquency, particularly stealing, was a group process rather than an individual experience. About 89 percent of the juveniles stole in groups of two or more associates. This group process of theft has been corroborated by other studies of delinquency in the urban community. Among 99 Ghanaian male delinquents for whom information was available, 94 percent were influenced by delinquent companions whom they knew and associated with prior to arrest (Weinberg 1964, p. 478). The modal clique size comprised two or three associates, again similar to the Shaw-McKay findings and consistent with other findings (Weinberg 1970; Short 1957). Thus, the transmission and execution of delinquency appear similar in these diverse cultural contexts.

## Delinquent Subcultures

Although the Shaw-McKay studies characterized delinquent subculture in detail, they did not explicitly categorize different delinquent subcultures. It is evident from their personal documents, however, that diverse life-styles among delinquents reflect varying delinquent subcultures (Cohen and Short 1958). One pervasive life-style among lower-class youths during the laissez-faire period of the twenties consisted of subsistence efforts through legitimate and illegitimate means. Thus, *Brothers in Crime* began their deviant careers with begging and stealing from people in middle-class neighborhoods. One of the brothers, James Martin, recalled that when he was six years old (Shaw, McKay, and McDonald 1938, p. 55):

> My brother Edward and a neighbor's kid, Joseph Wyman,
> taught me how to beg. I was so small and innocent looking that
> it was easy for me to deceive people. I would go to the door of a
> cottage or apartment.... If someone would answer, I would
> tell the person how poor my parents were. In this I was telling
> the truth. Seldom did I turn away without some money, food
> or clothing.

When no one responded to his knocking, ringing the bell, and
deliberate noise, he and his brother broke in the home to steal.
They used the money, frequently, for food and subsistence as well
as for treats, combining legitimate and illegitimate techniques to
attain subsistence and pleasurable ends. Brother Edward
recounts his home situation as follows:

> From my earliest recollection we were always in dire need.
> Our places of domicile were always of the cheapest, usually of
> the basement type. Many of the recollections of my childhood
> are of periods of sickness in these basement flats. From the
> smell of leaking gas to stinking garbage I pulled through it all
> until the age of seven when I received my first bath and first
> breath of clean fresh air at the Parental School. Although
> homesick for a while, I was made to feel at home there. To me
> it was better than home. The good food that I received there I
> never had at home (p. 130).

The fact that this punitive facility for wayward boys was a
desirable improvement over the boy's own home indicates the
extent of the poverty which was characteristic of many delinquents. The jack-roller fought with his stepfather and step-
brothers because they were abusive. In his fury at such mistreat-
ment, he fled from home, was caught, and was sent to the
Chicago Parental School. After serving his sentence, he experienced the same situation at home (Shaw 1930, p. 6):

> At the end of the first week I had a fight. I refused to sweep
> out the store when this fellow (stepfather) told me to, and he
> bawled me out. I couldn't do anything for him because of the
> way I felt about him and he got sore and started to grab me but
> I ducked and ran away. This time I was gone for three months,
> I didn't want to ever get back. When I was away this time I got
> in with two guys downtown and they started me in to picking
> pockets and making (shoplifting) in the Loop.

During his three-month absence from home, he was compelled to fend for himself. This precarious situation resembled that of the veranda boys in Accra, who also were on their own resources. As these boys grew older, stealing became a serious pursuit, a prospective mode of livelihood, a recourse for monetary gain rather than for pleasure or subsistence only.

These traits appear to characterize two delinquent subcultures. One way of life consisted of mischievous play and subsistence as a subculture among young delinquents. The other way was the contra-culture of crime as a source of livelihood among older delinquents and adult criminals.

While contemporary delinquents apparently do not resort to begging, they do participate in both subsistence and play activities. Some become more serious in their criminal behavior which then may be regarded as a potential source of livelihood. There is evidence that such activities sometimes assume the form of a systematic contra-culture (Cloward and Ohlin 1960; Short and Strodtbeck 1965).

The African delinquents, especially the veranda boys and others from poverty-ridden families, were akin to the American delinquents in the laissez-faire period as Shaw and McKay described them. Delinquents in both groups were concerned with subsistence, because they had to fend for themselves. Like American delinquents, the African boys combined legitimate and illegitimate techniques for subsistence ends, coupled with mischievous play. They worked at odd jobs, watched parked cars, and stole from the market stalls, from strangers in bus depots and cinemas, and at times hustled prospective customers for prostitutes.

As the African delinquents reached sixteen or seventeen, some began to conceive of a life of crime and to increase their contacts with adult offenders. They learned about fences for sale of stolen articles, about bribery of police, and about crime as a way of life and an occupation. This contra-culture seemed to specialize in machinery such as typewriters, recorders, sewing machines, and automobiles. But substantive differences between American and African delinquent subcultures reveal idiosyncratic aspects of delinquency in specific societies.

The West African delinquents used some hemp or marijuana but few, if any, were addicted to hard narcotics, such as heroin; they were similar in this respect to the delinquents characterized by Shaw and McKay. African delinquents also diverged from their American counterparts in that there were comparatively few gang fights and infrequent vandalism, rape, or assault.

Among African villages, urban areas within Accra proper, and the shantyville New Town, criminal and noncriminal groups of varying ages often existed together. Many African young delinquents apparently were unaware of older offenders and within their age-role orbit resorted to illicit capers for their own ends. It was only as they grew older that adult offenders and their contra-culture became known to these young men, who then would combine legitimate work with concerted efforts at theft. With unemployment high in these areas, unemployed migrants often lived with their relatives. Because of traditionally prescribed kinship obligations, these relatives grudgingly provided shelter. Many of these migrant adults were footloose and restless and prone to unorganized and petty thievery. A permissive attitude prevailed with respect to thievery from out-groups such as Europeans and strangers. Within the local area, one protected his property by vigilance and by juju, or black magic.

## Family Organization and Family Relations

The sociologist's concentration upon the influence of the peer group in delinquency has led to the neglect of systematic attention to the family's influence upon the onset of delinquency. The Shaw-McKay studies emphasized that the broken home is not a crucial influence in the onset of delinquency and that, while parent-child and father-son relations are fraught with conflict, these conflicts may or may not affect delinquency. They also made the point that older brothers and parents may contribute to the delinquency of younger boys by direct and indirect tutelage.

Subsequent studies of broken and intact families report that the broken family may affect personal offenders and young juveniles but has less influence upon property offenders, especially gang thieves (Cavan 1969). Miller argues that the single-parent, mother-dominated family is pervasive in the lower class, which is a generating milieu of delinquency (Miller 1958). Here the broken family is linked to delinquency by means of masculinity needs associated with family structure.

In slum areas of Ghana, as in the United States, parent-child conflict brought about alienation of boys from parents and greater responsiveness to street associates. But parent-child tensions and conflict must be differentiated in terms of the culturally prescribed Ghanaian family pattern, which is polygynous and matrilineal. Children live with the mother, and the father lives separately. The maternal uncle has authority over his sister's children. If our norm of family organization were applied to this maternal family pattern, which exists in many Ghanaian tribes, families would appear to be broken because of the absence of the father. Christian and middle-class families in Ghana generally accept the Western-style monogamous conjugal family pattern. Only 11.5 percent of the male delinquents and only 3 percent of the female delinquents resided with both parents. About 53 percent of the male delinquents and 64 percent of the female delinquents did not reside with either parent, but lived with a relative or alone. By contrast, of white and black American delinquents, according to Monahan (1957, pp. 230–58), 75 percent lived with both or one parent.

Broken homes were frequent among Ghanaian delinquents, as indicated by the estrangement or divorce of parents (41 percent) and by the death of one or both parents (21 percent) (Weinberg 1964). Thus, Ghanaian delinquents apparently had a higher broken-home rate than the delinquents studied by Shaw and McKay (1931) or those studied in contemporary society (Glueck 1950).

The extent and nature of such family influences cannot be fully ascertained. The young delinquents who resorted to illegitimate as well as legitimate activities appeared to be directly affected by estrangement from their families and by the lack of family control. But such family disorganization probably had less effect upon the more complex types of property offenders, who were more directly affected by their associates.

Shaw and McKay point out that, while some parents opposed the wayward behavior and thefts of their children, they lacked control. Other parents either did not know or pretended ignorance of such behavior. Some parents reacted by tacit acceptance or even encouragement of thefts (Shaw 1930). The jack-roller indicated that it was not unusual to find entire families stealing from freight cars, and he related the following:

> My stepmother sent me out with William (my stepbrother) to pick rags and bottles in the alleys. She said that would pay for my board and make me more useful than fretting and sulking at home. I did not mind that in the least. In fact, I enjoyed it because I was at least out of the old lady's reach. I

began to have a great time ... romping and playing in the
alleys and prairies gathering rags and iron and selling them to
the rag peddlers. . . . One day my stepmother told William to
take me to the railroad yard to break into box cars. William
always led the way and made the plans. He would open the
cars, and I would crawl in and hand out the merchandise. In
the cars were food stuffs, exactly the things my stepmother
wanted. We filled our cart, which we had made for this
purpose, and proceeded toward home. After we arrived home
with our ill-gotten goods, my stepmother would pat me on the
back and say I was a good boy and that I would be
rewarded. . . . After a year of breaking into box cars and
stealing from stores my stepmother realized that she could send
me to the market to steal vegetables for her (Shaw 1930, pp.
51–53).

This boy was left with almost no options to be law-abiding
unless he fled from home, an action which ironically would be
legally defined as truancy from the home.

Such patterns of parental influence upon delinquency were
also evident among delinquents in contemporary society. Among
Ghanaians the spectrum of parental attitudes also ranged from
those who completely resisted their children's effort at stealing to
those who virtually instigated such behavior. But few African
youths, as far as could be ascertained, were sent by their parents
to steal.

## Other Theoretical Formulations

The delinquent experiences described among the Ghanaians are
also relevant to other theoretical formulations of delinquent
behavior, particularly those developed by Cohen (1955) and by
Cloward and Ohlin (1960).

The Cohen version of delinquency as a process of inverting
middle-class values and emphasizing short-term hedonistic goals
seems only partially descriptive of delinquents in Accra. These
delinquents were relatively isolated from middle-class groups and
did not aspire for their acceptance. The middle class is proportionately smaller in Africa than in the United States and consists
primarily of white-collar workers, clerks, and supervisors in the
vast administrative bureaucracy, and of teachers and professionals. Although there was no direct evidence from the interviews
that the delinquent boys aspired to acceptance by middle-class
boys, short-term hedonistic pursuits were evident among some

delinquents who sought diversion by play from a boring stretch of free time during truancy from school. Instead of destructive vandalism or assault, their behavior took the form primarily of petty thefts. Of greater significance is the question of whether boys who are influenced by delinquents regarded their behavior as a "solution" to their problems. Perhaps their behavior may be a drift into a mischievous diversion to dispel their own boredom, as a basis for camaraderie, for the dare of an adventure, or in the search for food or treats. The view that a subculture is a standardized solution to a problem of subsistence or play is sustained. But recruitment and cultural transmission are related to the need for social acceptance by the individual and for new participants by the group.

The Cloward-Ohlin theoretical study (1960) is also fraught with problems. Although their version of legitimate and illegitimate means as opportunity systems toward given goals is logical, one significance of their contribution is the characterization of diverse delinquent subcultures. The applicability of their classification of subcultures is of little relevance to delinquency in Ghana. Two of their three subcultures, the conflict and the retreatist types, were not found in Accra. The existence of a criminal culture in slum areas in Accra could be discerned by the petty thefts from Europeans and strangers, which were tacitly approved by local residents, and by the concerted contra-culture of systematic thievery which was organized and secretive and at times, it appeared, in collusion with the police.

Whether individual characteristics attributed to group experiences are reductionistic depends upon whether the behavior of retreat has a shared motivational emphasis. Lindesmith and Gagnon (1964), for example, strenuously disagreed with the retreatist version of the drug addict's behavior. It would be of interest to ascertain what form of collective retreatist outlet could be found among youth prior to World War II, when drug addiction was minimal. In my study of schizophrenic youths in Chicago, I found that some resided in relatively high-rate delinquency areas where they were rejected by their delinquent peers and could not form friendships with conventional peers because they lacked the social skills to interact effectively. Hence they had become socially isolated (Weinberg 1967).

Generally, the sociological preoccupation with status and upward mobility among delinquents reflects the technologically advanced and highly mobile character of American society. But in technologically underdeveloped societies, as well as among some of the recent urban immigrants, the problems of subsistence and of economic needs are definitely of more immediate concern and of greater realistic importance than mobility.

Among people in Accra the ladders of mobility through legitimate means are more removed and inaccessible. The notion that organized criminal behavior may be a means for upward mobility, as it is in the United States, does not properly represent the situation. Many thieves, whether organized or unorganized, steal to supplement their legitimate means of livelihood, while for others stealing is their sole means of livelihood. If rackets exist in this developing society, they were certainly not widespread or visible.

## Conclusions

Despite differences, basic similarities in the rise and expression of juvenile delinquency in America and Ghana become promising points of departure for studying delinquency cross-culturally. Several hypotheses derived from Shaw-McKay have been investigated in other urbanized societies.

1. Juvenile delinquents who are detected and committed to rehabilitative or punitive institutions concentrate in disorganized slum areas.

2. Juvenile delinquents in slum areas experience lack of effective familial controls and tend to become estranged from the school.

3. Juvenile delinquency as expressed in stealing is learned informally from peer associates in the street and is executed predominantly as a group experience.

4. Delinquent experiences represent facets of a contra-culture the norms and goals of which tend to control and motivate the participants.

5. Delinquent subcultures vary in their motivating goals and include the subsistence-hedonic and career-oriented types.

These tentative cross-cultural hypotheses are amenable to revision, refinement, and elaboration by means of systematic inquiry in other urbanized societies. Hypotheses 1 and 3 have been seemingly confirmed in London (Scott 1956; Mannheim 1956), Paris (Vaz 1962), Berlin (Middendorff 1960), Mexico City (Hayner 1946), and Jerusalem (Reifen 1955).

Although H. C. Wilson (1958) has characterized delinquency

in Cardiff, Wales, as family-centered rather than peer-centered or community-centered, his inferences are derived from a clinical and individualistic perspective. By regarding delinquency as the outcome of emotional deprivation incurred from family relations, he does not analyze the influence of peers in the learning and development of delinquent behavior.

Generally considered, juvenile delinquency is a social phenomenon which is interwoven with the way of life in slum areas in different cultures. Hypotheses derived from Shaw and McKay are an important beginning for the research necessary to organize and verify knowledge of juvenile delinquency in diverse Western and non-Western urban cultures.

# References

Acquah, Ione
1958            *Accra Survey*. London: University of London.

Bloch, Herbert A., and Niederhoffer, Arthur
1958            *The Gang: A Study in Adolescent Behavior*. New York: Philosophical Library.

Burgess, Ernest W.
1925            "The Growth of the City." In *The City*. Edited by Robert E. Park et al. Chicago: University of Chicago Press.

Busia, Kofi
1950            *Report on a Social Survey of Sekondi-Takoradi*. Accra: Government Printing Office.

Cavan, Ruth
1969            *Juvenile Delinquency*. New York: J. B. Lippincott.

Chilton, Roland J.
1964            "Continuity in Delinquency Area Research: A Comparison of Studies for Baltimore, Detroit, Indianapolis." *American Sociological Review*. (February): 71–84.

Cloward, Richard A., and Ohlin, Lloyd E.
1960            *Delinquency and Opportunity*. New York: The Free Press.

Cohen, Albert K.
1955            *Delinquent Boys: The Culture of the Gang*. New York: The Free Press.

Cohen, Albert K., and Short, James F., Jr.
1958        "Research in Delinquent Subcultures." *Journal of Social Issues* 14: 20–37.

Gibbens, T. C. N., and Ahrenfeldt, R. H., editors
1966        *Cultural Factors in Delinquency*. Philadelphia: J. B. Lippincott.

Glueck, Sheldon and Eleanor
1950        *Unraveling Juvenile Delinquency*. Cambridge, Mass.: Harvard University Press.

Hayner, Norman
1933        "Delinquency Areas in the Puget Sound Region." *American Journal of Sociology* 39 (November): 314–28.
1946        "Criminogenic Zones in Mexico City." *American Sociological Review* 11 (August): 428–38.

Jonassen, Christen T.
1949        "A Reevaluation and Critique of the Logic and Some Methods of Shaw and McKay." *American Sociological Review*. (October): 608–14.

Klein, Malcolm W., editor
1967        *Juvenile Gangs in Context*. Englewood Cliffs, N.J.: Prentice-Hall.

Kobrin, Solomon
1951        "The Conflict of Values in Delinquency Areas." *American Sociological Review*. (October): 653–61.

Lindesmith, Alfred, and Gagnon, John
1964        "Anomie and Drug Addiction." *Anomie and Deviant Behavior*, edited by M. B. Clinard. New York: The Free Press. 174–85.

Mannheim, Hermann
1956        "Juvenile Delinquency." *The British Journal of Delinquency* 7 (June): 148–52.

Matza, David
1964        *Delinquency and Drift*. New York: John Wiley.

Middendorff, Wolf
1960        *New Forms of Juvenile Delinquency: Their Origin, Prevention and Treatment*. New York: United Nations, pp. 33–36.

Miller, Walter
1958        "Lower Class Culture as a Generating Milieu of Gang Delinquency." *Journal of Social Issues* 14 (3): 5–19.

Monahan, Thomas P.
1957            "Family Status and the Delinquent Child—A
                Reappraisal and Some New Findings." *Social
                Forces* (March): 230–58.

Reifen, S.
1955            "Juvenile Delinquency in a Changing Society."
                *The Jewish Social Service Quarterly* (Summer).

Robison, Sophia M.
1960            *Juvenile Delinquency*. New York: Holt, Rinehart
                and Winston.

Rosenquist, Carl M., and Megarzee, Edwin I.
1969            *Delinquency in Three Cultures*. Austin: The Uni-
                versity of Texas Press.

Salisbury, Harrison E.
1958            *The Shook-Up Generation*. Greenwich, Conn.:
                Fawcett Publications.

Scott, Peter
1956            "Gangs and Delinquent Groups in London."
                *British Journal of Delinquency* 7 (July): 4–26.

Shaw, Clifford R.
1930            *The Jackroller*. Chicago: University of Chicago
                Press.
1931            *Natural History of a Delinquent Career*. Chicago:
                University of Chicago Press.

Shaw, Clifford R., and McKay, Henry
1929            *Delinquency Areas*. Chicago: University of
                Chicago Press.
1931            *Social Factors in Juvenile Delinquency*. Report on
                the Causes of Crime. Washington, D.C.: U.S.
                Government Printing Office.
1949            "Rejoinder." *American Sociological Review*.
                (October): 614–17.
1969            *Juvenile Delinquency and Urban Areas*. Chicago:
                University of Chicago Press.

Shaw, Clifford R.; McKay, Henry, and McDonald, James F., eds.
1938            *Brothers in Crime*. Chicago: University of Chicago
                Press.

Short, James F., Jr.
1957            "Differential Association and Delinquency." *Social
                Problems* 4 (January).

Short, James F., Jr.; Rivera, Ramon; and Tennyson, Ray A.
1956            "Perceived Opportunities, Gang Membership and

Delinquency." *American Sociological Review* 30 (February): 56–57.

Short, James F., and Strodtbeck, Fred L.
1965          *Group Process and Gang Delinquency*. Chicago: University of Chicago Press.

Sklare, Marshall, editor
1958          *The Jews: Social Patterns of an American Group*. New York: The Free Press.

Spergel, Irving
1964          *Racketville, Slumtown, Haulberg*. Chicago: University of Chicago Press.

Sutter, Alan G.
               "Drug Use on the Street Scene." In *Delinquency, Crime and Social Process*, edited by D. R. Cressey and D. A. Ward. New York: Harper and Row.

Thrasher, Frederic
1927          *The Gang*. Chicago: University of Chicago Press.

Vaz, Edmund W.
1962          "Juvenile Gang Delinquency in Paris." *Social Problems* 10 (Summer): 21–23.

Weinberg, S. Kirson
1964          "Juvenile Delinquency in Ghana: Comparative Analysis of Delinquents and Non-Delinquents." *Journal of Criminal Law, Criminology and Police Science* 55 (December): 471–81.
1965*a*        "Urbanization and Male Delinquency in Ghana." *Journal of Research in Crime and Delinquency* 2 (July): 85–94.
1965*b*        "Urbanization and Delinquency in West Africa." In *Studies in Sociology* (9). Buenos Aires, Bibliografica Omega.
1967          "Social Psychological Aspects of Schizophrenia." In S. Kirson Weinberg, ed., *The Sociology of Mental Disorders*. Chicago: Aldine.
1970*a*        "Primary Group Theory and Closest Friendship of the Same Sex." In *Human Nature and Collective Behavior*, edited by Tamotsu Shibertani. Englewood Cliffs, N.J.: Prentice-Hall.
1970*b*        *Social Problems in Modern Urban Society*. Englewood Cliffs, N.J.: Prentice-Hall.

1973            "Female Delinquency in Ghana and West Africa: A Comparative Analysis." *International Review of Modern Sociology* 3 (March): 65-73.

Wilson, H. C.
1958            "Juvenile Delinquency in Problem Families in Cardiff." *The British Journal of Delinquency* 2 (October): 94-105.

# 7

## Community Organization and Property Crime
### A Comparative Study of Social Control in the Slums of an African City

*Marshall B. Clinard*
*Daniel J. Abbott*

Almost universally, the commitment to urbanization and industrialization in developing countries has been accompanied by sharp increases in property crime rates (see Clinard and Abbott 1973; Wolf 1971; Lunden 1962). Urban areas grow primarily by rural migration, in part a product of economic pressures at home and the search for a refuge from the dullness of village life and for the realization of new aspirations. The success or failure of the migrant's adaptation to this new urban world affects his chances of becoming a criminal offender. Of the many factors impinging on this outcome, the most important is the migrant's decision concerning place of residence within the city, although the majority has no alternative other than the slums.

In nearly all countries, regardless of development, most reported conventional property crimes are committed by urban slum residents, in the pattern described in the pioneer work of Shaw and McKay (1942, 1969; see also Morris 1958; Clinard and Abbott 1973). Some slum communities, however, are more successful than others in erecting barriers against property crime within their boundaries (Mangin 1967).[1] This study reports a comparative analysis of two local urban slum communities, one with a high crime rate and the other with a low rate. The study was conducted by the authors in Kampala, the capital and largest city of Uganda.[2] Uganda is a relatively small African country with a population of 9.5 million in 1969. Approximately 5 percent of the population live in urban areas, giving Uganda one of the lower rates of urbanization in Africa. The country's position on economic scales of development is comparatively low,

Marshall B. Clinard is a member of the Department of Sociology at the University of Wisconsin. Daniel J. Abbott is a member of the Department o Sociology at the University of New Orleans.

and it has primarily an agricultural economy. Political, commercial, and industrial activities are largely concentrated in Kampala, a city of 330,700 in 1969. The city reflects many of the problems associated with urbanization in developing countries—large, unskilled migrant population, extensive heterogeneity and cultural conflict, inability to provide adequate employment and housing, and an overrepresentation of young, unattached males. Although it possesses its own unique features, Kampala is representative of most of the developmental forces influencing the nature of criminality throughout the developing world.

The two slums studied in Kampala were similar in deteriorated physical conditions, but they had significantly different rates of property crime. Decisions on physical similarity and population size were simplified by a United Nations (1969) study of land use in Kampala. Population for one hundred subsections of the city was estimated with the aid of aerial photographs for less dense areas and individual canvassing in highly dense sectors. The United Nations researchers calculated each sector's population density and rated its physical condition on a three-point scale. Density of areas was classified as low (less than 20 inhabitants per acre), medium (20–60) and high (more than 60); general living conditions were designated as high, medium, or low, based on the quality of roads and lanes, water facilities, and living units in an area. The two sample communities were high on population density and low on general living conditions.

Two separate methods were used to assess the level of property crime in sixteen slum communities from which the two were selected: subjective ratings and official statistics. Supervisory police officers and probation officials were asked to rank the sixteen communities according to their degree of criminality. The rank numbers of eleven separate ratings for each area were added to give an overall index for ranking communities as to degree of criminality. In addition, rates of reported property crime were calculated for each subsection.

The average rate of property crime was 81.7 per 1,000 population for the high-crime slums and 10.7 for the low. The smallest reporting unit for criminal statistics was the territory covered by a police station, which always included several local areas in its jurisdiction. The only possible means of estimating rates was to consult the station records for all reported property crime in 1968; fortunately, place of offense was recorded by subarea, not by street address.

The high crime-rate slum area chosen for study was Kisenyi, an area which ranked first on subjective ratings of criminality and eighth on rate of reported property crime within the area. Kisenyi has been considered to be one of the most criminal areas in Kampala for many years, and it met the criteria of high density and poor physical conditions (see Southall and Gutkind 1957). Located adjacent to the bus station, major markets, and the business center, Kisenyi attracted many recent arrivals, especially those who had no relatives or friends to help them. It had the highest concentration of prostitutes in the city, a wide selection of bars with both legal and illegal beer, numerous gambling and dancing establishments, and an abundant supply of drugs (mostly marijuana).

Namuwongo, chosen for the low crime rate, is a highly dense peripheral area which ranked fifth on the subjective ratings of criminality and twelfth on rates of reported property crime. Its rate of 19.4 reported property crimes per 1,000 inhabitants was less than a third of Kisenyi's. Since its boundaries did not fall within the city limits until incorporation in 1967, Namuwongo had received little attention from agencies concerned with the physical improvement of urban conditions. A series of comparisons suggested that its living environment was worse than that of the more established Kisenyi.

### The Sample of Respondents

Two samples of males, one of men between eighteen and twenty-five and the other of men twenty-six and older, were selected from each community. Although both areas were densely populated, maps were available from the United Nations' study which identified each building, its use, the number of households, and the size of each household. All households in Kisenyi and Namuwongo, 1,914 and 2,314 respectively, were numbered, and samples of 350 for Kisenyi and 347 for Namuwongo were drawn from a table of random numbers, for which substitutions were provided.[3] To maximize the variance in age distribution and to avoid a sample of respondents that happened to be at home on a particular day, interviewers were instructed to seek the youngest male eighteen years or over in households with even code numbers and the oldest male in households with odd code numbers. Many of the difficulties typical of sampling in highly mobile slums were encountered, and the original sample of 697 was reduced considerably (see table 7.1). The final total of 534 cases, 250 from Kisenyi and 284 from Namuwongo, was divided by age into those between eighteen and twenty-five and those twenty-six or older. The results are shown in table 7.2. Each of these persons was interviewed with a schedule which took approximately one hour. The interviews were conducted by twelve advanced Makerere University students who had received extensive training and who were associated full-time with the project for several months (see Clinard and Abbott 1973).

TABLE 7.1    Outcome of Original Community Sample of 647 for Kisenyi and Namuwongo

|  | Kisenyi | | Namuwongo | |
|  | No. | % | No. | % |
| --- | --- | --- | --- | --- |
| Interviewed | 250 | 71.4 | 284 | 81.8 |
| Refused | 10 | 2.9 | 10 | 2.9 |
| Women only | 31 | 8.9 | 8 | 2.3 |
| Buildings vacant or destroyed | 5 | 1.5 | 9 | 2.6 |
| No African resident | 17 | 4.9 | 0 | 0 |
| Language problems | 8 | 2.2 | 0 | 0 |
| Never located | 29 | 8.2 | 36 | 10.4 |
| Total households | 350 | 100.0 | 347 | 100.0 |

TABLE 7.2    Age Distribution of 534 Males Interviewed, by Community

|  | Kisenyi | | Namuwongo | | | |
| Age | No. | % | No. | % | Total | % |
| --- | --- | --- | --- | --- | --- | --- |
| 18–25 | 100 | 40.0 | 106 | 36.9 | 206 | 38.6 |
| 26+ | 150 | 60.0 | 178 | 63.1 | 328 | 61.4 |
| Total | 250 | 100.0 | 284 | 100.0 | 534 | 100.0 |

## The Analytical Model and Results

It was hypothesized that effective control of property crime within a slum community requires sufficient knowledge of, and friendship among, neighbors so that: (1) there is a tendency to reject theft within the group, (2) neighbors will informally guard each other's property, (3) strangers can be readily identified, and

(4) residents will offer assistance if someone is attacked. These bonds must be firm because economic and other pressures to steal can be great among slum dwellers.

Certain social structures appear to facilitate the growth and maintenance of such bonds while others seem antithetical to their existence. Landecker (1951) suggested four types of integration characteristic of social groups: normative, cultural, communicative, and functional. While he did not suggest the direction of influence among the four types of integration, directionality is implied and specified in this study (see fig. 7.1). Consequently we have assumed that a high degree of communicative integration is expected to be associated with less crime. Persons with similar cultural backgrounds and experiences are able to communicate more effectively. While this does not preclude severe cleavages, in the heterogeneous urban environment, similarities are of importance as forms of support. High degrees of cultural integration increase the probabilities of friendships and a more solid communicative integration, all of which act as effective forms of social control over crime. Functional integration affects the degree of normative integration, as reflected in the rate of property crime in a community, in two ways: (1) persons are more likely to come into contact with unfavorable definitions of crime; and, (2) if a person has a job, power, or status through contacts outside the community, he will be less likely to jeopardize them by arrest and imprisonment.

Fig. 7.1

Cultural $\longrightarrow$ Communicative $\longrightarrow$ Functional $\searrow$ Normative Integration

## Normative Integration

Relying upon the work of Angell (1941), Landecker (1951) has suggested that a crime index can be used as a measure of normative integration, defined as the degree to which group conduct conforms to cultural standards. In this study normative integration was measured by rates of property crime and residents' perceptions of their communities. When asked about the likelihood of property being stolen in their communities, Namuwongo men felt that the danger was less than did those from Kisenyi. Respondents were also asked, "What do other

people think of this area?" and "What do you think of this area?"
Although slightly over half of the Namuwongo respondents
replied "Don't know" to the first question, the difference between
the responses was striking. In Kisenyi, the high crime-rate area,
83 percent of the men felt that outsiders' perceptions of their
community were negative (see table 7.3). The difference between
the high- and low-crime communities was also great for the
second question (see table 7.4). A much larger proportion of
respondents in Kisenyi, 44.4 percent versus 17.9 percent, felt that
their residential area was "not a good place to live." People's
perceptions of their surroundings develop from, and are influenced by, the nature of their interactions in their communities.
Kisenyi's residents saw their areas as being much more criminal

TABLE 7.3    Responses to: "What do other people think of this area?"

|  | Kisenyi | | Namuwongo | |
|---|---|---|---|---|
|  | No. | % | No. | % |
| 1. Bad place (drunkards, murderers, etc.) | 182 | 83.1 | 59 | 43.7 |
| 2. Not clean enough | 3 | 1.4 | 6 | 4.4 |
| 3. Good place | 29 | 13.2 | 27 | 20.0 |
| 4. Wish to improve it | 4 | 1.8 | 16 | 11.9 |
| 5. Good only for Luos | 0 | 0 | 22 | 16.3 |
| 6. Other | 1 | .4 | 5 | 3.7 |
| Total* | 219 | 100.0 | 135 | 100.0 |
| Don't know or no response | 55 | 22.0 | 156 | 55.0 |

* In several instances there were multiple responses to the item. All responses
were summed together, and totals are accordingly larger than the sample size.

TABLE 7.4    Responses to: "What do you think of your community?"

|  | Kisenyi | | Namuwongo | |
|---|---|---|---|---|
|  | No. | % | No. | % |
| 1. Good place | 56 | 24.3 | 80 | 37.0 |
| 2. Satisfactory | 23 | 10.0 | 29 | 13.4 |
| 3. Standard of living is too low | 4 | 1.8 | 15 | 7.0 |
| 4. Not a good place (dirt, theft, unemployment, underdevelopment) | 107 | 46.5 | 40 | 18.5 |
| 5. Improvements are necessary (lights, roads, buses, etc.) | 18 | 7.8 | 34 | 15.8 |
| 6. Nothing, except to live in | 22 | 9.6 | 18 | 8.3 |
| Total | 230 | 100.0 | 216 | 100.0 |
| Don't know or no response | 22 | 8.9 | 61 | 21.5 |

than did those in Namuwongo: the following comments are typical of the Kisenyi residents.

Each one looks after his property as best he can.
I have often been threatened by thieves in Kisenyi.
Each one guards his house in Kisenyi and theft is still rampant, particularly at night.
It teaches someone how to be tough and careful because one is constantly worried about his property.

On the other hand, comments such as the following were made about Namuwongo:

People like to stay here because there are few troubles, or at least few troubles like theft and fights.
There are fewer troubles like theft, quarrels, or drunkenness here.

## Cultural Integration

Cultural integration refers to the internal consistency of cultural standards within a group. Integration is lacking when group values and expectations make conflicting demands upon members. In most urban areas of African countries it is doubtful if many totally integrated communities exist, since culturally distinct ethnic groups are often clustered only in small pockets. If the local community is the unit of analysis, it is almost impossible to determine the internal consistency of each cultural subgroup. A more workable measure is the number and proportion of different cultural groups represented within the boundaries of the local community as a whole.

While similarity of cultural background is significant, success or failure in adjustment to an urban environment can also be affected by conscious attempts to preserve cultural beliefs and traditions. In the Mexico City barrio studied by Lewis (1965), residents survived the more disruptive aspects of urban life through emphasis on common traditions, aided by regular visits to their home villages. Similar results were found in a study of migrant adaptation in Brazil (Wilkening et al. 1967). Parkin's (1969) study of Kampala found that "the need for ultimate social security is one of a number of reasons for maintaining strong links with the rural home." Large regional associations have developed in Lima, Peru, to help the migrant adjust to city life (Mangin 1965).[4] Maintenance of kin and tribal ties could reduce the dissonance created by the many conflicting definitions of proper behavior with which the migrant must contend.

*Tribal Homogeneity.*   The principal means for measuring cultural integration in the two communities was the degree of tribal homogeneity, which refers to the number of tribes and their proportional representation within a local community. When there are fewer tribes, the chances are greater that individual members will receive more consistent definitions of traditionally accepted behavior. Other factors also determine whether the individual achieves a consistent and stable set of norms and values that might inhibit criminal behavior, such as frequent contacts with "kin" in both city and village. Interaction of this nature helps to reinforce basic traditions, and restriction of close friendships to members of one's own tribe may have the effect of reducing the normative dissonance characteristic of the city.

The degree of tribal homogeneity was calculated by a technique suggested by Lieberson (1969) which gives the probability of encountering two persons from a different tribe if they were randomly chosen from a specific community. The probability was much greater for Kisenyi (.906) than for Namuwongo (.724). Although this finding indicates greater homogeneity in Namuwongo, it understates the differences between the two communities. Men from thirty-four different tribes were included in the Kisenyi sample, compared to twenty-five tribes in Namuwongo. The dominant tribal group in Namuwongo, the Luo, represented 48 percent of the population in this area, whereas the largest proportion for any tribe in Kisenyi was 23.5 percent. Men in Kisenyi were aware that tribal heterogeneity was characteristic of their area, and they stated this clearly in the interviews. As one respondent said, "It is a place which brings all tribes together."[5]

*Tribal Diversity in Friendships.*   Restricting friendships to members of one's own tribe may reduce heterogeneous influences which lead to questioning important values or traditions opposed to property crime. Members of the same tribe have greater potential for exercising control over each other since they are much more likely to communicate with family members at home, and these ties with the village presumably provide a strong emotional force in the lives of African urban dwellers.

Respondents were asked to name the tribe of their three best friends, and a numerical scale measuring diversity of friendships was constructed.[6] The F score comparing the younger men from the two communities was not statistically significant, while for those over twenty-five it was highly significant. The older men from Kisenyi had close friends from a much wider spectrum of tribal groups than did those from Namuwongo. It might be argued that the more restricted friendship patterns among older males in Namuwongo would follow naturally from its greater tribal homogeneity. If this reasoning was valid, some difference would be expected between the young respondents. However, both groups were just as likely to have close friends from different tribal groups. The older men in Namuwongo served to strengthen cultural integration in the community by limiting contact with alternate definitions and values.

*Contact with Relatives.*    Members of each community were questioned as to whether they had relatives in Kampala and whether they had any form of contact with them, even if only on an irregular basis. There were no significant differences between the two slum areas for either age group. In all cases at least 90 percent of those who had kin in Kampala reported some form of family interaction (Parkin 1969). Such responses indicated the continued strength of family ties, even in urban areas. The interview item did not measure the relative closeness or importance of each relationship, but the data were adequate to suggest that this type of communication was not highly relevant for community crime control.

There was also no significant statistical difference between the two communities for either age group in the frequency of visits with relatives in the village. Of the total community sample, only 29 percent reported that they never visited relatives in their home villages. Although relations with family, both in the city and in the village, appear to be critical in the process of adjustment to urban living, they do not appear to be an important differentiating element in the role of community social organization in controlling property crime.

*Communicative Integration*

Communicative integration indicates the extent to which patterns of verbal exchange permeate the group. Communication patterns have been emphasized in studies of slum areas in the United States (see especially Suttles 1968). Communicative integration operates on both individual and organizational levels, but our use of the concept is more organizational than Landecker's (1951). At the individual level it refers to the everyday interactions which occur among residents of the community. The nature of these relationships can be analyzed on three dimensions— scope, depth, and exclusivity. Scope refers to the number of acquaintances an individual can relate to within the community on a basis that goes beyond simple recognition of a common geographical location. Depth, the degree of commitment members have to each other, is indicated by the degree to which people are willing to sacrifice or inconvenience themselves for another person. Exclusivity is defined as the degree to which close friendships are limited to members within the community.

The stability of a population affects its ability to sustain communication. In a case where a significant portion of the population remains only for a short period of time, formation of binding ties and commitments through organizations is severely hampered. Communication on a more formal level, that is, participation in voluntary organizations, can have a potent effect on the tone of the social environment (see Little 1965) by providing the opportunity for relationships to develop between groups within the total community.

*Community Selection and Mobility.*    One of the most critical decisions affecting the urban experiences of any individual is the selection of a place to live and the motivation behind the decision. Table 7.5 shows the reasons given for such choices by the sample from Kisenyi and Namuwongo. The men from Namuwongo much more frequently moved there because of friends or relatives (56.8 percent versus 36.8 percent). The factors surrounding the movement to Kisenyi more often reflected a response to the exigencies of urban life—employment, chance, and cheap housing. The men from Kisenyi apparently were more often compelled to establish a base from which they had little immediate support by relatives or friends.

High turnover in local population makes it difficult for a community to control residents' behavior and to develop stable lines of communication. The difference between the two communities on mobility, measured by the number of residence changes in Kampala, was statistically significant. This was true for both the younger and older groups, but it was stronger for those over twenty-five. The men from Kisenyi tended to change residence in the city more often than the men from Namuwongo. There were no significant statistical differences, however, between the two communities on length of residence. Only 30 percent in Kisenyi and 35 percent in Namuwongo had lived in their communities for more than five years.

TABLE 7.5    Responses to: "Why did you move to your community?"

|  | Kisenyi | | Namuwongo | |
|---|---|---|---|---|
|  | No. | % | No. | % |
| 1. To live with friend, or relatives | 92 | 36.8 | 153 | 56.8 |
| 2. Cheap housing | 61 | 24.4 | 60 | 20.9 |
| 3. Find a job | 26 | 10.4 | 17 | 5.9 |
| 4. Near place of employment | 47 | 18.8 | 19 | 6.6 |
| 5. Born there | 3 | 1.2 | 5 | 1.7 |
| 6. Chance | 18 | 7.2 | 4 | 1.4 |
| 7. Told it was a good place | 3 | 1.2 | 19 | 6.6 |
| Total* | 250 | 100.0 | 287 | 100.0 |
| Don't know or no response | 16 | 6.4 | 6 | 2.1 |

\* Multiple responses to open-ended questions were simply summed, and therefore the totals are frequently larger than the sample size.

*Individual Relationships.*    Effective control of property crime within a community depends, in part, upon mutual knowledge and friendship among members. Isolated individuals with few bonds to the people around them are less likely to support neighbors when trouble arises. As one respondent from Kisenyi stated, "Even when people see theft occurring they simply say that they are killing him and they go on their way. No help is offered. Each one to himself, that's what they do."[7] A large proportion of isolates in a community makes identification of strangers more difficult.

The scope of individual relationships was measured by asking "How many different places are there in your community where you know people and go by to visit every once in a while?" While the differences between the two areas were statistically significant for both age groups, they were much stronger for the older group. Men from Namuwongo reported greater visitation. The situation in Kisenyi was reflected in the comment of a respondent:

"No two neighbors can sit down and talk about how to reduce theft. Everyone is for himself."

Depth measured the strength of bonds among community members. Respondents were asked: "Will a person's neighbors give him any help if he loses his job?" and "Are the marriages or relations between men and women living together firm and lasting here?" The first item, reflecting responsiveness in time of financial crises, was chosen because the economic factor is one of the most critical uncertainties in the slum areas of all developing countries. Differences between the two communities on willingness to give financial help to others were not statistically significant for either age group. Only 20.8 percent of the men in Kisenyi and 33.8 percent of the men in Namuwongo stated that a man would receive help from his neighbors in any financial crisis. Even in Namuwongo, where the unity appeared greater, many were pessimistic about receiving help, one saying that people do not offer help "because everyone struggles for himself and they are people of my economic status." Another said that they give help only if they have been "very good neighbors." These answers are in sharp contrast to the village setting, where a man generally can expect help as his right.

The second question investigated not only the stability but also the strength of a primary bond, the family unit, on the assumption that more tightly knit families provide more effective resistance to the disorienting effects of urban life which impede the operation of informal social control. The differences in perception of permanence in the bonds between men and women were striking, both young and old in Namuwongo perceiving greater firmness and stability in relations between men and women in their community (85 percent in Namuwongo compared to 40 percent in Kisenyi). A Kisenyi respondent described the situation as: "A person married today will be a bachelor tomorrow. There is no love. People marry to get sexual enjoyment for a day or two." Another said that the family is weak because many women are not properly married, and there is a lot of prostitution. The strength of the family in Namuwongo stemmed in part from the value placed on marriage by the migrant groups living there. Informal social control of family members was enhanced by greater degrees of social cohesiveness in the community. A community leader in Namuwongo claimed that, if a man had a family back in the village and began to live with another woman in the city, leaders in the community would sometimes bring the family to Kampala.

The third area of individual relationships was exclusivity, that is, the degree to which close friendships were limited to members of the community. Respondents were asked where their three best friends lived. A four-point scale rating the individual on extent of exclusiveness was constructed by means of a mathematical technique developed by Lieberson (1969). There was no significant statistical difference on this scale between the communities in either age group. The distribution on the scale was almost evenly split in both areas—half had few friendships outside the community and the other half had many. Even though interaction among community leaders appeared to be higher in Namuwongo, many of their close friends lived outside the community. Perhaps mobility and work patterns had a more uniform effect on the locale of friends, and the pressure for living space forced close village friends to live in separate parts of the city. Thus the two aspects of individual relationships which considered the nature of interaction within communities (scope and depth) were statistically significant, but the variable which treated relations with outsiders (exclusivity) was not significant in affecting the degree of social control over property crime within the two communities.

*Participation in Organizations.*  Voluntary organizations are often an important part of African urban life, particularly West Africa; they include a wide range of activities such as self-help, recreational, political, ethnic, or religious groups. Respondents were asked to name their organizational memberships and were classified as active members if they had attended a meeting in the last six months.[8] Namuwongo was significantly higher than Kisenyi on participation in local community organizations, especially among older respondents. Twenty percent of the Namuwongo, but only 7 percent of the Kisenyi, respondents reported active participation in some local organization. Of particular importance are the tribal unions found in many parts of urban Africa (see Post 1964). The dominant group in Namuwongo, the Luo, has a strong union which provided numerous local community services for its members (see Jellicoe 1969). It established a credit union to help parents educate their children, organized sports teams, and even arranged for the dead to be buried in their tribal homeland. Thus the community with the lower crime rate appeared to have a higher degree of organizational unity.

Religion is an integral part of contemporary urban life in much of Africa (see Kuper 1965; Lloyd 1967; Wiley 1971). The data on attendance indicated that there were significant differences between the two communities, but there appeared to be a strong religious life in both communities. Although 66 percent of both age groups from Namuwongo claimed weekly attendance, so did 44 percent of the respondents in Kisenyi. Regular participation in religious services appeared to serve several functions, for example, interaction with other community members enhanced the sense of belonging, and noncriminal values were reinforced.

## Functional Integration

Functional integration was originally defined as interdependence of group members through a division of labor. This definition has limited use, however, within the boundaries of a small urban slum, as there is a limited degree of economic specialization within such local communities. The concept is more useful if modified to refer to integration into the larger urban society through participation in its organizations and institutions. Ties could develop through certain occupations, due to more education, or by membership in nonlocal organizations or political parties. In a study in Cordoba, Argentina, for example, DeFleur (1969, 1970) developed a theory of delinquency based on a series of concepts similar to this definition of functional integration. She hypothesized that the low institutional involvement of the lower class does not provide the experiences necessary to internalize societal norms. The lower class has low rates of participation in political, educational, economic, and religious institutions. The youth, as a result, do not have the necessary pressures brought upon them to restrict their contacts with delinquent boys.

Generally speaking, functional integration did not distinguish between high and low crime-rate communities. It was hypothesized that the community with a higher proportion of men functionally integrated into the large urban community would have a lower property-crime rate. This type of integration was divided into two parts, socioeconomic integration and participatory integration. Included in the first type were such variables as education and occupation; under the second were participation in urban organizations and civic participation.

*Socioeconomic Integration.* Education and occupation were the principal factors used to measure socioeconomic status. There were no differences between the two communities on the average education of the younger males, but there was a strong relationship for the older males. The older generation in the high crime community, Kisenyi, was better educated than the older men from the low crime community. Community cohesiveness apparently does not depend on a higher level of education among members. The lower educated group in the community sample, the older males from Namuwongo, was a primary source of unity and control in the low crime community. Perhaps the low level of education among the older men was related to attachment to traditional tribal ways. There was also a consistent trend for the respondents from the high crime community to have an equal or even a higher socioeconomic position as measured by occupation. The younger men from the high crime-rate community clearly tended to have higher occupations, but there was no significant difference between the two communities on the general occupations of either age group.

*Participatory Integration.*    Two separate approaches were used to investigate participatory integration in activities outside the community that would presumably reinforce conformity to societal values. The first was active membership in organizations such as labor unions, political parties, and various city-wide cooperatives which extend beyond the local community. The second, civic participation, was measured by asking the respondents such questions as whether they had attended an Independence Day ceremony or had spoken with a councilman about a problem. Seven items on civic participation were included in the interview schedule.

No significant differences were found between the two communities on participation in urban organizations for either age group. Twenty-two percent of the men in Namuwongo and 18 percent of the Kisenyi men reported active membership in at least one urban organization. There was also no significant difference between the two communities in civic participation for either the younger or the older groups.[9] The percent in the category for low civic participation was 64.5 for Namuwongo and 62.4 percent for Kisenyi. Except in the case of Independence Day ceremonies, minimal participation in activities of this type would be expected of a poorly educated migrant population. These general results fit somewhat the Mexican findings of Cavan and Cavan (1968) where the members of the barrio derived their strength and solidarity through their isolation from the dominant groups outside their communities. By remaining aloof they preserved customs and values contradictory to criminal involvement and gained a sense of purpose and belonging. This finding is also consistent with a study of three barrios in Colombia which differed in both age and internal cohesion. The measures of participation in nonlocal organizations did not distinguish between the three slums studied in the project (see Havens and Ugandizaga 1966).

## Conclusions

Some urban slums appear to be more successful than others in controlling criminal behavior. The two communities analyzed in this study, a high crime-rate community, Kisenyi, and a low crime-rate community, Namuwongo, in Kampala, Uganda, demonstrated a wide disparity in rates of property crime and in the residents' perceptions of local criminality. The men from the high crime community were much more likely to perceive frequent theft, fighting, and drunkenness in their immediate surroundings. Both statistically and perceptually there was a distinct behavioral difference between the two urban slums. On the other hand, no significant differences were found between either age group in the communities on the question of whether theft was wrong. The common disapprobation of theft suggests that, while most residents were opposed to stealing, one community was better structured to implement this opposition.

The explanation for the difference is imbedded in the differential social organization of the two communities. The low crime slum possessed higher degrees of both cultural and communicative integration. Namuwongo was tribally much more homogeneous, and its older generation selected their close friends from a limited variety of cultural backgrounds. The analysis of communicative integration indicated that in the low crime community, particularly among those over twenty-five, there was more visiting, less mobility, and greater participation in local community organizations, including religious groups. The high crime-rate area was less likely to report stable family relationships, and there was an overall impression of greater individual isolation. There was no difference, however, in the willingness to give financial help to others. A large, approximately equal proportion of both communities said that they would leave if they had an opportunity. Men from Namuwongo changed residence in Kampala less often than those from Kisenyi, but the average length of residence was quite similar. The low crime-rate area was able to maintain a sufficient degree of communicative unity to control property crime in spite of a fairly rapid turnover in population. In terms of functional integration there was no significant statistical difference in the links community members had with the larger urban areas for organizational and civic participation, and occupation and education, if anything, were negatively related to the crime level in a community. Occupation and education levels were significantly higher for young males in the high crime community.

Some tentative conclusions are of particular importance and thus warrant further investigation. First, while urbanization and industrialization erode traditional authority and negate the usefulness of the knowledge and experiences of older persons, those in the older group seem still to play a vital role in determining the character of urban slum communities. Second, a higher average socioeconomic status does not necessarily increase community members' ability to control behavior within its own areas, nor does a fairly rapid change in population destroy cohesiveness automatically. The latter finding may call into question some of the assumptions regarding the critical variables in city slum areas in both developed and developing countries. Finally, with respect to functional versus communicative integration and control of property crime, internal relations and patterns of behavior within the local community are the more important and appear to be somewhat independent of linkages outside the community.

This African community research study was greatly influenced by the work of Shaw and McKay in relating ordinary crime to the social and cultural factors operating within a local community. They shifted the emphasis away from the individual and the family to the process of urbanization and to the local community. This approach was confirmed in the African study. Yet there have always been many largely unanswered questions, in particular why slum communities vary so much in their crime rates, and why the crime rates of slum communities often change. It is possible that the findings of this research, while done in a less developed country, may in turn contribute to more sophisticated studies in developed countries of the relation of crime to cultural, communicative, functional, and normative integration in local communities.

## Notes

1. Property crime represents a more accurate index of the interaction between urbanization, community social organization, and criminality than crime against the person, for the principal response to urban growth is generally marked increases in burglary, robbery, and theft. Murder and assault most often grow out of personal disputes which, although related to subcultural definitions, need not directly reflect the processes of urbanization.

2. The research was carried out in 1968–69 (prior to the political takeover of the government by General Amin) at Makerere University under a teaching and research grant from the Rockefeller Foundation. Additional support was secured from the University of Wisconsin Research Committee. For a full account of the research, as well as data on crime in other developing countries, see Clinard and Abbott 1973.

3. There was considerable turnover of population, especially in the high crime community of Kisenyi. The United Nations' survey was conducted in August 1968, and by the time this research was begun, only six months later, fourteen buildings had been torn down or abandoned. Because of time pressure, two peripheral sections of Namuwongo were removed from the sample and the original number of households selected was reduced from 400 to 347.

4. Mayer (1962) describes how one portion of African migrants to the South African town of East London escaped disruptive influences of urban migration through frequent visits home and systematic rejection of contact with nontraditional influences.

5. The clustering of tribes within the communities was also distinctly different. Although Namuwongo contains a sizable number of tribal groups, there was a greater tendency for the Namuwongo migrants to gather into homogeneous enclaves than was the case in Kisenyi. Within some small sections of Namuwongo, Luos made up 75 percent of the respondents. In another small section of Namuwongo, representing 10.7 percent of the sample, the Banyaruanda totaled 78 percent of those interviewed. On the other hand, in no subsection of Kisenyi did one tribe comprise more than 57 percent of the sample.

6. Responses were coded 0 if no friend was mentioned, 1 if the friend was from the same tribe, and 2 if he was from a different tribe.

$$\text{Score} = \frac{3 \times (\text{Sums of responses})}{\text{Number of friends mentioned}}$$

It was necessary to develop the scale in this manner because some respondents mentioned only one or two friends.

7. In 1968, in a robbery in one of the more dense, heterogeneous slum areas of Kampala, a gang smashed the door with a rock, beat the occupants, and stole what they could find. No one responded to their pleas for help.

8. Organizations were classified into either "local" or "urban," urban implying that the membership was drawn from all parts of the city. Numerical scales were constructed for each category based on the number of active memberships. Attendance at a religious service was treated separately.

9. A scale of civic participation was developed by summing responses to the items and trichotomizing the scores into low, medium, and high participation. To a certain extent these findings confirm the validity of the scale. It was first used in a study of a slum and a more settled government housing estate in Mombasa (Stren 1968). The latter had a much higher rate of civic participation.

# References

Angell, Robert C.
1941            "The Social Integration of Selected American Cities." *American Journal of Sociology* 47:575-92.

Cavan, Ruth Shonle, and Jordan T. Cavan
1968            *Delinquency and Crime: Cross-Cultural Perspectives.* Philadelphia: J. B. Lippincott, pp. 45-49.

Clinard, Marshall B., and Daniel J. Abbott
1973            *Crime in Developing Countries: A Comparative Perspective.* New York: Wiley-Interscience.

DeFleur, Lois B.
1969            "Alternate Strategies for the Development of Delinquency Theories Applicable to Other Cultures." *Social Problems* 17 (Summer): 30-39.
1970            *Delinquency in Argentina: A Study of Cordoba's Youth.* Pullman: Washington State University Press.

Havens, Eugene, and Elsa Ugandizaga
1966            *Tres Barrios de Invasion.* Bogata: Ediciones Tercer Mundo, p. 74.

Jellicoe, Margaret
1969            "Credit and Housing Associations Among the Luo Migrants of Kampala." Kampala: Makerere Institute of Social Research, mimeographed.

Kuper, Hilda
1965            *Urbanization and Migration in West Africa.* Berkeley: University of California Press, p. 12.

Landecker, Werner S.
1951        "Types of Integration and Their Measurement."
            *American Journal of Sociology* 61:332-40.

Lewis, Oscar
1965        "Urbanization without Breakdown." In Dwight
            Heath and Richard Adams, eds., *Contemporary
            Cultures and Societies of Latin America*. New
            York: Random House.

Lieberson, Stanley
1969        "Measuring Population Density." *American Socio-
            logical Review* 34 (December): 850-62.

Little, Kenneth
1965        *West African Urbanization*. Cambridge: Cam-
            bridge University Press.

Lloyd, P. C.
1967        *Africa in Social Change: Changing Traditional
            Societies in the Modern World*. Baltimore: Penguin,
            pp. 258-60.

Lunden, Walter A.
1962        "The Increase of Criminality in Underdeveloped
            Countries." *Police* 6 (May-June): 30-34.

Mangin, William
1965        "The Role of Regional Association in the Adaptation
            of Rural Migrants to Cities in Peru." In Dwight
            Heath and Richard Adams, eds., *Contemporary
            Cultures and Societies of Latin America*. New York:
            Random House.
1967        "Latin American Squatter Settlements: A Problem
            and A Solution." *Latin American Research Review*
            2 (Summer): 65-69.

Mayer, Philip
1962        *Townsmen or Tribesmen: Urbanization in a
            Divided Society*. Capetown: Oxford University
            Press.

Morris, Terence
1958        *The Criminal Area: A Study in Social Ecology*.
            London: Routledge and Kegan Paul.

Parkin, David
1969        *Neighbors and Nationals in an African City Ward*.
            London: Routledge and Kegan Paul, p. 186.

Post, Ken
1964          *The New States of Africa.* Baltimore: Penguin
              Books, p. 80.

Shaw, Clifford R., Henry D. McKay, et al.
1942          *Juvenile Delinquency and Urban Areas.* Rev. ed.
1969          Chicago: University of Chicago Press.

Southall, Aiden, and P. C. W. Gutkind
1957          *Townsmen in the Making: Kampala and Its Sub-
              urbs.* London: Kegan Paul, Trench, Trubner.

Stren, Richard E.
1968          "Report on Housing Survey of Mombasa." Dar es
              Salaam: University College, mimeographed.

Suttles, Gerald D.
1968          *The Social Order of the Slum: Ethnicity and Ter-
              ritory in the Inner City.* Chicago: University of
              Chicago Press.

United Nations
1969          *Report on Survey of Present Land Uses and Master
              Plan Programme for Kampala.* Kampala: United
              Nations Regional Planning Mission.

Wiley, S. David
1971          "Social Stratification and Religion in Urban
              Zambia: An Explanatory Study in an African Sub-
              urb," Ph. D. dissertation, Princeton Theological
              Seminary.

Wilkening, Eugene, Joao Bosco Pinto, et al.
1967          "The Role of the Extended Family in Migration
              and Adaptation in Brazil." Research paper, Land
              Tenure Center, University of Wisconsin.

Wolf, Preben
1971          "Crime and Development: An International Com-
              parison of Crime Rates." *Scandinavian Studies in
              Criminology* 3:107–21.

# IV    Social Theory and Social Policy

# 8 Restraint of Trade, Recidivism, and Delinquent Neighborhoods

*Donald R. Cressey*

The organization of business corporations with reference to criminal violations of antitrust law is remarkably similar to the way slum areas of large cities are organized with reference to property crimes and delinquencies. Each form of organization is constructed on an ideology conducive to widespread law violation, including the notion that some crime is not crime, "really." And in neither the corporate world nor the ghetto world is there effective organization against crime, either in the form of institutions for aborting its development in the first place, or in the form of agencies for cutting off its head once it has appeared.

Because there are no accurate crime reporting systems, we cannot demonstrate conclusively that many or few corporations violate antitrust laws, or even that many or few slum boys violate larceny laws. Since no one knows the true rate of illegal restraint of trade or larceny—if indeed there is an identifiable reality to which the term "true rate" can logically be applied—there can be no index of a true rate. We can only *assume*, as I do, that restraint of trade is almost universal in the corporate world and that larceny, also, is much more frequent than crime statistics suggest. What can be *demonstrated* is that the corporate world contains patterns of criminalistic interaction that are remarkably similar to the patterns of criminalistic interaction noted years ago by Shaw and McKay in the world of the slum (Shaw et al. 1929; Shaw and McKay 1931; Shaw, McKay, et al. 1942).

Henry McKay (1949) has shown that, even in high delinquency areas, alternative educational processes are in operation, so that a child may be educated in either "conventional" or criminal means of achieving success. Certainly this generalization holds for the corporate world as well as for the neighborhood. Diffu-

Donald R. Cressey is a member of the Department of Sociology at the University of California, Santa Barbara.

sion of the ideologies and techniques of restraint of trade leads to restraint of trade, and diffusion of ideologies and techniques of larceny leads to larceny.

Note, however, that the legislative process of declaring an act to be a crime takes political power. The behavior of one set of persons is opposed by another set; a struggle for legislative or judicial dominance ensues, and victory in this struggle is won by those opposing the behavior. Any criminal statute, then, is necessarily an enactment by the more powerful for the regulation of the less powerful. Essentially the same process can be seen in enforcing or administering the criminal law—the certainty of being arrested for an outlawed act, and the severity of the punishment imposed, are both indexes of the degree to which someone with power wants the outlawed behavior to be crime, "really," and "after all."

In our urban and industrialized society, nonconformity, even in the form of street crime, does not encounter concerted and vigilant opposition. As the boundaries of social interaction have extended from local communities to large cities, regions, and nations, collective opposition to crime has diminished, for the effects of crime are diffuse and hidden, and the society as a whole is by no means certain (if it ever was) what acts should be considered as contrary to the general welfare. The welfare state became manifest when persons of power invented policemen and asked them, as government employees, to assume the last-resort responsibility for keeping the peace. In the nineteenth century, the welfare state blossomed as the economic competition symbolized in words like "free agent," "free competition," and "contract" (as opposed to "status") was extended into the political sphere (Rehbinder 1971; Childres and Spitz 1972). Businessmen publicly demanded free competition and cried out against governmental interference with it. But in their competitive efforts to acquire wealth, they discovered that advantages can be secured by patents, tariffs, trademarks, and other governmental privileges designed to restrict competition. It soon developed that the industries securing the most restrictive political regulation of competitors made the most money.

Admirably suited to such political restriction on competition was the "endocratic" corporation, defined as the "large, publicly held corporation, whose stock is scattered in small fractions among thousands of stockholders" (Rostow 1959). Later, this same form of organization became admirably suited to illegal restraint of trade, to violations of antitrust laws. Favorable legislation was piled on favorable legislation, monopolizers monopolized monopolies, and merged corporations merged with merged corporations, until "government" and "big business" have become at the highest levels one enterprise rather than two.

In 1941, two-thirds of the nation's industrial assets were held by the one thousand largest corporations; by 1971, this same proportion was held by two hundred corporations (Viorst 1972).

Between 1969 and 1971, the sale made by the nation's top one hundred corporations increased 12.5 percent, but employment in these companies dropped by 5.2 percent, or half a million workers (Vanik 1972).

In 1969, the corporate share of the federal income tax was 35 percent; it fell to about 26 percent in 1972 (Abel 1972).

Figures on the 1971 taxes paid by the top one hundred industrial corporations, as listed by *Fortune*, are available for only forty-eight of the one hundred. Of these, three made no profits and hence paid no taxes. But Vanik (1972) showed that five of the remaining forty-five corporations paid no taxes at all, despite the fact that they had taxable incomes ranging from $144 million down to $26 million, for a total of $382 million. They were Continental Oil, McDonnell Douglas, Gulf and Western, Aluminum Company of America, and Signal Oil.

These statistics, which are real but nevertheless merely symbolic, suggest that America's wealth continues to be increasingly controlled by fewer and fewer endocratic corporations, and that government privileges are both a cause of and an effect of this concentration. Corporations gain governmental privileges and then use them to gain still more privileges. As Senator Philip Hart of Michigan recently put it, "When a corporation wants to discuss something with its political representative, you can be sure it will be heard. When a company operates in thirty states, it will be heard by thirty times as many representatives" (quoted by Viorst 1972:38). One result of such legislative listening has been a fusion of endocratic corporation and government or, perhaps more accurately, transformation of the nation into a huge endocratic corporation, with a privately appointed board of directors at the top.

Ruby (1972) has noted the rewards to corporations of this

ultimate merger, and Representative Charles A. Vanik of Ohio (1972) drew the following conclusions about specific problems:

> The federal tax system is encouraging the growth of monopolies, conglomerates, and multi-national corporations. Many of the tax subsidies provided by Congress have outlived their usefulness and are now creating severe problems of inequity and injustice between corporations—both within the same industries and between different industries. The bigger they get the less they pay to the federal government.

There is nothing new in the observation that power begets power. This idea has long since been the subject of dissertations on politics, charts on the economy, essays on social organization, and newspaper columns on armies, the Mafia, church hierarchies, and almost every other enterprise in which men dominate men. But the venerable idea continues to have great relevance for those of us who would both develop and master a sociology of crime and delinquency, criminal law, criminal justice, punishment, and correction—all the concerns denoted by the word "criminology." This is true because the current state of affairs has been accomplished in large part by means of the same kind of corporate crime long ago studied by Edwin H. Sutherland (1940, 1941, 1945, 1949, 1956).

Those of us who have commented on Sutherland's work, and those of us who have done research on white-collar crime, have frequently missed the potent and profound implication, for considerations of relationships between "power politics" and crime, that Sutherland's research on corporate crime was not consistent with the research strategy implied in his definition of white-collar crime. He said (1941:9), "White collar crime may be defined approximately as a crime committed by a person of respectability and high social status in the course of his occupation."

By focusing on this definition, Edelhertz (1970:4) recently added his name to the long list of persons who have failed to note that what Sutherland *said* and what he *did* were two quite different things: "Sutherland was basically concerned with society's disparate approach to the crimes of the respectable and well-to-do on the one hand, and those of poor and disadvantaged on the other. His definition of white-collar crime concentrated, therefore, on characterizing violators rather than violations." All this is true. The implication of the definition is that sociologists-criminologists should get on with study of criminals who have traditionally been overlooked or ignored. But the fact is that Sutherland ignored his own definition and studied the crimes of the seventy largest manufacturing, mining, and mercantile corporations in the United States.

In the weird world of law, a corporation is technically a person, but it clearly was not this kind of person that was covered in Sutherland's definition. Further, Sutherland showed some concern for the criminality of the "persons of respectability and high social status" who directed the affairs of certain corporations. But he concentrated his research and his comments on the crimes committed by criminal organizations within corporations, not on white-collar criminals.

It is possible that this discrepancy arose because Sutherland was as much concerned with the injustice of what he called "private collectivism" as he was with criminality among the rich. He explicitly denied that his *White Collar Crime* was anything but a study in the theory of criminal behavior (1949:xiii): "It is an attempt to reform the theory of criminal behavior, not to reform anything else. Although it may have implications for social reforms, social reforms are not the objective of the book." Later on, however, he analyzes the war-time crimes of corporations, then severely attacks the criminals (1949:174): "The general conclusion . . . is that profits are more important to large corporations than patriotism, even in the midst of an international struggle which endangered Western civilization." Further, he says that one of the primary objectives of the book (1949:88) "is to show that large corporations have violated the antitrust laws with frequency and that these violations have been important in undermining our traditional institutions."

Even if presented in the name of scientific objectivity, Sutherland's data and analysis of corporate violations of antitrust laws called for radical reformation of American society, and he knew it. Witness this passage:

> During the last century [the] economic system has changed. . . . For free competition has been substituted a system of private collectivism. To a great extent prices, profits, the flow of capital and other economic phenomena are determined by formal and informal organizations of businessmen. In this private collectivism the public is not represented, and the interests of the public receive consideration primarily in the adver-

tisements issued by the corporations. This private collectivism is very similar to socialism in its departure from free enterprise and free competition, but differs from socialism in that it does not include representation and consideration of the public.

This change in the economic system from free enterprise to private collectivism has been produced largely by the efforts of businessmen. . . . The businessman has attempted to secure the privileges of free enterprise without meeting the obligations of free competition (1949:84–86).

Clearly, such an attack would not have been possible had Sutherland merely studied what he defined as white-collar crime—the individual criminality of business and professional men filing false claims for social security benefits, engaging in planned bankruptcy, real-estate fraud, charity fraud, or mail fraud, giving short weights and measures, chasing ambulances, violating financial trust, and all the other behaviors discussed in Gilbert Geis's reader (1968)—significantly titled *White-Collar Criminal* rather than *White-Collar Crime*.

Contemporary radical sociologists tend to insist that their elders used "scientific objectivity" as a red herring that enabled them to support the establishment. I myself can produce some examples of this kind of distraction. But it is possible that other sociologists used "scientific objectivity" as a screen behind which they could attack the establishment. Perhaps Sutherland was one of these. At any rate, as a Christian socialist and humanist he could not pass up the opportunity to do research bound to show that a good share of all Americans are excluded from the "private collectivism" which the establishment—in the form of corporations—has devised.

Neither could Sutherland resist pointing out that the establishment should be attacked, not supported. After saying the purpose of his book was not to suggest what ought to be done about the private collectivism he had been discussing, he went on to make some suggestions. He ruled out the possibility of returning to the individualistic and competitive system of earlier generations, "especially because the huge mergers cannot be unscrambled." He ruled out the possibility that the society could rely on the benevolence of the large corporations. He ruled out the possibility that we can depend on effective government regulation in a system of private capitalism. What is left is this:

We may adopt one of the collectivist systems in which the public has some representation: socialism, communism, fascism, or large-scale cooperative enterprises. In any case, we are in a transition from free competition and free enterprise toward some other system, and the violations of the antitrust laws by large corporations are an important factor in producing this transition (1949:88).

I shall later show how the organization of American corporate business both provides opportunities for monopoly and promotes inclinations toward monopoly. At the same time, American society is no more organized to discourage illegal practices in restraint of trade than the people living in the early "Chicago Area Project" communities were organized to discourage delinquency before Shaw, McKay, and others moved in (Burgess et al. 1937; Shaw and Jacobs 1939; Romano 1940; Alinski 1941, 1946; Sorrentino 1959; Kobrin 1959; Short 1969). If one takes diminished price competition as an index of socialism, then it is correct to say that America has developed a system of socialism for the rich, while retaining a system of free competition for the poor. Ghetto dwellers, behaving like the capitalists they are told to be, compete with each other for bread; corporation executives, behaving like the socialists they say they deplore, make illegal arrangements for restraining trade. In the process, both commit crimes.

There is need for further documentation of the nature and incidence of corporate antitrust law violations. But there is reason to believe even without such documentation, that the violation is higher now than it was at the time of Sutherland's study. Further, it seems reasonable to assume that for some time official action has been taken in a decreasing proportion of all incidents of antitrust law violation. Sixty of Sutherland's seventy large corporations had an average of 5.1 adverse decisions against them for illegal restraint of trade, with a range of 1 to 22, and it is probable that the other ten had violated the antitrust laws also. It can rightfully be assumed, but not demonstrated, that antitrust law violation is now practically universal among endocratic corporations. Certainly things have not changed much since 1947, when a member of the Federal Trade Commission said, "About the only thing that keeps a businessman off the wrong end of a federal indictment or administrative agency's complaint is the fact that, under the hit-or-miss methods of prosecution, the law of averages hasn't made him a party to a suit" (Mason 1947). The problem for theoreticians, now as then, is not that of explaining why some corporations violate the law and others do not. Rather, it is the problem of explaining why endocratic corporate organization and antitrust law violations are practically synonymous. Put another way, we must ask why the antitrust laws are violated with blatant impunity.

The balance between organization for restraint of trade and organization against restraint of trade has changed from time to time, and later I shall suggest that ever since the Sherman Antitrust Law was passed there has been an increasing degree of organization in favor of it, and a decreasing degree of organization against it. But before these general issues are considered, it should be noted that illegal restraint of trade does not occur randomly in the corporate community, even if it occurs frequently.

Years ago, Shaw, McKay, and their collaborators showed that children moving into a neighborhood take on the delinquency rate of that neighborhood, whether it be high, low, or somewhere in between. Despite methodological critiques (Rice 1931; Jonassen 1949; Morris 1958) this research finding has stood the test of time (Shaw and McKay 1949; Toby 1950; Morris 1958; Wilks 1967). By the same token, we should expect corporations moving into an industry to take on the crime rate of the industry. I have not been able to locate corporation histories which either support or negate this hypothesis. But Shaw and McKay demonstrated essentially the same point by showing that boys in similar neighborhoods have similar recidivism rates, and Sutherland's data suggest something comparable, namely that corporations in the same industry have similar recidivism rates.[1]

An industry is analogous to a neighborhood, a community, an urban area, but populated by corporations rather than by people. In this neighborhood, each corporation's recidivism rate—in terms of its number of adverse decisions for restraint of trade as discovered by Sutherland—tended to be similar to the recidivism rate of its neighbors. For example, neither of the two mail-order houses included in Sutherland's study were repeaters of the restraint of trade offense—Sears Roebuck had no adverse decisions against it, and Montgomery Ward had only one. But all three motion-picture companies had high recidivism rates—Paramount and Warner Brothers each had 21, and Loew's had 22.

Two dairy companies, Borden and National Dairy Products, had middle-range rates of 7 and 8. This patterning suggests that restraint of trade is a neighborhood (industry) phenomenon, and that—as in the case of delinquent boys—it is not merely a consequence of the individual characteristics of isolated actors. Sutherland (1949:263) attributed the patterning to conspiracy among the involved corporations, to diffusion of illegal practices, and to the policies of trade associations.

But there also were a few instances of wide scattering, among the corporations in a single industry, of the rates of adverse decisions for restraint of trade. One exception to the usual patterning was a high recidivism rate by a corporation surrounded by corporations with low rates. For example, United States Steel had 9 adverse decisions for restraint of trade, but the other nine steel companies included in the study had rates ranging between only 1 and 3. At first glance, this finding is similar to the "black sheep" delinquent in a middle-class neighborhood, or to a high-delinquency cultural island located in the middle of a low-rate area. In a study of violations of labor relations laws and of trade practices laws among 275 New England shoe manufacturing companies, Lane (1953) found that none of the firms in some cities had violated the labor relations laws, while in other cities almost half the firms got into trouble with the law. He attributed the difference to differential association with attitudes toward the government, the law, and the morality of illegality. But the variation in the recidivism rates of Sutherland's steel companies might more reasonably be attributed to the policies of the enforcing agencies. Decisions were in several instances rendered against United States Steel, as the dominant corporation in the industry, for illegal practices in which the smaller steel companies were also engaged. In what amounts to police crackdowns or to diversionary tactics, United States Steel took the rap for its neighbors. The morality of selective exemplary enforcement designed to maximize deterrence of criminal conduct has been defended by Andenaes (1970).

A second exception to the industry-based patterning of recidivism among Sutherland's corporations also is similar to variations noted in delinquent neighborhoods. This is the low recidivism rate in an area of high recidivism. For example, among the meat packing corporations, Armour and Swift each had 12 adverse decisions for restraint of trade, but Wilson had only 4.

There are several ways of explaining this deviance on the part of the Wilson corporation. In the first place, selective enforcement may have been involved. Second, the deviation may be considered analogous to the low delinquency rates of some boys living in delinquent neighborhoods (Mack 1964). Kobrin's study (1951) has become the classic in this field.

Third, the deviant rate may be considered analogous to the low delinquency rates of certain cultural islands surrounded by ghetto swamps of high delinquency. Hayner's early study (1933) of the low delinquency rates of the Japanese living in high delinquency areas of Seattle illustrated this phenomenon. The general point from such studies is that groups whose children are kept isolated from the delinquent boys of an area, and who are presented with antidelinquency patterns by members of their own group, will show low delinquency rates. Perhaps the Wilson corporation experienced something similar.

Fourth, Wilson's deviant rate might be considered a mere consequence of restricted opportunity to restrain trade at the level available to Armour and Swift. "Opportunity" refers here to the physical or other overt aspects of a situation which make specific crime possible. Blacks have a very low rate of embezzlement, as compared to whites, because they are seldom in the positions of financial trust that make embezzlement available to them as a crime. Restricted opportunity keeps United States Steel and General Motors from violating Pure Food and Drug laws. Armour, Swift, and Wilson, on the other hand, have many opportunities to violate those laws. But, so far as restraint of trade is concerned, "the industry" in which Wilson was participating might not really have been the same "industry" in which the other two delinquent corporations were participating, thus restricting Wilson's opportunities to restrain trade. Among other things, the Wilson company did not manufacture and distribute cheese; Armour and Swift did, and both had recidivism rates somewhat comparable to the rates of the dairy companies in the study.

Thirty-four of Sutherland's seventy corporations were "hardened," "unreachable," "habitual," or "recalcitrant" delinquents in the sense that they showed up at least three times in the legal settings designed for controlling conduct in restraint of trade, not counting adverse decisions for making illegal rebates. (If other law violations are counted, of course, the proportion of regular recidivism will increase—all but four of the seventy corporations had three or more adverse decisions of some kind.)

As is the case with juvenile delinquency and crimes such as larceny, theoretical statements accounting for high recidivism rates must necessarily be logically consistent with theoretical explanations of first crimes. I have argued elsewhere (Sutherland and Cressey 1970) that the best two-pronged principle of this kind was called "social disorganization" and "differential social organization" by Shaw and McKay and Sutherland. The essential point, oversimplified, is that both first crimes and recidivism are frequent when a society, community, or neighborhood is organized to produce them and is not organized to forestall them. Negatively, the incidence of first crime and the incidence of repeated crimes are both low when there is effective organization against them and only weak organization favorable to them. With reference to larceny, for example, we must be concerned with more than "law and order" repression of the crime, and even with the moral climate that discourages the crime; we must show concern for the social forces promoting larceny as well.

With reference to restraint of trade by corporations, similarly, we must be concerned with the elements of social organization which support monopoly, together with the relation between these elements and elements which, differentially, discourage monopoly. Among the many conditions favorable to illegal monopoly are business organization developed to obtain monopolies legally, and business and political organization designed to develop and maintain doubt about whether restraint of trade is crime, "really." Also relevant is ineffective organization, among consumers, against restraint of trade and, more generally, against a collectivism that gives greater relative wealth to the wealthy, greater relative affluence to the affluent, and greater relative poverty to the poor.[2]

## Organization for Monopoly

It seems reasonable to expect high crime rates and high recidivism rates when a widespread pattern of legal behavior is arbitrarily outlawed. For example, attitudes and behavior patterns supporting drug use seemed to carry over when drug use was declared illegal by the Harrison Act, just as drinking patterns carried over during the period of National Prohibition. A number of studies have shown that economic production and distribution patterns carried over when, during World War II, price control and rationing laws declared certain standard business practices to be crimes "for the time being" (Clinard 1946, 1952; Hartung

1950; Aubert 1952; Ball 1960; Levens 1964). Lane (1953) found, similarly, that 63 percent of the labor law violations occurring in the New England shoe industry between 1936 and 1950 occurred during the first three and a half years of the National Labor Relations Act. Consistently, it might be said that restraint of trade rates and recidivism rates are high because business patterns that developed when monopolies were legal carried over after the Sherman Antitrust Law was passed. American business was well organized for monopolistic practices before enactment of antitrust laws, and this organization has not changed significantly after the enactment of them.

Inelasticity of demand for a product and impediments to additional supplies of a product are both favorable to monopoly. For example, monopolies generally developed when there was a bottleneck at one or more points in the process of producing or distributing a product. By securing control of this bottleneck, a man or a corporation could legally arrange conditions under which his competitors ceased to be competitors. Put simply, when the opportunity for monopoly was present, monopolistic practices developed.

One kind of bottleneck is created by nature, as in the geographical limitation of the known sources of raw materials. For example, the known supply of bauxite was once limited to a few counties in Arkansas, and by purchasing that supply Aluminum Company of America was able to eliminate all competitors. Another kind of bottleneck is found in the patent, a product of legislation. About a third of Sutherland's corporations developed their power through control of patents. Among them were Singer Sewing Machine, Eastman Kodak, General Electric, Radio Corporation of America. A third kind of bottleneck is created by the character of certain commodities, especially perishable ones. For example, the demand for fluid milk is rather constant, but if a farmer has enough cows to meet the winter demand he will have a perishable surplus of milk during the summer, leading to a situation in which the surplus milk can be utilized economically only by corporations equipped to make cheese, evaporated milk, and other types of milk products.

Economic conditions such as the above can be considered as leading "naturally' to high violation rates after the legitimate monopolistic practices were declared illegal. Lane (1953) found that most businessmen, and most government officials for that matter, subscribe to such a "natural" economic explanation of business crimes: violation of the law occurs because the profits of corporations and industries will be increased by them. But the matter is not so simple. Obviously, when the antitrust laws were passed, the relevant corporations *could* have just closed their doors and abandoned their monopolistic control of bottlenecks, even if doing so meant losses of millions of dollars and loss of a high degree of economic efficiency. Even men convinced that "poverty causes crime" do not excuse the criminal acts of slum dwellers just because the criminal was in poverty. Neither do we—officially at least—excuse the crimes of corporations on the ground that, in games of economic decline versus crime, the latter wins.

Perhaps the persistence in outlawed behavior is related to the corporate form itself, as well as to the attitudes and behavior patterns of corporation directors. Thus, it is possible that corporation crime, like Cosa Nostra crime, persists because it is "organized," meaning that it is perpetrated by an apparatus rather than merely by individuals occupying positions in the division of labor constituting the apparatus (Cressey 1969, 1972). Support for this idea is found in the U.S. Justice Department's practice of finding corporations in violation of the law while acquitting the directors and executives (Dershowitz 1961). A corporation is rationality epitomized. It has no soul, no love, no moral inhibitions against law violation. If it is organized for monopoly it cannot easily be directed away from its rational pursuit when monopoly becomes illegal. It will persist in pursuing its rational objectives until it is dismantled, even if these objectives become illegal ones. As a system without a soul a corporation is not rehabilitatable.

Ideally, corporations are under the direction of boards or bodies, not of men. But the men on these boards are expected to contribute to the collectivity by making rational decisions about the possibility of profits. Half the 1,700 corporation executives polled in one study (Baumhart 1961) agreed with the following statement: "The American business executive tends to ignore the great ethical laws as they apply immediately to his work. He is preoccupied chiefly with gain." In opting for gain, corporate directors have increasingly attempted to restrain trade, even if doing so is in violation of the law, because it has become the nature of corporate business to do so.

Sometime in the nineteenth century, as was mentioned earlier, a changed notion of business competition provided for more explicit governmental manipulation of prices and other conditions so that prices would not be fixed by competitive conditions. Eventually, of course, this meant a merger of state and industry, and it was probably something along this line that President Eisenhower had in mind when he spoke of "the military-industrial complex." All economic enterprises now try to protect themselves from competition—endocratic corporations, labor unions, farmers' organizations, small businesses, even the learned professions. Such protection is, as indicated, the very essence of the welfare state. It seems rather naïve to expect, in this socialistic world, that endocratic corporations will conform to vestigial antitrust laws that demand capitalistic competition.

The rational development of private collectivism in the corporate world seems to have been supplemented by increasing control over manufacturing corporations by financial agencies such as banks, insurance companies, investment companies, trust companies. Sutherland did not study such agencies, which have interests in various corporations within one industry, and in various industries. The effect is that of a single domain, a single socialistic society, in which price competition and other frictions are avoided. If two corporations owned by an insurance company engage in a price war, the consumer benefits but the insurance company inevitably loses. Interlocking directorates tend to produce similar "neighborhoods." An integrated government-corporation complex develops, and in this socialistic world there is a patriotic effort to make the system work smoothly, to reduce waste and increase efficiency, to minimize competition, even if doing so is in violation of the law.

## Organization for Confusing the "Crime" Issue

The effects of continuing organization for restraint of trade can be observed in antitrust legislation itself, in court decisions about this legislation, and in the selection and funding of enforcement personnel. These effects, in turn, have become causes. That is, they signal corporations that restraint of trade is "all right," or at least "not bad," thus stimulating both extensive violations and extensive recidivism. All the consequences seem to flow from rational organization designed to keep vague the question of whether restraint of trade is or is not crime, "really."

The history of antitrust legislation suggests that American

policy regarding monopolistic activity has been both mushy and vacillating. Prior to the late 1880s, the only control of restraint of trade was through common law, under which contracts in restraint of trade could not be enforced in the courts, and a corporation making such contracts might be deprived of its charter. The impossibility of forestalling restraint of trade by these rules was realized by Thomas Jefferson, who expressed regret that the Constitution did not explicitly prohibit monopolistic combinations. Abraham Lincoln, similarly, was dismayed by the weak controls in the common law, and he voiced his fear that the time might come when "all the wealth is aggregated in a few hands and the republic is destroyed."

Fear of monopolies became both more general and more intense with the development of "trusts" in the 1880s. Legislation followed. The Interstate Commerce Act of 1887 prohibited rebates and the other unfair methods of competition used in the development of the Standard Oil Company. Six states enacted antitrust laws in 1889. The United States Congress, having failed to act on antitrust bills in the session of 1888, enacted the Sherman Antitrust Law in 1890. The bill passed the Senate unanimously, and there was only one dissenting vote in the House.

This overwhelming vote in favor of the Sherman Act has been taken as evidence of a popular belief that free enterprise should be preserved. Thus, it is said that the Act was prompted by widespread fear that trusts would ruin small business, would destroy the competitive system of business, would increase prices in the long run, and would destroy the democratic system of government. For example, Ball and Friedman (1965) say the Sherman Act was originally "the product of genuine public outrage," comparable to the occasional clamor against sex criminals, murderers, and airplane hijackers. Apparently such widespread fears and outrage existed. Nevertheless, the Sherman Law might have been enacted on the assumption, among congressmen and others, that it reduced competition rather than promoted it. That is, the law might have been considered simply as an extension of the socialistic system that favored restricting competition by governmental regulation, as in patents, embargoes, trade barriers, and so on.

But the overwhelming vote in favor of the Act also can be taken as evidence that Congress did not intend it to prevent restraint of trade at all and enacted it because it appeared to be only a pious resolution in favor of apple pie and motherhood. Some evidence favoring this interpretation is found in legislation that subsequently modified the Sherman Law, which presumably prohibited every restraint of trade, just as larceny statutes prohibit every larceny. Generally speaking, this new legislation did two things. It listed special forms of restraint of trade, and it restricted implementation of the Sherman Law by granting immunity to specific groups and commodities.

Price discrimination and price maintenance, for example, were presumably in violation of the Sherman Act if used to restrain trade, but the Act did not mention specific methods of unfair competition. Definitions of these methods were provided by the Clayton Act (1914) and the Robinson-Patman Act (1936), which prohibited price discriminations which tend to result in monopoly. Many states soon passed similar laws but, significantly, with no reference to monopoly. These laws were, clearly, socialistic designs for reducing price competition, not for encouraging it or preserving it.

Pressure groups managed to exempt railways, water carriers, motor carriers, marine insurance associations, labor unions, agricultural and fishing cooperatives, petroleum, coal, sugar, and other agricultural products. They even managed to shift the principle of legislation so that restraint of trade is *protected*, as in the creation of bureaus and commissions to fix commodity prices, and in fair trade laws that fix minimum retail prices. The latter laws are state laws (authorized by the Miller-Tydings Act of 1937) which prohibit price competition in a large area of business, increase the price of the articles whose price is regulated, increase manufacturers' profits, and support the whole socialistic policy of price agreements among manufacturers, a policy outlawed by the Sherman Act.

In view of such legislative confusion, it is no wonder that antitrust legislation has been repeatedly violated by endocratic corporations. The conflict in legislative principles also sheds light on why antitrust law violations cannot routinely be listed in sets of criminal statistics; we have declared restraint of trade a crime, but we also have made it a crime not to restrain trade by price maintenance.

Somewhat the same kind of conflict is also visible in court decisions. If this were a reasonable world, the courts would oppose violations of antitrust laws at least as vigorously as they oppose violations of larceny laws. As a matter of fact, the courts have on many occasions strained every point to permit corporations to escape the charges against them. By comparison, the more recent Mapp, Gideon, and Miranda decisions, which free criminals on so-called legal technicalities, are zealous cries for "law and order." For example, the Sherman Law says that every restraint of trade is in violation, and in the early days the courts interpreted this statement literally. But then the "rule of reason" was substituted. Under that rule, the Act prohibits only *unreasonable* restraints of trade. The U.S. Attorney General (1937) once complained that the courts refused to adopt the only practical criterion of restraint of trade—price uniformity and price rigidity—but insisted, instead, on trying to determine whether a fictitious personality has an evil state of mind. In the cultures of courthouses there was, and is, a sympathetic understanding of corporations.

Corporation executives often declaim to the effect that it is practically impossible to determine, even with expert legal assistance, whether a contemplated act will violate antitrust law. This point is plausible, but it also seems to be in part a camouflage for law violation. It is a bit like saying that a prospective robber cannot, even with legal assistance, tell whether the force he intends to use will make his crime robbery, kidnapping, assault, or something else. A large proportion of the cases studied by Sutherland involved rather obvious violations of law, about which no businessman of experience could be in doubt, regardless of whether he had any legal training. This was true, also, of the violations detected in the heavy electrical equipment industry a decade ago (Smith 1961; Watkins 1961; Hazard 1961; Herling 1962; Fuller 1962; Geis 1967).

Enforcement agencies, too, have been something less than vigorous proponents of law and order in the antitrust area. I am not at all convinced that it is necessarily bad practice, a sign of corruption, or a sign of inefficiency that only a small proportion of all arrested felons are sent to prison and that only a small proportion of detected antitrust law violators are punished. On the contrary, I have pointed out elsewhere (Cressey 1971) that gross injustices would be done if the criminal law machine mechanically ground up the soul of any man that violated a law, be it an antitrust law or a larceny law. The great injustices that would come from routine law-and-order processing of criminals are overlooked by those who, like Blumberg (1967), present out-of-hand condemnations of so-called "plea bargaining" in ordinary felony cases. It also is overlooked by those who present top-of-the-head condemnations of enforcement agencies that do not "get tough" with violators of antitrust laws.

But there are three points of difference between vigorous prosecution and punishment of street-crime felons and corporate antitrust violators. First, a corporation is a machine, not a person. Because it has no soul to be maimed or destroyed in punishment for committing a crime, it does not really suffer from the financial penalties imposed on it (Dershowitz 1961). Even dismantling a corporation—the equivalent of capital punishment— does not kill a human and thus does not produce in the executioner, or in the political personnel behind him, the bitter taste that accompanies the electrocuting, hanging, and gassing of men.

Second, there is more at stake in the regulation of corporations than there is in the regulation of street crimes. Corporate illegal restraints of trade are much more threatening to national welfare than are burglaries and robberies. What is at stake is democracy, not free enterprise, which long ago disappeared. As Sutherland put it (1956), "If the word 'subversive' refers to efforts to make fundamental changes in a social sytem, the business leaders are the most subversive influence in the United States." *Theft of the Nation* (Cressey 1969) could well be the title of a book about corporate crime rather than about organized crime. As a matter of fact, as I wrote that book I had an allegory in mind, but I presented it with such subtlety that few reviewers or readers saw it. I was pleading for understanding of the dangers of government-corporation organization, not just for understanding La Cosa Nostra's threats to democracy.

Third, it appears that the corporate world is a high delinquency neighborhood, and the need for democratic direction of this world—in the name of law and order if we can find nothing else—is great. The President's Commission (1967) put it this way: "Derelictions by corporations and their managers, who usually occupy leadership positions in their communities, establish an example which tends to erode the moral base of law and provide an opportunity for other kinds of offenders to rationalize their conduct."

Perhaps an analogy with blue-law violations is more appropriate than comparison of restraint of trade and street crimes. Lack of official sincerity about the criminality of antitrust violations is similar to the lack of official sincerity regarding the dastardliness of swearing, doing business on Sunday, or wearing skirts above the ankles. The lack of official concern lets corporations and persons violate the law as a kind of joke, coupled with a belief that the acts cannot be crimes, "really," because no one is arrested for performing them.

In the antitrust area, lack of official sincerity can be seen in the attitudes of enforcement personnel. For example, four of the first five attorneys general serving after passage of the Sherman Act were strongly opposed to it. According to Cummings and McFarland (1937:323) Richard Olney, attorney general at the time the infamous Sugar Refinery case was before the Supreme Court, wrote, "You will have observed that the Government has been defeated in the Supreme Court. I have always supposed it would be and have taken the responsibility of not prosecuting under a law I believe to be no good."

Lack of official sincerity also can be seen in the small appropriations for antitrust law enforcement. I cannot go into detail here, but it is clear that only the administrations of President Theodore Roosevelt and President Taft, and of President Franklin Roosevelt, have taken antitrust enforcement seriously. The Franklin Roosevelt administration vastly increased the budget and personnel of the antitrust staff in the Department of Justice. One consequence was Sutherland's finding that the number of decisions against his seventy corporations in the thirteen years of Franklin Roosevelt's administration was practically the same as the number of decisions against the same corporations in the entire forty-three years preceding the Roosevelt administration. But even this enforcement campaign was short-lived, interrupted by World War II, as Theodore Roosevelt's and Taft's less vigorous campaigns had been interrupted by World War I. During time of war, apparently, those who are powerful in American society want production by any means, including illegal monopoly.

In general, it appears that American society has not been organized to enforce the antitrust laws. Corporate organizations, on the contrary, have been continually fighting to secure the appointment of enforcement personnel who would be friendly and quiescent in the face of violations of law or, if action had to be taken, would act politely and considerately. The enforcement agencies have not had the funds or attitudes necessary to educate the public about the dangers of restraint of trade, even as they have—in several campaigns—tried to educate citizens about the dangers of organized crime. Neither have they had the funds, attitudes, and legal apparatus needed to protect the public against antitrust law violations. On the contrary, the enforcement agencies have waited for complaints of violations to come to them, even as the police were becoming proactive rather than remaining reactive.[3] They have given their official attention to only a small proportion of the violations, the "more pronounced" ones, even as the police were cracking down on street crimes. And they have instituted proceedings in only a small proportion of the few cases selected for official action, even as the Supreme Court was being angrily attacked for decisions that let some street criminals through the prosecutorial net.

The various forms of organization for confusing the issue of whether violation of antitrust laws is a crime have created an important criminological issue. I do not mean the old debate (Sutherland 1945; Tappan 1947; Caldwell 1958) about whether a violation of the criminal law is, by itself, evidence that a crime has been committed. Neither do I mean the issue of whether the use of criminal sanctions in antitrust cases is more or less effective than some other regulatory system might be (Kadish 1963). I mean the issue framed by Wilhelm Aubert (1952) and Egon Bittner (1957), both of whom have argued that Sutherland's important contribution was demonstration that a pattern of crime can be found to exist outside the focus of popular preoccupation with crime, and outside the focus of scientific investigations of crime and criminality. The important problem is not further demonstration that corporations illegally restrain trade, although this is essential. It is determination of the society's structural conditions which create differentials in the degree of public character of various kinds of offenses.

Years ago I argued (Cressey 1957) that vagueness in compilations of crime statistics is useful because it decreases the range of points at which nasty disagreements can occur. If this notion is extended to corporate violations of antitrust laws, we can argue that vagueness in deciding whether restraints of trade are crimes, "really," is a useful device for reconciling both the usual ideological commitments regarding the nature of crime and the broader ideological commitments regarding corporate and government enterprise. Some indication of the conflict and confusion in these ideologies can be given by asking the question in traditional form: "What causes violations of antitrust laws?" One part of the answer, it seems to me, is political organization, on a corporate base, for keeping interest groups, especially consumer groups, from making antitrust law violation a focus of popular concern.

## Lack of Consumer Organization

The general conclusion from the last section is that illegal restraint of trade has not been much more deterred or otherwise controlled under statutory law than it was under the common law criticized by Jefferson and Lincoln. The widespread violation rates and recidivism rates of corporations cannot be adequately explained by considering only the organization of special interests and the effects of this organization on the organization of the courts, the Department of Justice, the Federal Trade Commission, the Congress. The virtual absence of opposing organization must be considered also. Organizations of power have not insured that the legislative, executive, and judicial branches of government organize for enforcement of clearly stated antitrust laws. Accordingly, the perceived rewards for nonenforcement have been greater than the perceived rewards for enforcement.

All this is to say, simply, that citizens have not organized into pressure groups demanding law and order in the antitrust area, either in the interests of small businessmen or in the interests of consumers. Neither have they organized to prevent restraint of trade. The absence of any effective organization might be due to role conflicts among consumers—although they have common interests in low prices for consumer goods, some are also producers who have interests in high prices for one or another kind of consumer goods.

Sutherland's data provide clear evidence that when the consumers of a product are organized and powerful, producers are likely to avoid restraint of trade. For example, at the time of Sutherland's study about half the tires produced in the United States were purchased by automobile companies, and these companies made sure the tire manufacturers had low antitrust recidivism rates. The automobile companies even threatened to manufacture their own tires if prices were not reduced. Sutherland (1949:261) found no adverse decisions against any rubber corporations for conspiracy to fix uniform prices on automobile tires. Firestone, Goodrich, and Goodyear each had one adverse decision for restraint of trade and United States Rubber had six, but these were in reference to other rubber products, including golf balls, rubber hose, and rubber tubing. The conclusion is obvious. Combinations in restraint of trade are impractical when consumers are organizations of power.

In *White Collar Crime*, Sutherland (1949:230-33) made this point from the perspective of his earlier work on professional theft. Thus he pointed out that corporations, like professional thieves, select weak victims. Most consumers, investors, and stockholders are unorganized, lack technical knowledge about their own financial interests, have never heard of restraint of trade, and do not question whether price fixing and price maintenance practices work to their detriment or to their benefit. According to Viorst (1972), the *Antitrust Law and Economic Review* posed the rhetorical question: "Why does the American public tolerate the degree of monopoly we now have? The answer is that they don't know about it." Accordingly, illegal restraint of trade, resembling professional theft, is like stealing candy from a baby. It flourishes at points in the economic system where organizations with power encounter weak potential victims. Because of differences in the power between criminal and victim, the corporation enjoys relative immunity from detection, arrest, and prosecution. Further, it might be this difference in power that, basically, leads to the continual wonderment about whether antitrust violation is crime, "really."

It is not easy to determine why, on the one hand, the Sherman Act seemed to come to us from an organized segment of the public but, on the other hand, there has been no sizable or powerful segment of the public organized for enforcement of this legislation. Perhaps the theory and principles of psychology's modern behaviorism will shed some light on the question, especially if the behaviorists start analyzing political and economic power relationships. Certainly legislators, government executives, judges, and other public employees operate, like all animals, as their schedules of reinforcement and punishment have programmed them to operate. Like B. F. Skinner's trained pigeons, they push the levers that release their pellets of food. The man that rigs the program, the controller, has the power. In a democracy, the controller of governmental pigeons is supposed to be "the people"—electors are to devise the operant conditioning schedules of their public employees and representatives.

From this perspective, the basic idea at the base of the criminal law and criminal justice systems in democratic countries is that elected and appointed officials will be programmed by the voters, in a schedule of reinforcements and punishments, to in turn reinforce certain kinds of citizen conduct and punish or extinguish other kinds of conduct. The trouble is that "the voters" or "the people"—if there is such a thing—do not know who, or what, to reward. They reward an official with prestige and a salary on the contingency that he somehow "be good" or "do good" and occasionally "be efficient," and let it go at that.

But businessmen, especially those sitting on the boards of endocratic corporations, know a great deal about human performance. Even if they have never heard of operant conditioning, they deal in reinforcements and punishments on a daily basis. In popular parlance, "money talks." In the language of what I call an "atmospheric theory of human conduct," they exert "pressures." In more meaningful language, they arrange delicious and specific rewards for the pigeons that push the proper specified levers, and no rewards and even punishments for the pigeons that push the wrong ones. That is what leads us to say that some persons and special groups have power. Whoever puts the food pellets in the box and rigs the program for the pigeons has the power, and nowadays the "person" with the pellets is a corporation.

So far as antitrust behavior is concerned, at least, businessmen train governmental officials to train "the people," rather than "the people" training officials to train businessmen. As a noted political columnist (Viorst 1972) recently put it, "How can one expect an administration—any administration—to curb the power of the giant corporations that are its chief source of political financing?" With the melding of corporations and government, the controllees have become controllers.

The pressing problem of our time is not that of dismantling the socialistic system which the corporate controllers have demanded and created. The problem is to get the people, especially the poor people, into it.

## Notes

1. The penultimate draft of Sutherland's *White Collar Crime* (1949) contained court and commission citations and, thus, identified the corporations involved. The manuscript, which I possess, also contains information on the histories of some of the corporations. The following consideration of corporate industries as neighborhoods relies on this manuscript.

2. The following discussion is based on unpublished materials assembled by Professor Sutherland and once in my possession. In 1961–62, when I was Visiting Fellow in Cambridge University's Institute of Criminology, I used these materials to prepare a paper, "White Collar Crime and Social Structure," which I delivered to the "Cambridge Sociology Group" on February 14, 1962. I used a copy of that paper in preparing these pages, but am unable to locate its sources. The style and content of my 1962 paper—of which this chapter is an updated and shortened version—convince me that the principal source was an unpublished Sutherland draft, but I can find no such draft in either the papers Sutherland gave me when I assisted him on his white-collar crime project or in the papers I inherited from him.

3. I have borrowed these terms from Bordua and Reiss (1967:40). Wilson (1968:83–89) uses a different terminology—"police-invoked action" and "citizen-invoked action"—to indicate these two kinds of order maintenance.

## References

Abel, I. W.
1972        "A Lop-sided Tax Structure." *Viewpoint*, An Industrial Union (AFL-CIO) Department Quarterly 2 (Third Quarter): 1–4.

Alinsky, Saul D.
1941        "Community Analysis and Organization." *American Journal of Sociology* 46 (May): 797–808.
1946        *Reveille for Radicals*. Chicago: University of Chicago Press.

Andenaes, Johannes
1970        "The Morality of Deterrence." *University of Chicago Law Review* 37 (Summer):649–64.

Aubert, Vilhelm
1952        "White Collar Crime and Social Structure." *American Journal of Sociology* 58 (November):263–71.

Ball, Harry V.
1960        "Social Structure and Rent-control Violations." *American Journal of Sociology* 65 (May): 598–604.

Ball, Harry V., and Lawrence N. Friedman
1965        "The Use of Criminal Sanctions in the Enforcement
            of Economic Regulation: A Sociological View."
            *Stanford Law Review* 17 (January):197–223.

Baumhart, Raymond C.
1961        "How Ethical Are Businessmen?" *Harvard Business
            Review* 39 (July-August): 6–19, 156–76.

Bittner, Egon
1957        "White Coat Crime." Research Studies of the State
            College of Washington 25 (June):200 (abstract).

Blumberg, Abraham
1967        *Criminal Justice*. Chicago: Quadrangle Books.

Bordua, David, and Albert Reiss, Jr.
1967        "Environment and Organization: A Perspective on
            the Police." In David Bordua, ed., *The Police: Six
            Sociological Essays*. New York: John Wiley, pp.
            28–40.

Burgess, Ernest W., Joseph D. Lohman, and Clifford R. Shaw
1937        "The Chicago Area Project." In *National Probation
            Association Yearbook*, pp. 8–28.

Caldwell, Robert G.
1958        "A Re-examination of the Concept of White Collar
            Crime." *Federal Probation* 22 (March): 30–36.

Childres, Robert, and Stephen J. Spitz
1972        "Status in the Law of Contract." *New York Univer-
            sity Law Review* 47 (April): 1–31.

Clinard, Marshall B.
1946        "Criminological Theories of Violations of Wartime
            Regulations." *American Sociological Review* 11
            (June): 258–70.
1952        *The Black Market: A Study of White Collar Crime*.
            New York: Rinehart.

Cressey, Donald R.
1957        "The State of Criminal Statistics." *National Pro-
            bation and Parole Association Journal* 3 (July):
            230–41.
1969        *Theft of the Nation: The Structure and Operations
            of Organized Crime in America*. New York:
            Harper and Row.
1971        "The Role of Discretion, Diplomacy and Sub-
            cultures of Justice in Crime Control." In Jon Palle

et al., eds., *Festskrift Til Folketingests Ombudsman Professor, Dr. Jur. Stephan Hurwitz.* Copenhagen: Juristforbundets Forlag.

1972        *Criminal Organization: Its Elementary Forms.* London: Heinemann. American edition by Harper Torchbooks, New York, 1972.

Cummings, Homer S., and Carl McFarland
1937        *Federal Justice.* New York: Macmillan.

Dershowitz, Alan M.
1961        "Increasing Community Control over Corporate Crime: A Problem in the Law of Sanctions." *Yale Law Journal* 71 (September): 289–306.

Edelhertz, Herbert
1970        *The Nature, Impact and Prosecution of White-Collar Crime.* Washington, D.C.: U.S. Government Printing Office. (National Institute of Law Enforcement and Criminal Justice.)

Fuller, John G.
1962        *The Gentlemen Conspirators.* New York: Grove Press.

Geis, Gilbert
1967        "The Heavy Electrical Equipment Antitrust Cases of 1961." In Marshal B. Clinard and Richard Quinney, eds., *Criminal Behavior Systems.* New York: Holt, Rinehart and Winston, pp. 139–50.

Geis, Gilbert, ed.
1968        *White-Collar Criminal: The Offender in Business and the Professions.* New York: Atherton.

Hartung, Frank E.
1950        "White-collar Offenses in the Wholesale Meat Industry in Detroit." *American Journal of Sociology* 56 (July): 25–34.

Hayner, Norman S.
1933        "Delinquency Areas in the Puget Sound Region." *American Journal of Sociology* 39 (November): 314–28.

Hazard, Leland
1961        "Are Businessmen Crooks?" *The Atlantic* 208 (November): 57–61.

Herling, John
1962        *The Great Price Conspiracy.* Washington, D.C.: Luce.

Jonassen, Christen T.
1949        "A Re-evaluation and Critique of the Logic and
            Methods of Shaw and McKay." *American Socio-
            logical Review* 14 (October): 608–14.

Kadish, Sanford H.
1963        "Some Observations on the Use of Criminal Sanc-
            tions in Enforcing Economic Regulations." *Univer-
            sity of Chicago Law Review* 30 (Spring): 423–49.

Kobrin, Solomon
1959        "The Conflict of Values in Delinquency Areas."
            *American Sociological Review* 16 (October):
            653–61.

Lane, Robert E.
1953        "Why Businessmen Violate the Law." *Journal of
            Criminal Law, Criminology, and Police Science* 44
            (July-August): 151–65.

Levens, G. E.
1964        "101 White Collar Criminals." *New Society*
            (March 26): 6–8.

Mack, John
1964        "Full-time Miscreants, Delinquent Neighbour-
            hoods, and Criminal Networks." *British Journal
            of Sociology* 15 (March): 38–53.

Mason, Lowell B.
1947        "Comment." *Nation's Business* 35 (January): 38.

McKay, Henry D.
1949        "The Neighborhood and Child Conduct." *Annals
            of the American Academy of Political and Social
            Science* 261 (January): 32–42.

Morris, Terrence
1958        *The Criminal Area.* London: Kegan Paul.

President's Commission on Law Enforcement and Administration
of Justice
1967        *Task Force Report: Crime and Its Impact—An
            Assessment.* Washington, D.C.: U.S. Government
            Printing Office.

Rehbinder, Manfred
1971        "Status, Contract, and the Welfare State." *Stanford
            Law Review* 23 (May): 941–55.

Rice, Stuart A.
1931        "Hypotheses and Verifications in Clifford R. Shaw's
            Studies of Juvenile Delinquency." In Stuart A.

Rice, ed., *Methods in Social Science: A Case Book*. Chicago: University of Chicago Press, pp. 549–65.

Romano, Fred A.
1940          "Organizing a Community for Delinquency Prevention." In *National Probation Association Yearbook*, pp.1–12.

Rostow, Eugene V.
1959          "To Whom and for What Ends Is Corporate Management Responsible?" In Edward S. Mason, ed., *The Corporation in Modern Society*. Cambridge: Harvard University Press, p. 303.

Ruby, Michael
1972          "Global Companies: Too Big to Handle?" *Newsweek* (November 20): 96–104.

Shaw, Clifford R., with the collaboration of Frederick M. Zorbaugh, Henry D. McKay, and Leonard S. Cottrell
1929          *Delinquency Areas*. Chicago: University of Chicago Press.

Shaw, Clifford R., and Jesse A. Jacobs
1939          "The Chicago Area Project." In *Proceedings of the American Prison Association*, pp. 40–53.

Shaw, Clifford R., and Henry D. McKay
1931          *Social Factors in Juvenile Delinquency*. National Commission on Law Observance and Enforcement, Report no. 13, vol. 2. Washington, D.C.: U.S. Government Printing Office.

Shaw, Clifford R., and Henry D. McKay
1949          "Rejoinder." *American Sociological Review* 14 (October): 614–17.

Shaw, Clifford R., and Henry D. McKay, with the collaboration of Norman S. Hayner, Paul G. Cressey, Clarence W. Schroeder, T. Earl Sullenger, Earl R. Moses, and Calvin F. Schmid
1942          *Juvenile Delinquency and Urban Areas*. Revised
1969          edition, with a new introduction by James F. Short, Jr., and new chapters by Henry D. McKay. Chicago: University of Chicago Press.

Short, James F., Jr.
1969          "Introduction." In Clifford R. Shaw and Henry D. McKay, *Juvenile Delinquency and Urban Areas*. Revised edition. Chicago: University of Chicago Press.

Smith, Richard Austin
1961     "The Incredible Electrical Conspiracy." *Fortune* 63 (April-May): 132–37; 61–164 ff.

Sorrentino, Anthony
1959     "The Chicago Area Project after 25 Years." *Federal Probation* 23 (June): 40–45.

Sutherland, Edwin H.
1940     "White-collar Criminality." *American Sociological Review* 5 (February): 1–12.
1941     "Crime and Business." *Annals of the American Academy of Political and Social Science* 217 (September): 112–18.
1945     "Is 'White-collar Crime' Crime?" *American Sociological Review* 10 (April): 132–39.
1949     *White Collar Crime.* New York: Dryden. Reissued, with a new forward by Donald R. Cressey, by Holt, Rinehart and Winston, New York, 1961.
1956     "Crime of Corporations." In Albert Cohen, Alfred Lindesmith, and Karl Schuessler, eds., *The Sutherland Papers.* Bloomington: Indiana University Press, pp. 78–96.

Sutherland, Edwin H., and Donald R. Cressey
1970     *Criminology.* Eighth edition. Philadelphia: Lippincott.

Tappan, Paul W.
1947     "Who Is the Criminal?" *American Sociological Review* 12 (February): 96–102.

Toby, Jackson
1950     "Comment on the Jonassen-Shaw and McKay Controversy." *American Sociological Review* 14 (February): 107–8.

U.S. Attorney General
1937     *Annual Report.* Washington: U.S. Government Printing Office.

Vanik, Charles A.
1972     "The Great Corporation Sport—Evading Taxes." *Viewpoint,* An Industrial Union (AFL-CIO) Department Quarterly, 2 (Third Quarter): 8–12.

Viorst, Milton
1972     "Gentlemen Prefer Monopoly: The Impotence of Antitrust Law." *Harper's Magazine* 245 (November): 32–38.

Watkins, Myron W.
1961            "Electrical Equipment Antitrust Cases—Their Implications for Government and Business." *University of Chicago Law Review* 29 (August): 97–110.

Wilks, Judith A.
1967            "Ecological Correlates of Crime and Delinquency." Appendix A, in President's Commission on Law Enforcement and Administration of Justice, *Task Force Report: Crime and Its Impact—An Assessment*. Washington, D.C.: U.S. Government Printing Office.

Wilson, James Q.
1968            *Varieties of Police Behavior: The Management of Law and Order in Eight Communities*. Cambridge, Mass.: Harvard University Press.

# 9     The Labeling Approach
## Problems and Limits

*Solomon Kobrin*

      The rise to prominence of labeling theory in recent years represents a major development in the analysis of deviant behavior. The particular contribution of the theory has been to call attention to the fact that deviant behavior is always and necessarily a joint product of acts and the definition of acts, of the conduct of actors and the definition of that conduct by others as contravening some set of social norms. This would appear to be perfectly obvious, but it has proved to be one of those patent features of social life often obscured by ideological bias. Durkheim (1938) had long since demonstrated the role of the defining group response in establishing the deviant character of acts. Despite this, deviant behavior had been commonly and persistently viewed as a property either of individual actors or of defective social arrangements for the communication and inculcation of prevailing conduct norms. The unexamined operating assumption had been that the social norms of a society were relatively fixed, coherent, and invariant; that the norms were universally known and respected; and that the failure of the person to guide his conduct in accordance with them betokened some defect of personal or social function.[1]

Beginning with the early work of Lemert (1951), labeling theorists have sought to elucidate the effects of the societal response on the probability that persons engaging in deviant acts will become permanently and inescapably identified as deviants. The focus in much of this work has been on the details of a developmental process having as its end product the establishment of categories of deviants of various kinds, walled off from association with any but those of their own kind and viewed by others solely in their role as deviants. This process is seen as an effect of sustained negative labeling, principally by social control

Solomon Kobrin is a member of the Department of Sociology and Anthropology at the University of Southern California.

agents operating as surrogates of public opinion, that communicates to identified deviants the content of their identity.

The analysis of the process through which human beings are transformed into deviants, as presented in the work of Lemert (1951),[2] Becker (1963), Scheff (1966), Lofland (1969), and especially that of Goffman (1959, 1965),[3] represents without question a major enlargement of our understanding of how deviants come into existence as social categories. However, this demonstration of the manner in which the societal response may literally create deviant persons inadvertently redefines the problem of deviance as one of conflict between protagonists of opposing normative systems, the conventional and the deviant. Without explicitly doing so, labeling theory seems to claim for deviant normative systems something of the same validity possessed by conventional ones as a source of human potential and capacity.[4] The implicit nature of this claim is revealed by the fact that the precise form of deviant behavior, whether or not it victimizes others, is rarely specified in the formulations of the labeling theorists. The closest approach to an explicit recognition of this feature of the theory came in Becker's (1967) essay: "Whose Side Are We On?" Becker was concerned principally with the methodological issue of the perspective to be adopted in achieving an accurate description of the experience of deviants as they are processed by nondeviants and their agents. But there remains the overtone that the deviant adaptation, being "natural," possesses a kind of legitimacy. The point to be made is that labeling theory assimilates the problem of deviance to the general class of the phenomena of social opposition.

In thus redefining deviant behavior as a product of conflict process, labeling theory has converted the study of deviance into a special branch of the sociology of conflict. It may be argued that the conversion has produced illuminating analyses. Conflict theorists like Coser (1962) have seen in deviant behavior the source of constructive social change. Those who have taken their cue from Durkheim's functionalism, for example, Erikson (1966), regard deviant behavior as performing the essential function of defining the boundaries of the social space inhabited by groups. In their need to make manifest their own distinctive character and identity, societies are driven, in this view, to establish categories of deviants representing what the respectable members are not. Conflict is consequently seen as integral to the maintenance of social groups and is commonly expressed in the creation of labeled deviant categories whose treatment as opponents symbolically affirms the validity of the official normative structure.

However, while conflict is indubitably entailed in both the genesis and the treatment of deviance, the problem field cannot be encompassed by a simple sociology of conflict without further specification of its distinctive elements. Much of ordinary social conflict concerns opposition among normatively conventional groups, and there remain aspects of deviance phenomena for which conflict theory appears irrelevant. In applying the conflict assumptions of the labeling approach it is above all necessary to attend to distinctions among types of deviant behavior (for example, those that violate the widely supported norms of the criminal law versus those that offend norms whose legitimacy is in dispute). And, as will be seen, it is also necessary to note the distinctions among stages in the deviance-making process in which the impact of labeling may be differentially prominent, have quite different consequences for deviant careers, and involve patterns of conflict specific to identifiable elements of group and institutional structure.[5]

With an eye to such distinctions, we may now ask what the contribution of labeling theory has been to our understanding of the delinquency problem. It can hardly be doubted that its main impact has been to focus attention on the effect of stereotypic categorizing on the behavior of young law violators. It is by now an item of common knowledge and conviction that insistence on perceiving and treating the young person in his often transient role as an offender can only result in his exclusion from groups of normals and his enforced association with similarly excluded others. In thus fastening on him the label of "delinquent," the youngster is in effect constrained to construct an identity as a delinquent and consequently to increase both the frequency and seriousness of his delinquent acts. The crucial agents in promoting this transformation are, moreover, the functionaries with official responsibility for maintaining social control—police, courts, and correctional workers. Representing as they do the dignity and power of the total society, they convey to those whom they define and deal with as delinquents the weight of collective judgment. Thus labeled, the young offender is confronted by what must seem to him incontrovertible evidence of who and what he is and by the task of constructing a life organization on the basis of this identity. In brief, labeling theory has without question provided an accurate description of how the institutional machinery devised to prevent and control the deviance we call delinquency in fact fosters such deviance by unavoidably treating youngsters as categorical objects.

Indeed, the insights provided by labeling theory have so far carried the day that they form the basis of what are viewed as the most promising new programs in the delinquency field. Labeling theory has been directly and explicitly implemented in current "diversion" programs.[6] Their stated aim is to divert from official juvenile court processing youth who have encountered trouble with the law. As an alternative, these programs attempt to induct young offenders into existing or newly developed programs. In concept, diversion programs are designed to accomplish the same aims of reformation for which juvenile courts were originally established. But because the activities of diversion programs are conducted in settings free of the ambience of authority, sanction, and coercion that clings to courts and their functionaries, reformative aims may presumably be pursued without risking the danger of the stigmatizing label.

An assessment of the likelihood that the movement for the diversion of juvenile offenders will enjoy notable success offers an opportunity to identify at the same time some of the limits of labeling theory. Among the difficulties that diversion programs encounter, two deserve special attention. The first is the explicit requirement imposed on those who operate diversion programs that they suspend or inhibit the spontaneous tendency to see the basic attributes of persons in terms of the moral meanings of their actions, in brief, to forego the native impulse to form social judgments. This becomes particularly difficult when the acts in terms of which personal attributes are imputed involve predatory and other victimizing behavior. The difficulty posed by this requirement is that the labeling response is in some part an irrepressible feature of human interaction in that persons perceive and identify one another by employing culturally standardized cognitive categories. One can concede that a stigmatizing label carrying an official stamp, and imposed in the course of the impressive social ceremony of a court procedure, may be more insidious and inescapable in its effects than that which occurs in more casual and informal settings. But, and this is the second difficulty encountered by diversion programs, such programs are far from informal or casual in that they are required to function with an eye to public accountability. They can operate only with authority implicitly borrowed from the official control agencies.

Evidence already has surfaced, indicating that diversion programs are evolving in a number of directions, none of which promises success in avoiding the labeling process. The first, and probably most subversive of the aim of labeling avoidance, is the tendency for diversion programs to develop a clientele composed exclusively of juveniles referred by control authorities—school personnel, police, and juvenile court functionaries. The initial labeling instituted by selection for referral is then compounded by membership in programs whose sole participants are thus already stigmatized and recognizable as such.

A second direction taken by some diversion programs is heavy reliance on the clinical model. While individual psychotherapy may have its constructive uses, the clinical model tends to preempt efforts to incorporate young offenders into groups of conventional youngsters, where exposure to prosocial norms is most likely to promote reformation. Finally, a third tendency evident in diversion programs, antagonistic to their labeling reduction aim, is the use of coercion. Referral out of the juvenile justice system usually has the character of a probationary sentence. The implied agreement is that official action will be stayed so long as the juvenile participates in the assigned program and its activities and refrains from committing further acts of delinquency. The "behave or else" climate of many diversion programs can only reinforce the person's sense of his labeled status.[7] It is not too far off the mark to characterize many diversion programs as extensions of the reach of the juvenile justice system. The use of coercive authority is masked, but it is emphatically present. In brief, then, there exist latent tendencies of diversion programs to foster the segregation of delinquents, to neglect the use of group experience in favor of individual-treatment methods, and to employ coercion in maintaining program membership. The effect of these tendencies is to reinforce rather than to reduce the impact of labeling.

If this assessment of the prospects of diversion programs is valid, it points also to what is most problematic in labeling theory. Its principal shortcoming is not evident in what the theory asserts, which seems unexceptionable, but in certain of its unexamined implications. The first of these has already been mentioned, namely, the unspoken assumption that the tendency to impose negative labels may be brought under control through awareness of its destructive consequences. However, the use of negative labels is but one side of a more general disposition to define persons in terms of culturally established social categories. The information content of such categories, whatever their accuracy, facilitates the anticipation of behavior: we name or label people in order to know in advance what their actions are likely to be.[8] Labeling in the interest of this need is not only negative. It may also be positive, and as such can as often be as inaccurate and misleading as are negative labels. In short, the labeling process in human groups, whether for good or ill, remains a fixed feature for a species extraordinarily dependent on symbolic modes of communication. What has only to be added here is that in complex urban societies, with their predominance of transient and impersonal relationships, the accuracy of information forming the basis of labeling is increasingly attenuated.

Second, from the standpoint of a sociology of knowledge, labeling theory had its source in a growing acceptance of the pluralism of contemporary urban societies, accompanied by what Matza (1969) has called an attitude of "appreciation" for cultural diversity. With this has come an increasing restiveness with the traditional "moral absolutism" which forms the basis of laws administered by official control agencies. Labeling theory may be seen as an expression of social criticism directed against what is perceived as an archaic body of moral principles. In their application under contemporary social conditions, these principles are seen as unjustly condemning many to pariah status. It is no accident, consequently, that the focus of labeling theory, and particularly its thrust with reference to social policy, has been on the operations of the agents of formal social control. There seems to be a fairly clear implication in labeling theory that the only, or the only important, context in which negative labeling occurs is in the course of confrontation with those possessing formal control authority. Indeed, in its earliest statement, that of Tannenbaum (1938) concerning "the dramatization of evil," this was explicitly indicated. Relatively neglected, although not totally ignored, is the fact that whole classes of agents of informal social control are likely to have been involved earlier in imposing negative labels on those whose behavior has been, over time, either disruptive of normal social routines or, more seriously, predatory and destructive. These classes of informal control agents include parents and other relatives, neighbors, teachers, other children, storekeepers, and many others with whom routine contact is unavoidable. The intrusion of the formal agents of control into the picture usually comes as the capstone of a labeling process that is likely to have been under way for some time.

Third, the theory fails to differentiate among conditions in which the use of negative labeling may have variously constructive or destructive consequences. This is an enormously complex problem, but both systematic as well as commonsense observation suggests that under some conditions the experience of being negatively labeled is a significant factor in the socialization of the young. In behavioristic terms, involved here is the probability of aversive conditioning to forms of behavior to which penalties are attached. While little of a generally valid nature is known regarding the mechanisms of deterrence, it is hardly to be doubted that responsiveness to the threat carried by negative labeling has its foundation in prior personal experience of having been negatively labeled.

Labeling, both positive and negative, is an intrinsic feature of all human interaction. Labeling is unquestionably more pervasive, and more often inaccurate, unjust, and destructive in complex societies than in simple ones, and in impersonal bureaucratic contexts than in those of the small group. Precisely because of the enhanced scope of labeling activity in contemporary societies, however, it would seem the more unwarranted to expect its reduction by fiat. By the same token, it seems unrealistic to expect success in programs based on the assumption that negative labeling can be avoided, particularly with respect to those who, like most clients of diversion programs, have already been identified as in need of their special ministrations. At that point it is late in the day to reverse a process already initiated and altogether too likely to run all or part of the course of a self-fulfilling prophecy.

If not diversion programs, with their foundation in labeling theory, what then?

Labeling theory usefully applies a conflict interpretation in illuminating the dynamics of the relationship between formal control agents and self-identified groups of deviants. But to be useful in this context, conflict theory must be elaborated to disclose the conditions in which the conflict has had its origins; specifically, it must define by hypothesis the conditions that generate a population prepared to engage formal control agents as antagonists.

A theoretical formulation is needed that takes as its starting point the typical institutional settings in which the early formation of a civic identity occurs. The question of civic identity is crucial because delinquent behavior and the delinquent role impart to the person his unique relevance as an actor on the public stage. The problem the theory must explicate concerns the elements of institutional structure which, in the dynamics of their relationships, tend systematically to create civic identities of the delinquent variety. What is begun in this setting is then nurtured to full fruit by the labeling process, but the labeling does not initiate it.

It is possible to indicate the general outlines of such a theory in a set of summarily stated propositions. The central proposition of the theory asserts that initial (primary) deviance is a response to a structurally determined tendency of institutions to restrict the variety and scope of official values and, consequently, to reduce the number and types of roles accorded legitimate status. Stated formally, the greater the restriction in the range of official values, and the fewer the types of legitimate roles available, the larger will be the number of individuals constrained to engage in deviant conduct and the more frequent will be their forays in this direction—all of this on condition that membership in the institution is compulsory rather than voluntary.

The first assumption of the theory, that institutions move toward increased restriction in the variety and scope of their official values, is based on a set of common and accessible observations. In the contemporary rational-legal order, all groups beyond the level of primary-group association, and particularly those that are instrumentally oriented with reference to the accomplishment of social tasks, move over time in the direction of increased bureaucratization. Internal competitive pressures around issues concerning appropriate modes of achieving institutional goals tend to be resolved in bureaucratized institutions on the basis of their hierarchical authority structures. The social values, of which specific institutional tasks are the concrete representation, are typically and necessarily formulated in general and global terms (for example, the general welfare, control of crime, education of the young, and so forth). They require reduction or transformation into specific program elements. In effect, then, what comes to represent the set of social values of which the institution is the embodiment are those modes of their implementation that come to be authoritatively established as appropriate. In this process, however, alternative means of implementing these values, extending the range of their expression in action, tend necessarily to be eliminated as subversive of the authority structure. Hence, the more mature an institution in its evolution in a bureaucratic direction, the greater the restriction in the variety and scope of its official values.

The second assumption of the theory is that increased restriction in the variety and scope of official values reduces the number and types of roles accorded legitimate status. The latter would seem to be a straightforward consequence of the former. Roles having relevance to the accomplishment of institutional tasks are necessarily keyed to operating assumptions as to how these tasks are best accomplished. To use a common and overworked example, if institutions of public education (and school systems provide an exemplary case of the processes here summarized) determine that the social value of educating the young is best accomplished by bringing students up to some standard of academic proficiency, then the only roles accorded legitimacy will be those seen as serving that purpose. But, by the same token, whatever other roles the clients of the institution may develop that are either irrelevant to or that interfere with this highly restrictive expression of the social value as implemented cannot be granted legitimate status. The denial of legitimacy to roles that are not in conformity with narrowed conceptions of how social values may best be implemented represents the basic condition for the inception of deviance.

A further structurally derived determinant of restricted access to institutionally legitimated roles is the purely mechanical fact that the number of members who may occupy each of the legitimate roles is limited to the number of task or performance types established as expressive of the role in terms of a technical division of labor. Whether these are task roles or roles oriented to expressive aims, they tend over time to be organized as a limited number of performance types and can be increased only through the imaginative elaboration of the meanings of official institutional values. But as Sorokin (1937–41) has observed with reference to entire civilizations, there is a tendency for "cultural exhaustion" to overtake the impulse to discover new meanings in roles that have become traditional.

The structural model outlined suggests a need for new imagery with which to project those features of institutional order crucial for generating deviance. Somewhat metaphorically, we may speak of a group, whatever its degree of institutionalization, as possessing a "value space." That space is in one sense filled by the complement of established (legitimate) roles whose enactment constitutes the group's round of activities in pursuit of its goals. Given an advanced degree of institutionalization exacerbated by bureaucratization, the "value space" tends both to contract and to be organized in sharply hierarchical form. Roles are evaluated, assigned status positions, on the basis of the degree to which they exemplify, or express, the restricted operational version of official values.

The image that would seem most aptly to represent this situation may be rendered as the "moral ecology" of the group or institution. The thrust of the term "ecology" in this context is to specify the fact that each member of the group, of the institution, or of the social order (to give the argument greater generality) is by virtue of his role or roles literally differentially placed with respect to his access to the limited supply of social virtue or honor. Just as in the natural order the ecological organization of a plurality of units is determined by placement with respect to limited sources of sustenance, determining rates of survival and morbidity, so in the moral order of human groups placement with respect to similarly limited sources of social virtue may determine rates of deviant behavior. In the symbolic coin of human interaction, deviant behavior is to the coherence and unity of the human group—in brief, to its vital signs—what morbidity is to biological units.

I do not intend to insist that ecological processes are literally definitive of operations in the moral sphere but only to exploit them as a model in the sense that, as both Rudner (1966) and Kaplan (1964) have suggested, a model may generate new theoretical perspectives. It is a fact, after all, that human beings bring to the moral life of society all of their biological properties, not the least of which is the drive to compete for survival as social beings. It is possible that a wide range of ecological processes may prove to have their homologues in the moral sphere, in purely formal terms, as for example in the suggestive similarity between symbiosis and identification.[9]

The implications of this line of speculation for the deviance problem remain to be stated. The source of conflict, of which deviant behavior is the expression, is to be found in the "moral ecology" of any group as that group acquires institutional form. To the extent that its "value space" is so organized as to reduce the number of legitimate roles, and to reduce the number of potential incumbents of those roles, the number of deviants and the frequency of deviant acts will be increased as a function of their exclusion from access to the limited supply of social virtue. Those group members who are confronted by the threat of exclusion as a result of competitive disadvantage, limited personal resources, or whatever, find that the essential grounds of their membership in the group or institution have been rendered uncertain and ambiguous. They face the threat of exclusion from a share in advancing collective goals and aims, and therefore of exclusion from sharing in the stock of collective honor.

Those subject to an experience of this kind may respond in a variety of ways, all of which are necessarily implicitly or openly oppositional. The necessity of an oppositional stance, however muted in the interest of avoiding painful sanction, stems very simply from the elemental investment of affect in the social self. As an object of primary value to the person, that self has its source in allocation to a role category within the complement established by the group as legitimate. The existence of the self as an object of experience is sustained by continual reaffirmation in the responses of others to the role content of the self. The effort to *avert* the threat of social death, to put the matter in its most extreme terms, is commonly expressed in random, anxiety-based activity in search of some grounds on which to assert a claim to a self whose legitimacy, if marginal, has a recognizable source in the ambiguities of common culture values. As Cohen (1955) has pointed out, such activity is commonly conducted in concert with others similarly situated. But precisely because the self-actuated rescue operation must resort to what is most uncertain, ambiguous, and problematic in the common culture values, the implementation of these values in conduct norms amounts, in fact, to the invention of roles that have already been excluded from the complement of those deemed legitimate. Thus, the response to the threat of exclusion tends to take the form of opposition to and conflict with the incumbents of legitimate roles.

The extension of a conflict sociology to the structural sources of deviance may offer some suggestions for social policy. With respect, specifically, to the problem of delinquency, intervention efforts keyed to a reversal of negative labeling promise limited success. The analysis presented here suggests a need for an intervention strategy that is both more realistic and, in every sense of the word, including its political sense, more radical.

What seems to be called for is closer attention to the kinds of institutional processes that have been described, those in particular associated with bureaucratization and its often arbitrary and sometimes mindless narrowing of the "value space" within which the firm attachment of the young to institutional goals and aims may take place. Inevitably, one is brought to a consideration of that primary "institutional home" of the young in the advanced industrial societies, the public schools. They stand as an apt illustration of an institutional order that has been brought into crisis as a consequence of increasing restriction in modes of implementing the general social value represented by the education of the young. It is no accident that the field of education is currently inundated by a wave of uncertainty and soul-searching, expressed in innovation in some places and in revolutionary change in others. The most profound of the changes that are likely to have relevance for delinquency control are not those concerned with the technology of instruction but those that provide for its clients an increased number of honored and respected places in the form of legitimate roles.

The accomplishment of this aim poses difficult and complex problems, which cannot here be considered, but there is some evidence that ingenuity for their solution will not be found wanting.[10] The best current example of such ingenuity is provided by the movement for the expansion of work roles in the human service industry. Designed to contribute to the solution of one aspect of the poverty problem, which is in part a problem of restriction in the availability of legitimate work roles, the paraprofessional movement, whatever its current vicissitudes, stands as an indication of the direction in which a solution may be sought for the more general problem of humane and constructive social control.[11]

## Notes

1. For an early critical appraisal of these views, see Mills (1943) and Davis (1938).

2. Lemert's subsequent writings present elaborations and refinements of his initial theses respecting the labeling process. See his (1967) collection of essays and research reports.

3. While Goffman's work is concerned primarily with strategies of identity presentation and management, the dynamics of the labeling process are implicitly assumed.

4. The polemical stance of many of the early labeling theorists, Lemert aside, seemed to discount the possibility of substantial pools of normative consensus in even the most pluralist of societies. For a current systematic statement which denies substantial normative consensus, see Douglas (1970:3–30). On the other hand, in his recent reassessment of the claims of the labeling approach, Schur (1971), himself prominently identified with this school, has provided a balanced appraisal of its values and limits.

5. Progression through stages in the development of deviant identity was particularly emphasized by Lemert (1951) in distinguishing between primary and secondary deviance. However, his attention and interest were directed to the latter. Primary deviance was treated as analytically nonproblematic random variation in adaptive behavior. This approach suggests reluctance to push social structural analysis into a problem domain claimed by experts in individual psychology.

6. For the content of some of these programs, see United States Department of Health, Education, and Welfare (1973).

7. Lemert (1972) calls attention to the focus on potential misbehavior usually found in programs and institutions whose clients have been "selected in" by virtue of their past misbehavior. In the extreme case of the juvenile reformatory this takes the form of detailed regulation of activities normally reserved to individual choice and discretion.

8. The threat of stigma under conditions of mutual trust may, however, promote normalization, but its severity requires careful calibration to induce cognitive dissonance. Limited experimental evidence supports the claim that deviant behavior is more readily given up under conditions of mild rather than severe threat (Festinger 1957; Aronson 1966).

9. To explicate the homology: in symbiosis, units provide each other with life-sustaining utilities, such as protection and nutrition. In psychological identification, the self of one is built up of elements appropriated from but not depleting the self of another. Both are instances of mutual support, and in neither case does the survival of one unit entail the destruction of the other.

10. A review and analysis of problems encountered in school-centered programs of delinquency prevention may be found in Lemert (1972). Although he makes a strong case for the potential capacity of educational programs to normalize deviant conduct, Lemert regards Ameri-

can schools as currently too crisis-ridden to be expected to undertake this task.

11. For a description of the origin, career, and problems of this movement, see Pearl and Riessman (1965).

# References

Aronson, Elliott
1966        "Threat and Obedience." *Trans-action* 3 (March-April): 25–27.

Becker, Howard S.
1963        *Outsiders.* New York: The Free Press.
1967        "Whose Side Are We On?" *Social Problems* 14 (Winter): 239–47.

Cohen, Albert K.
1955        *Delinquent Boys.* Glencoe, Ill.: The Free Press.

Coser, Lewis A.
1962        "Some Functions of Deviant Behavior." *American Journal of Sociology* 68 (September): 172–81.

Davis, Kingsley
1938        "Mental Hygiene and the Class Structure." *Psychiatry* 1 (February): 55–65.

Douglas, Jack D., ed.
1970        *Deviance and Respectability.* New York: Basic Books.

Durkheim, Emile
1938        *The Rules of Sociological Method.* New York: The Free Press.

Erikson, Kai T.
1966        *Wayward Puritans.* New York: John Wiley.

Festinger, Leon
1957        *A Theory of Cognitive Dissonance.* Stanford: Stanford University Press.

Goffman, Erving
1959        *Presentation of Self in Everyday Life.* Garden City, N.Y.: Doubleday.
1965        *Stigma: Notes on the Management of Spoiled Identity.* Englewood Cliffs, N.J.: Prentice-Hall.

Kaplan, Abraham
1964        *The Conduct of Inquiry.* San Francisco: Chandler Publishing Co.

Lemert, Edwin
1951        *Social Pathology*. New York: McGraw-Hill.
1967        *Human Deviance, Social Problems, and Social Control*. Englewood Cliffs, N.J.: Prentice-Hall.
1972        *Instead of Court: Diversion in Juvenile Justice* USDHEW Publication No. (HWM) 72-9093. Washington: Government Printing Office.

Lofland, John
1969        *Deviance and Identity*. Englewood Cliffs, N.J.: Prentice-Hall.

Matza, David
1969        *Becoming Deviant*. Englewood Cliffs, N.J.: Prentice-Hall.

Mills, C. W.
1943        "The Professional Ideology of Social Pathologists." *American Journal of Sociology* 49 (September): 165–80.

Pearl, Arthur, and Frank Riessman
1965        *New Careers for the Poor*. New York: The Free Press.

Rudner, Richard S.
1966        *Philosophy of Social Science*. Englewood Cliffs, N.J.: Prentice-Hall.

Scheff, Thomas
1966        *Being Mentally Ill*. Chicago: Aldine.

Schur, Edwin M.
1971        *Labeling Deviant Behavior*. New York: Harper and Row.

Sorokin, Pitirim
1937–41     *Social and Cultural Dynamics*. 4 vols. New York: American Book Co.

Tannenbaum, Frank
1938        *Crime and the Community*. Boston: Ginn and Co.

United States Department of Health, Education, and Welfare
1973        *Better Ways to Help Youth: Three Youth Service Programs*. Washington: Government Printing Office.

# 10 Marginal Workers
## Some Antecedents and Implications of an Idea from Shaw and McKay

*Daniel Glaser*

### McKay, Shaw, Burgess, and the Future Roles of Sociologists

My first contact with the ideas of Henry McKay and Clifford Shaw came in 1938, as an undergraduate at the University of Chicago, when we read their books and heard them as guest speakers in a course taught by Ernest W. Burgess. My postwar studies began with Clifford Shaw's course on juvenile delinquency at the university's downtown campus. These contacts have been followed by over two decades of basking, whenever possible, in the friendship and stimulation radiated by Henry McKay and his Institute for Juvenile Research associates. What role models for sociologists have they provided?

Ellsworth Faris, head of the university's Department of Sociology in the 1930s and himself a former religious missionary in Africa, informed us that sociology disproportionately attracted persons whose initial occupational orientation was to the clergy. In the troubled Depression years it was also evident that many students sought careers as sociologists after earlier dreams of leading humanity to salvation by social revolution or, at least, by drastic social reform. They were repeatedly disillusioned, of course, when left-wing parties failed to gain political power in this country, and were even more discouraged when revolutionary leaders who gained power in other countries became more repressive than the tyrants they had replaced.

For many of these erstwhile preachers, revolutionists, or reformers, McKay, Shaw, and Burgess represented a viable alternative, that of applied social science. Not only had these men pioneered in theory and research on juvenile delinquency, but they had also moved via the Chicago Area Projects to do something significant about it. This was the path most of us wished to follow in addressing all social problems.

Daniel Glaser is a member of the Department of Sociology and Anthropology at the University of Southern California.

To what extent did Burgess, Shaw, and McKay provide the optimum role model for today's sociologists? It seems to me that each of these three occupied a different position on a still important continuum from the ivory tower of academia to the workaday world of high crime-rate neighborhoods where events obscure abstract causal patterns.

Burgess we recall with respect and affection chiefly in the ivory tower, which is important as a base for reflection and data analysis. He was famed as the man who became an expert on marriage without getting married and on urban crime without residing outside of university communities (or, earlier, the prairies). Shaw, on the other hand, was the Chicago probation officer who found support in Burgess and other sociologists at the university for his effort to address delinquency as a collective condition rather than as a collection of individual case problems. He was especially preoccupied with the organization of action. Henry McKay shared these action responsibilities, and my impression from a variety of sources is that he has been particularly effective in cutting across two sociocultural worlds and linking two types of specialization. He is in the middle of our continuum from the field of action to the halls of academe and thus could most readily help each to comprehend the other.

To McKay and Shaw we owe what I believe is the most important idea in the field of crime prevention and correction. This is the concept of the marginal worker—one who has been enculturated in two different social worlds, one who can therefore help those in each of these subcultural settings to blend the language, norms, and values of their sphere with those of the other. Henry McKay has been most outstanding as the marginal worker integrating crime prevention activity with social science, thereby benefitting both.

It is important to recognize that this type of role, which Henry McKay created for himself as a sociologist, is now probably the most rapidly growing role in our discipline. During the 1960s universities produced Ph.D.'s at a phenomenal rate to meet the demands of an academic marketplace inflated when the postwar baby boom crowded campuses. Today the demand for Ph.D.'s for college faculties has dropped markedly, but Ph.D.'s are still created at a high rate. Also, today as in the 1930s, our students are overwhelmed by the failings of our society. They are especially disturbed by the moral cost and ineffectiveness of all our recent wars, including our war on poverty, our war on crime, and our war on drugs. This experience has given our new Ph.D.'s an orientation to social action and has made them increasingly receptive to careers of research—research that will guide policy-makers in social change and in treatment agencies of all types. More and more sociology Ph.D.'s will be marginal workers, between academia and the world of action. Thus, in the 1970s and 1980s more than ever before, Henry McKay's career can be a model for the modern sociologist.

The marginal worker idea has been widely applied over the years but often under other labels, and frequently in a distorted, subverted, or corrupted form. Now, however, it is developing in a form closer to the original Area Project concept, although still under different labels. Why did this idea emerge in the Chicago Area Projects during the 1930s? To answer this question we must examine a bit of the history of American sociology and of social work and corrections in the United States.

## Social Darwinism, American Sociology, and Delinquency Theory

Thomas S. Kuhn, in his modern classic *The Structure of Scientific Revolutions* (1970), advises that sciences grow by leaps of conceptualization, by periodically accepting dramatic new ways of thinking about the phenomena that puzzle them. Each of these radically new and basic ideas, which Kuhn calls "paradigms," is resisted at first (some laymen still resist, as did scientists earlier, Darwin's theory of evolution, or even Pasteur's germ theory of disease). When such a paradigm is eventually adopted by most scientists, however, it becomes part of what Kuhn calls "normal science." The paradigm then underlies the thinking of scholars without their being aware of it, and they often even forget the nature and origins of the basic conceptual leap as they become preoccupied with its less dramatic elaboration, specification, and qualification.

Sociology is to a large degree what Kuhn calls a pre-paradigmatic science, "characterized by continual competition between a number of distinct views of nature, each partially derived from, and all roughly compatible with, the dictations of scientific observation and method" (1962:4). The American and British sociology and anthropology that evolved in the nineteenth century and became institutionalized academically in the twentieth century had developed paradigms with which to account for the diversity of customs and beliefs in strange societies that the older discipline of ethnography was mapping. These paradigms, collectively labelled "social Darwinism," not only included a variety of short-lived and competing simplistic theories of social and cultural evolution but also an enduring principle of cultural determination of behavior, with its corollaries of cultural diffusion and cultural relativity. The nonevolutionary components became an automatic part of American social-science thinking as the diffusionist viewpoint began to dominate anthropology early in the twentieth century and anthropological writings were widely read.

Culturally deterministic thinking was especially propelled in the United States by William Graham Sumner's *Folkways*, the first and longest best seller of American social science in this century. First published in 1906, it was still the book most influential in making people think sociologically throughout the 1920s and 1930s, when Shaw and McKay were conducting their delinquency research and the Area Projects were launched.

Sumner himself was an arch-conservative, opposing social reform efforts with the slogan "stateways cannot change folkways." His appeal in the 1930s was greatest, however, to students eager for change. Sumner's assertion that "the mores can make anything right," buttressed by his evidence on the multiplicity of creeds, moral standards, taboos, and tastes in the world, meant that the status quo was not sacred and that customary beliefs could be questioned. Indeed, his sloganistic phrases became ideological foundations for challenging prior verities and for explaining deviance, especially that which Chicago researchers were finding disproportionately concentrated just outside the business areas of the city.

The essence of cultural determinism and cultural relativity, those parts of social Darwinism which became the underlying paradigm of "normal" sociology and anthropology, involved a view of the world as one in which cultures have three key characteristics: they determine what people regard as proper and improper behavior; they change continually; they are acquired by social contacts and, hence, are distributed by social diffusion. This view of culture implies a basic law of sociology and anthropology: *social separation produces cultural differentiation*.

This principle, which I call the "law of sociocultural relativity," probably is the most powerful explanatory proposition in our discipline, but sociologists and anthropologists seldom are aware that they are employing lawlike principles, and they often fail to appreciate the utility of the laws which have become normal to their thinking. In the 1920s, however, cultural determinism was more salient in the work of American sociologists than now because the preceding seventy years of accelerating immigration had made our cities and rural areas mosaics of neighborhoods with contrasting languages, foods, festivals, faiths, and other culture components. Much sociological work consisted of studying such communities in a manner resembling the method of ethnology much more than does most sociological research today.

With this preoccupation normal to sociological thinking in this period, Shaw and McKay, mapping Chicago delinquency rates in the 1920s, explained the variation of these rates by neighborhood as due to social separation producing cultural differentiation. Switching from statistics to tracing the "natural history" of delinquent careers, however, they found the social separation and cultural differentiation not only between neighborhoods but also within the high delinquency neighborhoods. Those who had settled the urban areas as adult immigrants maintained the low crime rates of their former locales, except for certain customs then illegal in the United States, notably alcohol consumption. What fostered persistently high delinquency rates in these areas of first settlement for new and poor immigrants was social separation from children and adults elsewhere. In the streets, schools, and youth hangouts of neighborhoods that had long had high delinquency rates, as well as in the hangouts of adults who had grown up in these neighborhoods, there was continuity in the diffusion of norms, values, and rationalizations conducive to delinquency and crime, just as there was continuity in the contrasting cultures of youth and adults in suburban and rural communities.

During the 1950s the habit of thinking in terms of the paradigm of sociocultural relativity diminished in American sociology. Instead, analysis was done by speculative postulation of functions which, as philosopher of science Carl Hempel (1959) points out, is at best a heuristic assumption of interdependence that in itself conveys no image of the world reducible to testable propositions.

Much of the research on delinquency during that period failed to focus on such analytic variables as social separation, cultural diffusion, and differential opportunities. Yet in today's delinquency, with its emphasis on drug use, the primary importance of the law of sociocultural relativity as an explanatory principle is more evident than ever before. The social separation, hence cultural differentiation, of today's youth from the adult world can be shown to be greater than ever was demonstrable formerly, by comparisons of either official or admitted rates of deviant behavior. Surveys which ask people if they have used marijuana or "speed" (methedrine), or if they know people who use these drugs, usually yield affirmative answers from a majority of our seventeen to twenty-year-old population, but from less than five percent of those over forty. Indeed, the frequency of acquaintance with such drugs is often fifteen to twenty or more times as great among older juveniles and youth as among our middle-aged or older population. In the light of such evidence, it is clear that those who refer to adolescent subcultures as a myth are either oblivious to relevant data on age-group differences in norms or have only a mythical claim to be thinking sociologically.

## Simmel, American Sociology, and the Marginal Worker Idea

The sociological frame of reference which Shaw and McKay acquired in their close relationships with the Department of Sociology of the University of Chicago was most fully summarized in the Park and Burgess text, *Introduction to the Science of Sociology*, first published in 1921 and for over a quarter century thereafter the model for most textbook formulations of the elements of sociology. The most frequently cited author in this Park and Burgess work was the German sociologist Georg Simmel. His writings were then read mainly in translations made twenty years earlier by Albion W. Small and were in much more meaningful English than that in which Simmel is now most readily available. At any rate, Simmel sensitized sociologists to the dynamics of interaction across group lines. He noted how conflict with an outgroup unified an ingroup and how conflicts were accommodated by social stratification within and between groups. He observed the significance of sociability, of interaction for its own sake, in developing ties between persons. He also observed the knowledge-gathering advantage of being a friendly but nonjudging stranger, noting that such strangers often gained confidential information that their informants would withhold from intimate acquaintances.

Such sensitivity to the subtleties of social interaction, combined with focus on interaction as the independent variable by which culture is transmitted, is reflected in McKay and Shaw's delinquency causation theory, field research methods, and action programs, but especially in the idea of the marginal worker as change agent. Implicit in this idea is recognition, first, that the persons most effective in bringing delinquents from one culture to another are those who have recently made this transition themselves. Second, the marginal worker idea implied that mutual trust and commitment to both giving and receiving help comes from demonstration of personal concern for someone else, through acts and gestures which go beyond the routine requirements of bureaucratic roles.

The ideal marginal worker in delinquency prevention, as originally conceived in the Area Projects, was a person who had been involved in delinquency and crime, had been helped by residents in the Area Project in obtaining self-sufficiency in a noncriminal life, and felt committed thereafter to help others make this transition. This combination is illustrated by the following statement of one such marginal worker:

> I was in Joliet for nine years. . . .
> After four years, nine months and fifteen days I was eligible for parole. My sister came down and went to the Parole Board and my parole was denied. Each time for the next five years my parole was denied to me and it made me feel bitter. . . .
> The last time my sister came down . . . she told me she saw someone belonging to the Russell Square Community Committee [an Area Project]. The first time the members of the Committee appeared before the Parole Board, I got a year's continuance. . . . I had just about given up hopes of ever getting out when my sister told me that a couple of members of the Committee were interested in helping me. When they appeared in my behalf and things looked pretty favorable, I was given a new lease on life because someone was fighting for me who didn't always remind me that I had served time. Finally, I was paroled to the Committee and they got me a job with a local company.
> . . . When I got out everyone treated me like an old friend. If I had any problems, some of the members of the Committee would always give me a helping hand. . . . Whenever I needed money, I could borrow it from some of the Committee. I wasn't ashamed to ask for it. I made up my mind to go straight as long as I had a few friends. . . .

Since I've been paroled I spent a lot of my time in the club
operated by the Russell Square Community Committee,
helping with the program. I go around with a neighborhood
man employed by the Chicago Area Project. We're out
together two or three times a week (Shaw 1944: 8–9).

During the 1950s, when delinquent-gang fights reached a peak
of intensity, the failure of traditional settlement-house delinquency prevention methods was apparent. The Area Projects were
by then nationally known. When other types of private and public
agencies were pressured to do something about gang fights, they
borrowed the marginal worker idea. A new position was established in many of these organizations, variously called "detached
worker," "extension youth worker," "gang worker," and finally
the now most standard term, "street worker."

Street workers sound much like marginal workers, as when
Spergel, in a leading social-work training manual, asserts that
such a person "belongs to two worlds. He is of the delinquent
group and its subculture, but also of the world of respectable and
conforming people" (1967: xiii). When street worker appoint-
ments require a Master of Social Work or other college degree,
however, the worker is less likely to be "of the delinquent group
and its subculture" than are the ex-offender marginal workers of
the Area Projects. College-trained street workers are often mis-
sionaries from the middle class, to which they usually return
daily. Of the street-work pattern during the 1950s, Spergel says:

social work agencies with roots outside of the neighborhood
were subjected to pressure to do something about blatant
delinquency problems. Attention was . . . directed to gang
fighting. The middle class orientation abhorred violence, and
the supportive psychoanalytic and limited social science
tradition of the agencies saw the origin of social disorders in the
dysfunctioning of individuals and small groups. . . . the
agencies' response to pressure for control was to assign special
youth workers to gangs in an attempt to redirect their energies
into more constructive channels (1967: xvii).

This description has also been valid for much use of street workers
since the 1950s.

Repeatedly, research to test the effectiveness of street workers
has found that, while they often intervene successfully to negotiate
the cessation or avoidance of gang fights, they fail to alter rates of

theft, burglary, robbery, or drug offenses by gang members. Malcolm Klein (1971), whose review of research by others and by himself provides the most careful evaluation available on this topic, concludes that street workers do not reduce delinquency and often increase it.

Frequently street workers provide "fun and games" which make the gangs more attractive but sometimes increase the social separation of delinquents from people in the legitimate adult roles that youth must adopt if they are to achieve independence in a noncriminal way of life. The law of sociocultural relativity has been inexorable: increasing the social separation of juveniles and youth from adults increases the differentiation of their culture from that which is dominant in adult society. Conversely, Klein's study and others, such as that of Elliott (1966), indicate that getting delinquents into adult work-roles decreases their commitment to delinquent subcultural values.

The new marginal workers, those who now most closely approximate this role as originated in the Area Projects, are generally not the graduates of group-work curricula in our schools of social work but are paraprofessionals in a variety of agencies who are recruited mainly from ex-offenders. These workers most effectively link two cultural worlds when they are employed as part of a team with a professional social worker, sharing a common caseload. The paraprofessionals are initially more expert in direct communication with clients and their families and friends, while the more educated professional is more expert at communication with higher officials or with other agencies, but all the team members can learn from each other if they collaborate; eventually they can substitute for each other and thus be more available in crises. This has been illustrated in the Chicago Federal Probation Office's Case Aide Project (cf., Beless et al. 1972), which employs part-time paraprofessionals, and even more so in the Harambee, RODEO, and other projects of the Los Angeles County Department of Probation, which employs full-time paraprofessionals in casework teams.

## Marginal Workers and the Future

As society becomes more complex, a larger amount of schooling is required as a prerequisite for most of the types of employment which provide average or higher compensation. For decades, studies have found school maladjustment to be one of the best predictors of a subsequent delinquent or criminal record (e.g., Glueck and Glueck 1950; Empey et al. 1971). My impression is that this relationship is becoming more marked as the years pass. Stinchcombe (1964) demonstrated that it is the youth for whom school seems irrelevant as both present and future gratification who are most attracted to rebellious activity.

The importance of the school as a bridge between childhood and adulthood cannot be overstressed, but to keep adolescents on this bridge until they can get off with a secure adult foothood requires new kinds of activity on the bridge, as well as new kinds of off-ramps from it, at new locations. New architects of school programs are needed much more than new architects of school construction. Perhaps most of all, if the school is to bridge childhood to adulthood successfully, there must be new jobs for marginal workers to keep adolescents from straying off this bridge on roads to delinquency and crime. We need imaginative new ways of using these workers to apply the law of sociocultural relativity constructively by reducing the social separation of the generations, so that they are less contrasting in culture. A few of the many relevant but still too few and scattered steps in this direction, in addition to those already mentioned, are the following.

1. Employment of parents or other adults from the school children's neighborhood as part-time voluntary or paid aides or supplements to teachers, and also employment of older students to help younger ones. Much of this activity can occur outside of regular school hours, some of it outside the school building, and it can provide mixtures of education, employment, and recreation for students, increasing the employment component as they grow older, especially in poor neighborhoods.

2. More apprenticeship of youth to adults in jobs of all types, preferably on a part-time and paid basis, as a matter of public policy rather than of economy, hence perhaps more government-subsidized part-time jobs in private business.

3. More involvement of youth from early adolescence on with adults in political activities, including campaign work, lobbying, and other forms of democratic action. Lowering of the voting age to eighteen seems to have encouraged this involvement, and in some areas it has been stressed in high delinquency neighborhoods rather than just in suburban high schools.

4. The replacement of all large correctional institutions by

community correctional programs of diverse types for all who can fairly safely be placed in them, with small custodial establishments available when needed before or between community correctional efforts. Massachusetts has pioneered in this by closing all its correctional institutions for juveniles (Bakal 1973). The main advantage of smallness is its facilitation of personal communication between staff and members, and thus its enhancement of the staff's ability to become marginal workers.

5. More utilization of casework teams in all aspects of corrections, the teams to consist of personnel of diverse background and age, rather than just single caseworkers with separate caseloads. The increasingly widespread recruitment of retired persons as volunteers or as paid part-time workers in court probation offices can well be combined with the already described recruitment of young ex-offenders as paraprofessionals, all as members of teams sharing a common caseload, hence more readily available for crisis intervention, when help can be most strategic. The Connecticut School for Boys (recently combined with the School for Girls) had an interesting practice of including an older woman and a young woman and an older man and a young man in the staff of at least four persons assigned to each cottage; each of these diverse personnel had communication advantages for some of the boys which the other staff lacked. Together, such a staff group simulates more closely than homogeneous personnel of identical background the outside world into which the inmates must successfully assimilate if they are to associate less exclusively with peers who exert pressures for conformity to delinquent subcultures.

None of the foregoing methods of generating marginal workers is a panacea, of course, and it should also be noted that acculturation is a two-way street. Just as the descendants of early settlers in the United States added pizza to their cuisines while giving Italian immigrants the English language and American life-styles, so those who now conform to adult subcultural standards may learn some things from youth. It will be especially fruitful for all if they learn from the youth culture more permissiveness toward letting individuals "do their own thing" as long as they do not harm others. We can prevent an appreciable proportion of what is now deemed delinquency and youth crime by ceasing to define it as criminal. I refer here especially to the consumption of substances, such as marijuana, the possession of which is often a felony even though, according to clear predominance of rigorous research, its use is less harmful than a comparable intake of alcohol.

Throughout history marginal men have been the source of great new ideas, for they have what has been called a "double vision," seeing both the perceptions of their immediate associates and the perceptions of the culturally different persons in whose groups they also participate. Those who most adequately achieve the McKay and Shaw ideal of a marginal worker, who are at home in both delinquent and nondelinquent social circles, may be our greatest hope in reducing the human costs of crime and delinquency.

## References

Bakal, Yitzhak
1973          *Closing Correctional Institutions.* Lexington, Mass.: D. C. Heath.

Beless, Donald W., William S. Pilcher and Ellen Jo Ryan
1972          "Use of Indigenous Nonprofessionals in Probation and Parole." *Federal Probation* 36 (March): 10–15.

Elliott, Delbert S.
1966          "Delinquency, School Attendance and Dropout." *Social Problems* 13 (Winter): 307–14.

Empey, LaMar T., and Steven G. Lubeck, with
Ronald L. LaPorte
1971          *Explaining Delinquency.* Lexington, Mass.: D. C. Heath.

Glueck, Sheldon and Eleanor T. Glueck
1950          *Unraveling Juvenile Delinquency.* Cambridge, Mass.: Harvard University Press.

Hempel, Carl C.
1959          "The Logic of Functional Analysis." Chapter 9 in Llwelyn Gross, ed., *Symposium on Sociological Theory.* Evanston, Ill.: Row, Peterson.

Klein, Malcolm W.
1971          *Street Gangs and Street Workers.* Englewood Cliffs, N.J.: Prentice-Hall.

Kuhn, Thomas S.
1970        *The Structure of Scientific Revolutions*. 2nd Edition. Chicago: University of Chicago Press.

Park, Robert E., and Ernest W. Burgess
1921        *Introduction to the Science of Sociology*. Chicago: University of Chicago Press.

Shaw, Clifford R.
1944        "Methods, Accomplishments and Problems of the Chicago Area Projects: A Report to the Board of Directors of the Chicago Area Project" (mimeographed).

Spergel, Irving
1967        *Street Gang Work*. Garden City, N.Y.: Doubleday-Anchor.

Stinchcombe, Arthur J.
1964        *Rebellion in a High School*. Chicago: Quadrangle.

Sumner, William Graham
1906        *Folkways*. Boston: Ginn and Co.

# 11 Seriousness of Crime and a Policy of Juvenile Justice

*Marvin E. Wolfgang*

## Measuring Seriousness

In 1964 Thorsten Sellin and I published *The Measurement of Delinquency*, the result of a research project supported by the Ford Foundation. Six years later, with Robert Figlio, we published *Delinquency in a Birth Cohort*, based on research sponsored by the National Institute of Mental Health and conducted through the staff of the Center for Studies in Criminology and Criminal Law at the University of Pennsylvania. These two studies are linked together by reason of what we have called "the seriousness scores" of delinquency and crime.

In this chapter I should like to describe briefly the linkage of these two studies and to propose an experimental program in juvenile justice that has been generated by them, though it was not originally a part of either. I shall omit technical and methodological details from the descriptions of these studies, for those details are located in the published volumes.

The primary purpose of *The Measurement of Delinquency* project was to develop a more refined index of delinquency than crudely existed in the FBI Uniform Crime Reporting system. The result was a new type of index which we claimed to be as applicable to adult crime as to juvenile delinquency. Evaluating the many limitations of the UCR system, we sought to develop an index that built upon the varying degrees of seriousness of acts defined as violations of the law. We noted that the UCR masks offenses by counting only the most serious offenses in a complex event that may have more than one criminal law violation, thereby underreporting some crime. And, although there is a hierarchy of seriousness in the UCR system, such that criminal homicide is viewed as more serious than the other six crimes in the index, nonetheless the complete tally of so-called "serious" crime

Marvin E. Wolfgang is a member of the Department of Sociology at the University of Pennsylvania.

or "major" crime produces a crude crime rate per 100,000 that fails to take into account the variations and the degrees of seriousness between homicides, aggravated assaults, rapes, robberies, burglaries, larcenies, and automobile thefts. We took the position "that judged seriousness of delinquency is the homogeneous dimension which can allow for quantitative measurement of this phenomenon and that there are ways of ascribing values to the magnitudes in this common medium of seriousness" (Sellin and Wolfgang 1964:338).

The system we used for weighting the relative seriousness of each offense included in a penal code was derived from psychophysical scaling.[1] Hundreds of police officers, judges, and university students were asked to assign numerical weights to 141 offenses. On the basis of these weights a set of scale scores denoting the relative mathematical weights of the gravity of different crimes was developed. Part of the testing procedure was to obtain category scales, or equal interval units, on the one hand, and magnitude estimation scores, on the other, allowing for freedom of choice from any number above zero and less than infinity. The magnitude estimation scores represented a ratio scale which permitted us, by a variety of computations and division by a common denominator and rounding to produce scores such that a murder is generally over twice as serious as a rape; an aggravated assault, depending on the medical treatment necessary, may be two or three times more serious than auto theft, and so on. A homicide, for example, is given a score of 26, forcible rape a score of 10, an assault involving hospitalization for the victim 7, an assault requiring medical treatment by a physician but no hospitalization 4, and a minor injury having no treatment a score of 1. Property offenses were also scored by the amount of damage or theft.

The study has been repeated from Canada to China, England to Africa, usually with similar results (Sellin and Wolfgang 1969:8-9, n.3). Trends produced by counting the seriousness of crime with these weights can be dramatically different from those based on the UCR system. The accompanying diagram (fig. 11.1) shows estimated robbery trends in Philadelphia between 1960 and 1966 using the UCR index rate, with the simple count of robberies per 10,000 population, and the weighted index that incorporates seriousness scores computed from the detailed facts of each case. The two trend lines are very dissimilar. Most

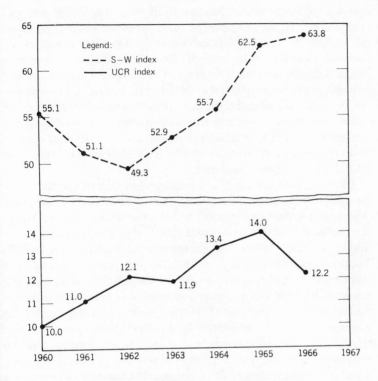

Figure 11.1

Fig. 11.1 Trends in robbery known to police in Philadelphia as shown by the weighted and UCR indexes: 1960 to 1966 (rates per 10,000 total population according to census adjustments).

Source:   André Normandeau, "Trends in Robbery as Reflected by Different Indexes," in *Delinquency, Selected Studies*, edited by T. Sellin and M. Wolfgang, (New York: John Wiley, 1969), p. 151.

noticeably, the UCR index indicates that reported robbery per 10,000 was about the same in 1962 as in 1966. Yet the weighted index rate reveals a clear increase in seriousness over the period. Further analysis revealed that the amount of property stolen was substantially similar over the seven-year period and that the reason for the rise in the weighted rate was the increase in injury to robbery victims (Normandeau, in Sellin and Wolfgang, eds., 1969:150–57).

The FBI method of counting crimes underreports multiple events. When more than one kind of crime is committed, the FBI asks the police to count for the UCR only the "most serious" criminal act. If, for example, an offender commits forcible rape, burglarizes the house, physically assaults the victim, and steals the victim's automobile, only the forcible rape is to be reported by the police to the FBI. The amount of physical harm or the loss or damage to property is not counted as such, and many acts are not recorded statistically. In our system, which is weighted for seriousness, underreporting and incompleteness are eliminated. For each criminal act that occurs during an event, the number of times it is committed is multiplied by the weight of the crime, and a total score is then calculated.

The weighted system is not without limitations, as has been indicated by Gordon Rose (1968), Alfred Blumstein (1974), and others. But a modified version was recommended to the FBI by the National Crime Commission (1967) and the National Commission on the Causes and Prevention of Violence (Mulvihill, Tumin and Curtis 1969). Whether "disutility units," such as were mentioned in the reports of the Science and Technology Task Force of the President's Crime Commission (1967), or some other derivation from the initial psychophysical scaling might be employed is not the important issue. The significant feature is that there is general agreement that some form of measuring the seriousness of crime is an important and useful goal in developing a better understanding of the amount and character of crime in a nation, state, or community.

The seriousness scores were used in the recent project that resulted in *Delinquency in a Birth Cohort*. The statistical process through psychophysical scaling permitted us to assign scores to the offenses committed by members of the birth cohort and to assign cumulative scores to the biography of each offender, to average seriousness by race, socioeconomic status, age, and other variables.

## Scoring Delinquents

In 1964 the National Institute of Mental Health sponsored a unique study of delinquency in the United States. Under the direction of Professor Thorsten Sellin and myself, the Center for Studies in Criminology and Criminal Law at the University of Pennsylvania launched a program to capture and analyze a group of boys born in 1945 who lived in a given locale (Philadelphia) at least from their tenth up to their eighteenth birthdays.[2] This group constitutes a birth cohort. Our main interest was to determine a fact thus far unknown, namely, the probability of becoming officially recorded as a delinquent. Only in Norway (Christie 1960) and England (Mulligan, Douglas, Hammond, and Tizard 1963:1083–86; Douglas, Ross, Hammond, and Mulligan 1966:294–302) had efforts been made to discover this datum; nowhere had a study been so elaborately designed and executed. All previous criminology research had been retrospective, that is, looking backward on a group of known and recorded delinquents of varying ages to determine their age of onset of delinquency (as the Gluecks [1930, 1934, 1937, 1940, 1943, 1950, 1968, 1970] at Harvard have so often done), or prospective, that is, looking forward from a group of delinquents of varying ages to describe their adult patterns of criminality. Neither of these types of cross-section studies validly provides proper probability statements concerning the chances of becoming delinquent or an adult criminal. Neither can offer valid assertions about patterns of delinquent behavior by specific ages, about the onset of criminality, desistance (stopping delinquency), or about relative degrees of seriousness of offensivity.

Through school, police, and Selective Service files we traced 9,945 boys, or all those born in 1945 who lived in Philadelphia at least from ages ten to eighteen. From this total birth cohort universe, 35 percent became delinquent, that is, had at least one contact with the police for something other than a traffic violation. The 3,475 boys committed 10,214 offenses up to the end of the juvenile court statute age of seventeen.

Our figure of 35 percent delinquent needs further clarification. First, it has commonly been said that in any given calendar year only about 2 percent of juveniles are arrested, and that probably no more than 10 percent are ever arrested. Hence, the probability that 35 percent of urban males will be arrested before their eighteenth birthday is comparatively high. Second, race is one of the most significant variables in this analysis. Nonwhites make up 29 percent of the birth cohort, but 50.2 percent are recorded delinquents; whites are 71 percent of the cohort, 29 percent of whom are delinquent. The 50 percent and 29 percent delinquent populations may be used as probability statements because we have longitudinally traced the entire universe through their juvenile years, thus indicating significant racial differential probabilities of becoming labeled delinquent. Major differences in the proportions of nonwhites and whites in other cities, assuming relative constancy to the delinquent probabilities, could make for lower or higher general probabilities of delinquency.

It should be clearly understood that the offense histories we have analyzed are derived from police arrest records. We are aware of the concept and studies of "hidden delinquency" (Wolfgang, Figlio, and Sellin 1972:15–16, nn.32, 34) or the "dark numbers" of crime,[3] which refer to illegal acts unknown or unrecorded by official agencies. For certain types of offenses, usually the less serious, racial and socioeconomic disparities found in official police records are often reduced among self-reporting studies from anonymous questionnaires or interviews. There may also be race differentials in police arrests. Therefore, we generally use the phrase "having a police record" or a "police contact." When the term "delinquent" or "delinquency" is used, officially recorded persons and acts are described. If society is concerned about the process of labeling persons as offenders and providing dispositions through our justice systems, it is important that we know who these persons are and what their probabilities are for being so processed.

Finally, there is the issue of the generalizability of a birth cohort. Each cohort is in a sense unique, time-bound, as the demographer Norman Ryder (1955) has demonstrated. How representative a single cohort may be for other communities, for different birth cohorts, for females, can only be conjectured. Cohort subset comparisons as, for example, delinquents with nondelinquents, on the basis of social, economic, and personality variables, may be representatively valid and reliable beyond the single cohort itself. Moreover, the career patterns of the delinquent group, the character of their delinquency, a probability model that forms a dynamic typology of movement from one stage to another—all of these empirical findings may be converted to conclusions for other cohorts. Minimally, every finding from this cohort has the posture of a hypothesis for testing on other cohorts elsewhere and at other times.

After examining the relationship between such background variables as race, socioeconomic status (SES), types of schools attended, residential and school moves, highest grade completed, IQ, achievement level, we concluded that the variables of race and SES were most strongly related to the offender-nonoffender classification. The remaining variables in the school records had little or no relationship to delinquency status. For example, although high achievers are much less likely to be classified as offenders than are low achievers, the relationship between race and achievement is such that most of the variance between achievement and delinquency status is explained by race, for being a poor achiever is highly related to being nonwhite. This relationship also exists between race and the remaining background variables.

The 3,475 boys in the cohort who are recorded delinquents were responsible for 10,214 delinquent acts through age seventeen. Whites were involved in 4,458, or 44 percent, and nonwhites in 5,756, or 56 percent of these offenses. The offense rate, of course, is different from the offender rate. When the rate of delinquency is computed on the basis of the number of boys ever recorded as having had a delinquency contact with the police, the offender rate is 349.4 per 1,000 cohort subjects. But this kind of computation ignores the number of offenses committed by statistically treating alike each boy, regardless of the number or types of acts committed. An offense rate, computed for the birth cohort by using the number of events as numerator and the 9,945 boys as denominator, times the constant 1,000, yields a cohort rate of 1,027.

The nonwhite crude rate (1,983.5) is 3.1 times as great as the white crude rate (633.0), but the rate when seriousness scores are considered is 4.4 times as great for nonwhites (2,585.9) as for whites (587.8). Among index offenses (injury, theft, or damage), the nonwhite crude rate is 2.4 times as great as the white rate, but the weighted rate is 4.6 times as great. Among nonindex offenses, nonwhites have a crude rate 2.6 times and a weighted rate 3.7 times as great as the respective white rates. These figures reveal that nonwhites proportionately commit not only more offenses but more serious offenses than do whites.

Among the 5,756 offenses committed by nonwhite cohort boys, 2,413 were index offenses with a mean seriousness score of 265.0. Among the 4,458 offenses committed by white cohort boys, only 1,400 were index offenses, with a mean score of 243.3. Incidence and average seriousness make for considerable difference in the computed rates for whites and nonwhites. Nonwhites committed 3,343 nonindex offenses, with a mean seriousness score of 33.2; whites had 3,058 nonindex offenses and a mean score of 24.0.

Another way to view the weighted rates is in terms of cumulative scores for the offenses and the total amount of social harm inflicted on the community. For example, nonwhites inflicted on the city 750,433 units of social harm or seriousness points— 639,455 of which were from index offenses and 110,988 from nonindex offenses. If a 10 percent reduction, not of all nonwhite offenses but of index offenses, were shifted to a 10 percent increase in nonindex offenses, the corresponding reduction in seriousness units would amount to 72,777. That is, index gravity units would dip to 565,501, and nonindex gravity units would increase to 122,087—a socially favorable trade-off. The overall crude rate of 1,983 would remain the same, but the reduction of 72,777 seriousness units (or a weighted rate reduction from 2,585.91 to 2,403.81) would be equivalent to the elimination of 28 homicides, or 104 assaults that send victims to hospitals for treatment, or 181 assaults treated by physicians without hospitalization.

In short, if juveniles must be delinquent, a major thrust of social action programs might be toward a change in the character rather than in the absolute reduction of delinquent behavior. It could also be argued that concentration of social action programs on a 10 percent reduction of white index offenses ($N = 1,400$; $WR = 483.63$) would have a greater social payoff than a 10 percent reduction of nonwhite nonindex offenses ($N = 3,343$; $WR = 382.45$). To inculcate values against harm to others, in body or property, is obviously the major means to reduce the seriousness of delinquency, both among whites and nonwhites. We are simply faced with the fact that more social harm is committed by nonwhites, so that the resources and efforts of social-harm reduction should be employed among nonwhite youth, especially the very young.

Although delinquency in a birth cohort has been analyzed in many other ways, including juvenile justice dispositions (Thornberry 1973:90–98) that reveal significantly more severe sentences for nonwhite offenders (even holding constant seriousness of offenses and number of prior offenses), perhaps the most important and new analysis is of the dynamic flow of delinquency.

By benefit of a birth cohort, we have been able to consider offenses as a stochastic process or, more specifically, whether the commission of delinquency and the types of delinquent acts are a function of frequency and the preceding history of delinquency.

If offensivity is independent of time and not a function of prior offense types, the result may be designated, mathematically, as a Markov chain. Essentially, we compared the instant, or last offense (kth offense) with the immediately preceding one (k-1st offense), and then the empirical transitions between offense types for the first through the kth (in our case, the fifteenth) offense. Five offense types were clustered and classified as Injury, Theft, Damage, Combination, or Nonindex. A sixth opportunity was Desistance. Assessing the k-1st and kth offense as well as all k-1st and kth offenses presented problems of distributions and trend analysis. Later we were able to examine shifts from one type of offense to another as the cohort passed from the first to their fifteenth offense.

We visualized the progression from birth to the first offense, then to the second, to the third, and so on as pathways along the branch of a tree with six alternative paths of offenses or desisting at each juncture. Each point of departure becomes the probability of arriving at a given location, having come from the offense type at the origin point along the path. After any offense, or from birth, one may desist from delinquency and thus become "absorbed" into the state of desistance. We call this analysis a branching probability model of offensive diversity.

We have noted that the probability of committing a first offense of any type is .3511. The likelihood of a second offense is .5358, but if a second offense is committed the probability of a third of any type is greater, .6509. Beyond the third offense the likelihood of further offenses ranges from .70 to .80.

Besides these probabilities are those concerned with moving from one type of offense to another. Does the type of offense that a cohort member committed at the k-1st offense number have any bearing on the probability that he will commit a certain type of offense at the kth number? Analysis of our data for offense switching generated a set of matrices, or transition configurations, that provided an answer.

The typical offender is most likely to commit a nonindex offense next (.47 probability), regardless of what he did in the past. He is next most likely to desist (.35), commit a theft (.13), an injury (.07), or combination (.05). With the exception of the moderate tendency to repeat the same type of offense, this pattern obtains regardless of the type of previous offense.

Knowledge of the immediate prior offense type (k–1st) does aid slightly in the prediction of the kth type, for there is some tendency to repeat the same type of offense. But this inclination is not strong. It is clear, however, that the offense history up to the immediately previous offense, or prior to the k-1st offense, has no bearing on the observed probabilities of committing the kth offense. That is, knowledge of the number and type of offenses prior to the k-1st gives us no aid in predicting the type of the next offense. Because the same process operates at each offense number, we suggest that an offender "starts over," in a sense, each time he commits an offense and that there is no specialization in offense types. Thus the transition probabilities associated with commission of juvenile offenses may be modeled by a homogeneous Markov chain.

We can now arrive at a social-intervention policy suggestion: recall that 46 percent desisted after the first offense, 35 percent after the second, and approximately 25 percent at each remaining step after the third offense. In short, a stability of stopping delinquency occurs after the third act. At what point, then, in a delinquent boy's career should an intervention program occur? Our answer would be that the best time is that point beyond which the natural loss rate, or probability of desistance, begins to level off. Because 46 percent of delinquents stop after the first offense, a major and expensive treatment program at this point would be wasteful. Intervention could be held in abeyance until the commission of the third offense. We would thus reduce the number of boys requiring attention in this cohort from 3,475 after the first offense, to 1,862 after the second offense, to 1,212 after the third offense, rather than concentrate on all 9,945 or some large subgroup under a blanket community action program.

## Adult Crime

Since 1968 the Center has been engaged in a follow-up of the original birth cohort. A systematic 10 percent random sample yielded 974 subjects. An effort was made to locate and to interview as many as possible. At the time of this writing, the follow-up study is in the data processing, data analysis stage, but a few basic statistical findings about the birth cohort in adulthood, from ages eighteen to twenty-six, can be reported. The chance of ever having an official arrest record before reaching age twenty-seven is .4308 (table 11.1). This 43 percent probability is based on juvenile as well as adult police data and is considerably higher than most of us suspected. Having previously reported that there is a .35 probability of having a police record prior to age eighteen, we may now note that an additional 8 percent of the cohort, who had no previous juvenile arrest record, became adult offenders.

Yet another way to question the data is to ask about the probability of becoming an adult offender from among those members of the cohort who escaped being arrested up to age eighteen. That probability is .1218. The chances of being an adult offender, regardless of juvenile record, is .2320. Calculation of this last probability is based on the number of previously known juvenile offenders plus new offenders in adulthood (≥18), divided by the total cohort. But most of the contribution to this relatively high rate of adult offensivity comes from persons who also had a juvenile delinquency record. Of the total adult offenders (226), 66 percent (149) had also been arrested under age eighteen, whereas only 34 percent (77) were new recruits into the arrest file after age eighteen.

Perhaps the most disquieting, albeit not unexpected, finding is

TABLE 11.1   Age of Offenders and Nonoffenders,
before Age 18, Age 18 and Over

|  |  | Age 18 and over offender | nonoffender |  |
|---|---|---|---|---|
| Under | offender | 149(A) | 193(B) | 342(A+B) |
| age | nonoffender | 77(C) | 555(D) | 632(C+D) |
| 18 |  | 226(A+C) | 748(B+D) | 974(E) |

Probabilities of being a:

1. Juvenile offender (<18)    $= .3511 \left( \dfrac{A+B}{E} \right)$

2. Offender (≤26)    $= .4308 \left( \dfrac{A+B+C}{E} \right)$

3. Adult offender only (>18 to ≤26)    $= .2320 \left( \dfrac{A+C}{E} \right)$

4. Adult offender,
   having been a juvenile offender    $= .4357 \left( \dfrac{A}{A+B} \right)$

5. Adult offender,
   *not* having been a juvenile offender    $= .1218 \left( \dfrac{C}{C+D} \right)$

that the chances of becoming an adult offender are much higher for persons who had a delinquency record than for those who did not. The probability of being arrested between eighteen and twenty-six years of age, having had at least one arrest under age eighteen, is .4357, which is three and one half times higher than the probability (.1218) of being arrested as an adult, having had no record as a juvenile. This is another way of saying, with new precision, that the chances of recidivating from a juvenile to an adult status are higher than commencing an adult arrest record— at least up to age twenty-six. These observed data conform very closely to the curvilinear probability expectations we projected from our earlier Phase I study of the birth cohort. It should be no surprise, therefore, if we find in later projections that half of the entire cohort had an offense record by age thirty-five.

By examining age-specific probabilities of ever being arrested, or of having a first offense, some interesting new information can be reported (table 11.2). Age seventeen has the peak probability

TABLE 11.2   Age, Probability of Arrest by Age, Proportion Arrested by Age, and Cumulative Probability of Arrest

| Age $(x_i)$ | N | Frequency $(x_i)$ | (a) $(P_i = \dfrac{x_i}{N_i - 1})$ | (b) $(P\, x_i / N)$ | (c) $(\Sigma P\, x_i / N)$ |
|---|---|---|---|---|---|
| 7 | 974 | 0 | 0 | 0 | 0 |
| 8 | 973 | 1 | .0010 | .0010 | .0010 |
| 9 | 971 | 2 | .0020 | .0020 | .0030 |
| 10 | 966 | 5 | .0051 | .0051 | .0081 |
| 11 | 952 | 14 | .0145 | .0144 | .0225 |
| 12 | 925 | 27 | .0284 | .0277 | .0502 |
| 13 | 896 | 29 | .0314 | .0298 | .0800 |
| 14 | 857 | 39 | .0435 | .0400 | .1200 |
| 15 | 799 | 58 | .0677 | .0595 | .1795 |
| 16 | 735 | 64 | .0801 | .0657 | .2452 |
| 17 | 661 | 74 | .1007 | .0760 | .3212 |
| 18 | 631 | 30 | .0454 | .0308 | .3520 |
| 19 | 614 | 17 | .0269 | .0174 | .3694 |
| 20 | 596 | 18 | .0293 | .0185 | .3819 |
| 21 | 581 | 15 | .0252 | .0154 | .4033 |
| 22 | 572 | 9 | .0155 | .0092 | .4125 |
| 23 | 569 | 3 | .0052 | .0031 | .4156 |
| 24 | 563 | 6 | .0105 | .0062 | .4218 |
| 25 | 556 | 7 | .0124 | .0072 | .4290 |
| 26 | 555 | 1 | .0018 | .0010 | .4300 |

(a)   Probability of first arrest by given age.
(b)   Proportion arrested by given age.
(c)   Cumulative probability of arrest by given age.

of having a first arrest (.1007). Up to age seventeen, the probabilities increase monotonically from age eight (.0020), for example, to age twelve (.0284) and age sixteen (.0801). They also decrease from age seventeen in nearly a monotonic fashion through age eighteen (.0454), age twenty (.0293), age twenty-two (.0155), and age twenty-six (.0018). However, the cumulative probabilities of ever being arrested rise much more rapidly and dramatically up to age seventeen than they do after that age. For example, the probability of at least one arrest jumps from .0502 at age twelve to .3511 at age seventeen, which is an absolute 30 percent increase, or seven and one-half times greater. However, this probability of ever being arrested climbs much more slowly after age seventeen and reaches, as we have observed, .4300 by age twenty-six, an absolute 8 percent increase, or only one and one-half times as great. Thus, based on these and other data, we know that the probability of ever being arrested, as well as committing offenses generally, declines with age, beginning with the eighteenth year. Hence, maximum efficiency and effectiveness of an intervention program should occur prior to age eighteen, or within the juvenile justice system.

## A Point System of Juvenile Justice

How do these two studies, which are mostly descriptive, permit us to make inferences about a social policy for the juvenile justice system?

We are now provided with several important pieces of information, each one of which builds upon the preceding item that leads us to the policy assertion. These relevant data items are as follows.

1. Offenses can be scored or mathematically weighted for seriousness.

2. Individuals, longitudinally followed, can be assigned cumulative scores over time.

3. Probabilities are known about having an official arrest and adjudication record.

4. Seriousness of crime and probabilities of a record can be combined.

5. Probabilities of desistance can be calculated over age and time.

6. The probability of desistance is highest after the first offense, decreases to the third offense, and then remains stable out to the fifteenth offense.

7. At present, there appears to be little relationship between the gravity of the sanction (that is, intervention process) and the probability of recidivism or desistance after any frequency of offenses.

The inference one draws, then, is that little or nothing in the form of social intervention should be done until the third recorded offense, unless the first or second are of a very serious quality; but that the accumulation of seriousness scores should be maintained in the files of the system to be used as a basis for determining the moment and gravity of sanctioning intervention. In short, we are referring to a point system of juvenile justice which, as Larry Schultz and others have suggested, would "make the severity of penalties against children who violate criminal laws vary primarily according to the seriousness of the crime proved" (Schultz 1973:429).

We have become so accustomed to the notion of "individualized treatment" that we fail to recognize that for many youths the juvenile justice system has really become individualized justice. Beccaria and Voltaire wrote poignantly against judicial caprice, and in *Crime and Punishment* Beccaria called for a scale of crimes and punishments. The rigidity of the classical system became muted by mitigating circumstances. But besides the child-saving humanitarianism that brought paternal judges, the system of diagnosis and adjudication became burdened with the sheer weight of numbers. Young deviant humanity now passes impersonally through the dossiers and desks of people of good will but little time. And with more alternatives for disposition available to bureaucrats, including juvenile court judges, a pretentious system has developed. On the manifest level that system appears to disperse justice with variations to fit the individual, but on the latent level it is plagued with inconsistencies, vagueness, and institutionalized anxiety for each recipient of societal response (Platt 1969).

I am not about to suggest a return to undifferentiated treatment. We still need research to fit the best treatment strategy to the personal reactions of the individual. What I am suggesting, however, is a modest system that promotes clarity, both to the social agents of response and to the youthful deviants, about where a young person stands in the social scale of adjudged harmfulness to the community.

I suggest something akin to the motor vehicle violation point-system used in some states. The first need in this system is a scale of seriousness of the social harm inflicted on a community. By assigning offense scores to offenders, cumulative scores over time can be obtained for each offender. Thus, many minor offenses may add up to the same score as a single major offense in the record of a juvenile offender.

The system can be used to alert young offenders to the degree of collective response (à la Durkheim) the community feels about their delinquency. This kind of knowledge should be clearly and loudly announced, proclaimed with much more precision than now exists in the wrist-slapping episodes at youth study bureaus or juvenile courts. Failure to know where one stands in the hierarchy of harm promotes further testing of the system, the reduction of fear, or cautious anxiety. A point system shows the delinquent just how seriously society takes the deviance, offers guides to the future reaction to violations, tells the offender his position in the domain of deviance, and provides a rational basis for consistency to the response. It would work as follows.

Under the assumption of appropriate evidentiary material to indicate that the juvenile has committed the act in question, he would be informed by the police or the juvenile court that he now has X number of points against him. Some cut-off point must be established which permits the police up to that point to function as the principal agents of disposition. After that numerical point the juvenile court would be called into action as the agent of disposition, just as now occurs without much precision or clarity.

We are not here making judgments about how serious a single offense or series of offenses committed by a person should be before the disposition agent is the court instead of the police. Nor are we making assertions about sanctions relative to seriousness. Rather we are suggesting a point system that would be widely known to all in the community and used as a basis for establishing sanctions with more consistency than now exists.

The juvenile offender whose offense scores reach a certain point would know that he would be subjected to a specific penalty in the graduated scale of sanctions. He, his family, the police, the intake interviewers at a youth center, the court officials, and everyone else in the response agencies would know how to respond.

Dispositions now in use—a warning and return to custody of parents, probation, out-patient clinical care, restitution, detention and commitment to an institution, and so on—would be invoked in relation to a given accumulated seriousness score. Rigidity can be tempered, of course, but essentially the system would have to be adhered to with regularity. Perhaps even greater care than now exists would have to be given to protect young offenders against abuses of the system; that is, if the police arrest a juvenile with little evidence and the juvenile court gives little attention to the defense, justice would be sacrificed to precision of the instruments. But errors are abundant now and need correction. The problems of inappropriate labeling and adjudication of juveniles are separate issues and do not affect the merits of the rationale for the point system briefly outlined here.

Exceptions to the rule should be minimal.

Finally, it should be kept in mind that the introduction of a point system is suggested within a juvenile court philosophy that includes a juvenile public defender system and the admission into juvenile court of only serious cases. A *serious* case, we suggest, requires further clarification and precision by means of special local or regional surveys. But, equally important, a *case* can be viewed either as a single juvenile criminal event or the accumulated set of juvenile criminal events that reach a given point of seriousness, to be equated with the single serious event and hence to be taken to the juvenile court.

Such a system of consistency between the scales of crime seriousness and sanctioning could have the following advantages which, of course, have the posture of testable hypotheses.

1. A high potential for deterrence results from foreknowledge of more precise and consistent social response.

This hypothesis assumes that there is some relationship between cognitive awareness, risk-taking, the probabilities of apprehension, and the likelihood of given sanctioning responses. There will always be something less than certainty ($< 1.0$) in being arrested and adjudicated delinquent, or in being convicted as an adult. These probabilities will most likely be unchanged in the future, for our efforts to effect change here seem unsuccessful. But it is possible to effect change in the type and moment of sanctioning once offenders are proved to be law violators. By increasing the likelihood (certainty) of given sanctions, scaled to the seriousness of crime, we should expect cognitive and concerted efforts by potential offenders to reduce their chances of being arrested, either through not committing crime or through more clever techniques of avoiding arrest. If the former, society experiences reduced crime; if the latter, the offender escapes stigmatizing labeling and may thereby escape a future criminal career.

2. Consistency of sanctioning reduces the injustice of judicial disparities and thereby reduces a major grievance of adjudicated offenders.

Under this system, the sanction is administered not in relation to a specific offense at a given moment but in relation to the accumulated social harm over a given period of time (three years? five years?). The sum of many minor acts becomes equivalent to the sum of a few major acts. Additivity is, of course, an important ingredient of the scoring system. But the system is a function of the people's perceptions, the societal will, about seriousness and social harm, and it benefits from clarity and consistency of the response to that harm. The sheer regularity of the crime-sanction system contains an element of justice that is lacking in the capricious vicissitudes of current operation of the administration of the courts and sentencing procedures. The major loss to the adjudicated offender could be his capacity to nullify or neutralize his guilt by blaming the system for the injustice or disparity of his sentence compared to that of other persons (Mahoney 1972). But the gain from consistency could promote respect for the system and techniques of avoiding contact with the system.

There are clearly aspects to this point system that are vulnerable to criticism: questionable additivity; its automaticity; the need for consensus about categories of accumulated points; matching of the two scales of crime and sanction; whether there are more deterrent potentials; whether punitiveness exceeds reformativeness; and so forth.

As is usual with new proposals of this kind, previous research evidence that might bear upon the proposal should be mustered to shed empirical light on the adequacy of the logic. (For example, how well does the point system for traffic violations in various states function?) And if the proposal survives that kind of cross-examination, a pilot experimentation in a given jurisdictional territiory should be made, with a complete as possible test of the hypotheses and an evaluation of the results.

## Notes

1. We built mostly upon the work of S. S. Stevens at the Psychophysical Laboratory, Harvard University.

2. Much of this and the subsequent section of the chapter is extracted from my paper delivered at the April 1973 meeting of the American Philosophical Society and published as "Crime in a Birth Cohort," *Transactions of the American Philosophical Society*, 117, no. 5, pp. 404–11.

3. The term "dark number" is more commonly used in Europe and covers a broader range of offenders (adults as well as juveniles) and acts.

## References

Blumstein, Alfred
1974          "Seriousness Weights in an Index of Crime." Paper
              prepared for Urban Systems Institute (January).

Christie, Nils
1960          *Unge Norske Lorovertredere.* Oslo: Universitets
              forlaget, 1960.

Douglas, J. W. B., J. M. Ross, W. A. Hammond, and D. G.
Mulligan
1966          "Delinquency and Social Class." *British Journal of
              Criminology* 6 (July): 294–302.

Glueck, Sheldon, and Eleanor T. Glueck
1930          *Five Hundred Criminal Careers.* Millwood, New
              York: Kraus Reprint Company.
1934          *One Thousand Juvenile Delinquents.* Millwood,
              New York: Kraus Reprint Company.
1937          *Later Criminal Careers.* Millwood, New York:
              Kraus Reprint Company.
1940          *Juvenile Delinquents Grown Up.* Millwood, New
              York: Kraus Reprint Company.
1943          *Criminal Careers in Retrospect.* Millwood, New
              York: Kraus Reprint Company.
1950          *Unraveling Juvenile Delinquency.* Cambridge,
              Mass.: Harvard University Press.
1968          *Delinquents and Nondelinquents in Perspective.*
              Cambridge, Mass.: Harvard University Press.
1970          *Toward a Typology of Juvenile Offenders.* New
              York: Grune and Stratton.

Mahoney, Anne Rankin
1972          "Youths in the Juvenile Justice System: Some
              Questions about the Empirical Support for
              Labeling Theory." Paper prepared for the Juvenile
              Justice Standards Project.

Mukherjee, Satyanshu
1971          "A Typological Study of School Status and Delin-
             quency." Ph.D. dissertation, University of
             Pennsylvania.

Mulligan, Glenn, J. W. B. Douglas, W. A. Hammond, and J.
Tizard
1963          "Delinquency and Symptoms of Maladjustment:
             The Findings of a Longitudinal Study." *Proceedings
             of the Royal Society of Medicine* 56 (December):
             1083-86.

Mulvihill, Donald J., Melvin Tumin, and Lynn Curtis
1969          *Crimes of Violence*. Task Force Report, Volume
             11, of the National Commission on the Causes
             and Prevention of Violence, Washington, D.C.:
             Superintendent of Documents, pp. 25-30.

Platt, Anthony
1969          *The Child Savers*. Berkeley: University of Cali-
             fornia Press.

Rose, Gordon
1968          Report to the Council of Europe on "The Merits
             of an Index of Crime of the Kind Devised by Sellin
             and Wolfgang." Given at Strasbourg, 14 October.

Ryder, N. B.
1955          "The Influence of Declining Mortality on Swedish
             Reproductivity." *Current Research in Human
             Fertility*. New York: Milbank Memorial Fund,
             pp. 65-81.

Schultz, Larry
1973          "The Problems of Problem Children." *The Nation*
             (October): 429.

*Science and Technology*
1967          *Task Force Report of the President's Commission
             on Law Enforcement and Administration of Justice*.
             Washington, D.C.: Superintendent of Documents,
             p. 56.

Sellin, Thorsten, and Marvin E. Wolfgang
1964          *The Measurement of Delinquency*. New York:
             John Wiley.
1969          *Delinquency: Selected Studies*. New York: John
             Wiley, pp. 8-9, n.3.

Thornberry, Terence P.
1973          "Race, Socioeconomic Status and Sentencing in the

Juvenile Justice System." *Journal of Criminal Law and Criminology* 64 (March): 90–98.

Wolfgang, Marvin E., Robert M. Figlio, and Thorsten Sellin
1972        *Delinquency in a Birth Cohort*. Chicago: University of Chicago Press.

# 12 Reflections of a Former Prison Warden

*Hans W. Mattick*

Three years as a professional worker in a large, maximum security, state prison, followed by four years as the assistant warden of a large, maximum security, urban jail, may not do much for a man, but it is an experience that can lead to reflection on "the prison problem." An adequate analysis of the American prison and its problems in the final quarter of the twentieth century must begin far from the prison gate. Of fundamental importance is a contradictory complex of utilitarian and religious ideas of eighteenth- and nineteenth-century origin, debased into a mélange of twentieth-century "high school thought," which now serves as the "intellectual basis" for what passes as our penal policy. It is, for the most part, a policy of isolation and punishment, accompanied by the rhetoric of rehabilitation, which results in the chronic underfinancing, inadequate staffing, deflected sexuality, and general lack of resources and poverty of imagination that characterize our prisons and jails. For the past two hundred years, neither the American prison nor its prisoner have been deterred by a continual demonstration of failure, and both have been recidivating as if incapable of learning from experience. While nothing can be done to alter the history of American penal practice, it may be instructive to place the prison and its problems into a larger social and political context through which they can be better understood. Whether understanding can lead to change must remain an open question.

## The Traditional Criminal Legal Process

To begin with, it must be clearly understood that the prison is the ultimate stage in a highly selective process of social control. It is the repository of those who "fail" at every previous stage of

Hans W. Mattick is the director of the Center for Research in Criminal Justice at the University of Illinois at Chicago Circle.

the traditional criminal legal process—a process which, in sum, constitutes the criminal justice system. The traditional criminal legal process, which serves the ambiguous function of distinguishing the "innocent" from the "guilty," tends, more frequently than not, to distinguish those who can and cannot mobilize social, economic, and legal resources. When not aborted by the clearly demonstrable innocence of the accused, a serious error of the authorities, or one of the many discretionary alternative dispositions legally available, an "ideal-typical" description of the traditional criminal legal process includes the following stages: (1) a preexisting definition in the criminal law designating some act of commission or omission as illegal; (2) a preexisting definition in the law of criminal procedure describing the legal response that may be made to conduct so defined; (3) an allegation based on observation or report that an illegal act has occurred; (4) the physical arrest of a suspected or accused person by the police; (5) the official placing of a criminal charge against the accused; (6) remanding the defendant to the police lockup, detention quarters, or local jail; (7) a preliminary hearing before a local magistrate to determine if there is probable cause to justify the charge, to determine whether the defendant may be released on his own recognizance or on deposit of cash bail, or if denied release, he is to be remanded to custody to await legal processing; (8) the indictment of the defendant on the basis of a criminal charge through either the grand jury process or by the filing of an information by the prosecuting authorities; (9) an arraignment hearing before a judge to determine the nature of the defendant's plea—guilty or not guilty—and the assignment of a trial date and court; (10) the trial proper, either before a judge alone (the so-called bench trial that processes the overwhelming majority of cases) or trial by jury; (11) a finding of guilt, hearing in mitigation or aggravation, and pronouncement of sentence; (12) remand to jail to await transportation; and (13) imprisonment.

At every stage both formal and informal bargaining takes place between and among the actors representing the defense, the law enforcement authorities, the prosecution, bondsmen, custodial agents, court bailiffs and clerks, the judiciary, the victims of crime, and a potential variety of less visible "outsiders"—all attempting to influence the outcome at every decisional stage, or the ultimate disposition of the case. The informal bargaining processes which are not made a matter of record are the real substance of the scenarios enacted in the more formal public dramas that are made a matter of record. Quite apart from innocence or guilt, a great deal depends upon the ability of the defendant to mobilize social, economic, and legal resources, and upon the amenability of the authorities to be responsive, for whatever reason, to such mobilization. It is not so much a question of official corruption out of either venal or sentimental motives, as it is of differential vulnerability and general ethnocentrism. As a formal system of social control the process seems rational enough, provided the basic premises and sequential stages are accepted and acted upon. As a human process of social justice, however, the informal practice is discretionary, arbitrary, and discriminatory. The traditional criminal legal process that makes up the criminal justice system has none of the virtues of statistical randomness and all the faults that discretion and bargaining power will admit.

## Selecting Prisoners from Criminals

This rather harsh view of American criminal justice clearly requires elaboration and supporting argument. In the past twenty-five years, surveys, self-report studies, peer nomination cross-checking techniques, and victim surveys have repeatedly demonstrated that *behavior* defined as criminal is distributed fairly evenly across the entire social structure, class and race differences notwithstanding. The most recent survey by the Institute for Juvenile Research (1973) also indicates an increasing equality of criminal behavior as between the sexes. This is not to say that different kinds of crime are not differentially distributed as between the young and the mature, the white and the nonwhite, and the rich and the poor. There are few young price-fixers and few mature vandals. Whites are more likely to embezzle, while nonwhites snatch purses. The rich violate the antitrust laws more often than the poor. But the "surreptitious entry" of the Watergate electronic eavesdropper is almost indistinguishable from the breaking and entering of a burglar who is also a Peeping Tom. Some middle-class housewives shoplift, while their businessmen husbands pad their expense accounts and attempt to evade taxes. This is not an argument that everyone is a criminal; rather, it is clear that the level of criminal behavior in society is more evenly distributed across the population than is suggested by official criminal statistics.

The proportion of criminally defined behavior that comes to the attention of the authorities is simply unknown. Current scientific techniques have cast little light on the so-called "dark figure of crime" problem, although it is clear that a great deal of crime—even the crime of the young, the poor, and the non-white—goes unreported. Moreover, there is absolutely no warrant for drawing any kind of proportional inference about the relationship between crimes known or reported to the police and the amount of unreported crime. What are popularly referred to as "crime statistics" are more accurately described as a mathematical representation of some of the activities of the law enforcement agencies as they try to come to grips with the crime problem.

If we restrict ourselves to that 20 percent of crime known to the police that is considered serious and is designated by the *Uniform Crime Reports* of the Federal Bureau of Investigation as "Index Crimes" (murder, rape, robbery, assault, burglary, larceny, and auto theft), we note a high rate of case mortality. For every one hundred such serious crimes known to the police, only twenty-five arrests are made, only twelve convictions are sustained by the courts, and only three persons are imprisoned. There is obviously something seriously wrong with such a rate of attrition. While there may be many reasons for the fact that the police arrest only twenty-five persons for every one hundred serious crimes known to them, it is more difficult to explain the difference between twenty-five and three. Moreover, although about half of those arrested for serious crimes are convicted, the convictions include fines, suspended sentences, probation, terms of less than a year in a local jail—most of which indicate that felonies have been "bargained down" to less serious charges, for all Index Crimes are chargeable as felonies meriting more than a year in prison. The police are either arresting the wrong people or charging them with more serious offenses than they should; or the standards of the prosecutors and the courts are so much higher than those of the police that half the cases are "thrown out." Finally, while the 3 percent of serious offenders who "failed" at every prior stage and who were, therefore, convicted and sent to prison, quite probably were convicted validly, they are also a highly select group. They represent only one out of a potential thirty-three such groups whose members might have been convicted and sent to prison. Clearly, it is not the fact of guilt, alone, that distinguishes the imprisoned 3 percent from all the others. Somehow, for every serious offender who wound up in prison, twenty-five eluded arrest and another three managed to avoid imprisonment after conviction. It should be no occasion for wonder that a criminal justice system so selective and apparently arbitrary generates more resentment than satisfaction on the part of both the public and those who are prisoners. The criminal justice system should not resemble a thinly veiled instrument of class and cultural warfare.

## The Public, Mass Media, and Politics

General public knowledge of imprisonment is limited and stereotyped. By and large, the public has been taught to view crime, criminals, and the legal process as a contest between the forces of good and evil. The mass media report crime and its immediate consequences, and the public participates, vicariously, as the forces of law and order go about the business of bringing criminals to justice. There is high interest in the details of the crime, suspense while the criminal is sought, and some interest in police procedures, trials, and sentences. At that point, for the public, the drama is over and, presumably, justice has been done. In the process many people have played their roles and commented on the crime, the criminal, and how the criminal justice system has functioned. Mass media reports of these matters form a major basis for public opinions about the crime problem and how it is being dealt with.

If all crime known to the police were to be classified into two major classes, crimes against the person and crimes against property, the former would account for only about 15 percent of the total. Because of their focus on news and human interest, the mass media produce an image of crime that virtually reverses the percentages of these two classes of crime. Both print and electronic media, in both news and entertainment programming, create the impression that the vast majority of crime consists of murder, rape, assault, and armed robbery. There are, of course, good reasons for such selection. Violent crimes involve personal injury and fear, and the public can readily identify with the victims. But such crimes are limited in their social consequences and involve relatively few persons. In 1973, *Uniform Crime Reports* reported a total of 9,027,700 arrests. Of these, 1,833,300 (20 percent) were for the more serious Index Crimes, and 380,560 (4 percent) were for violent crimes. Whether the crimes of these 4 percent are as serious in their social consequences as the larger-scale white-collar, corporate, and organized crime is, at least, debatable. The focus of the mass media is not likely to contribute to this debate, however. The commercial exploitation of a sedulously cultivated public interest in violent crime increases public fear, encourages scape-goating, fosters vicarious participation in a criminal mythology that is partially cathartic and partially protective of other socially important crime, and generally supports the false notion that criminal behavior is characteristic of the young, the poor, and the nonwhite, that is, those who are vulnerable to arrest. Meanwhile, the mature, the wealthy, and the white, that is, those who are less vulnerable to arrest in their criminal behavior, are represented as the pillars of society. It is not that violent crime is of little import or that it can be ignored or tolerated; rather, one kind of criminal behavior should not be allowed to become a public diversion that distracts attention from another kind of crime. If the criminal justice system is used preponderantly to deal with the crimes of the lower classes, rather than as an instrument of justice that acts without fear or favor, we should not be surprised at an increasing cynicism about "law and order."

Generally speaking, there is very little appreciation on the part of the public that this "contest between good and evil," and the whole "drama of crime," takes place within the larger arena of our political system. This, in turn, helps to determine public opinion about the nature of the crime problem and the kinds of responses that ought to be made to it. Since 1964, many candidates have run for public office on the "law and order" issue (with detente the "anticommunist" issue is beginning to lose some of its political utility). A strong, usually simpleminded, and cheap "anticrime" stance is politically *de rigueur* for the ambitious candidate.

The political relevance of crime is nothing new, it has merely become popular. The mayors of our towns and cities, their assemblies and councils, through the police chiefs they appoint and the policemen they employ, have always been tied directly to the lowliest criminal who breaks the law. The public interest is involved in the response of these official actors. Similarly, public prosecutors, judges, and governors, are involved. Directors of corrections and parole boards are appointed and prison wardens and guards employed. All these public officials may find their political fortunes tied directly to the conduct of the lowliest of inmates in the prison most remote from the state capitol. The state legislatures, too, through the appropriations they vote for police, courts, and corrections, and the contract possibilities accompanying such appropriations, are intimately related to criminal justice. All of these functionaries and many others have a great stake in how the crime problem, and responses to it, are perceived by the general public. Politics and crime are intimately related.

Insofar as recurrent crises in the crime problem dictate the amount of time and space that the mass media devote to it, the least likely situation for giving the public accurate information and rational knowledge is created. The news has to be reported as it is developing, regardless of what is said and done in the process, even if this is arrant nonsense. In an atmosphere of crisis the sensational value of a crime is confused with seriousness; a prominent cause of prison riots is agitators or militants; all escapees are described as dangerous and may be armed; and all ex-convicts on parole are potential recidivists. While there may be some truth in all these assertions, the distinctions that have to be made in particular cases are just as likely to result in an untruth. But people acting in crisis situations have to say something; and what they say is reported to the public and enters into the common fund of information, whether it is true or not. The more dispassionate accounts of these events, in the form of feature articles, educational TV specials, or wrap-up presentations are buried in the back pages of the newspapers or are slotted for 6:00 A.M. Saturdays in public-service air time. They are neither designed to capture the public imagination nor do they in fact. They are designed to meet a reluctant public responsibility, but they tend to miss the public.

It is not only the atmosphere of crisis that surrounds the crime problem, and the resultant misinformation, that deprives the public of an understanding of crime and criminals, prisons and prisoners; there is also a more pedestrian cause. As long as the public continues to view crime as a simple moral problem, that is, as "a contest between good and evil," their interest extends only to the apparent point of public resolution, if there is one. And the apparent point of public resolution is the conviction which brings the public drama of a trial to an end. They seem to forget, altogether, that life goes on in prison and beyond. Such a morally simplistic view of the crime problem and the criminal justice system results in a mass delusion which punishes society along with the convicted criminal. In the political arena, the struggle for place, power, patronage, and public-relations dominance also plays an active part in sustaining this mass delusion that imprisons the general public. It would, perhaps, offend the public— to say nothing of the actors in the criminal justice system—if they were told that the genius of American penology lies in the fact that we have demonstrated that eighteenth- and nineteenth-century methods can be forced to work in the last quarter of the twentieth century. Few other fields of human endeavor can lay claim to such an accomplishment; but we achieve it at considerable cost.

Despite spiraling crime rates, malfunctioning prisons, and persistently high recidivism rates, we persevere in the same old ways with the same results. With a few notable exceptions, legislators, lawyers, law enforcement officials, judges, and, indeed, many of those working in prisons, parole, and probation are stuck on dead center. The mass media, which are prone to confuse incumbency with competence, because they are more interested in the drama of the news than in educating the public, gather their information about imprisonment from those who happen to be spokesmen when some news event occurs. Thus the blind and the interested lead the blind and the disinterested. The spokesmen, caught up in the froth of a newsworthy current event, pontificate with their fund of eighteenth- and nineteenth-century notions about the treatment of crime and criminals, and the mass media represent these notions to the general public where they are taken as twentieth-century gospel. This completes the cycle of manufacturing the mass delusion that victimizes us all.

There are, of course, a few knowledgeable and competent people working in the field of corrections—legislators, lawyers, law enforcement officials, judges, prison administrators, probation officers, and parole agents—but there is no necessary relationship between incumbency and expertise. Similarly, although there may be ignorance, laziness, opportunism, and venality among some of those working in the field of corrections, such qualities of character are no more prevalent in this field than in any other. The peccadillos or ravages of the private sector are merely less open to public scrutiny.

We are not indicting the motives of all the people in corrections or of the people working in the mass media. We are, rather, addressing ourselves to human limitations that work to the general disadvantage of society. Prison administrators, for example, should not be blamed for the high recidivism rates among their discharged inmates, if their prisons are not financed, staffed, and equipped to rehabilitate inmates, and if their inmates are simply returned to the crimogenic environments that produced them. If neither of these conditions is changed, what else should one expect? What prison administrators should be blamed for is keeping quiet about conditions that make rehabilitation impossible. Similarly, the mass media should not be held responsible for reporting the content of the news, even if that content happens to be nonsense asserted by someone. But the mass media ought to be blamed for asserting the same nonsense editorially and for failing to cultivate a healthy skepticism when complex matters are represented as simple, or are presented only from the official point of view. Just as there is no necessary relationship between incumbency and competence, there is also no necessary relationship between what is reported as news and accurate information. And, as a series of official reports should have taught us by now—the Wickersham Commission, the Katzenbach Commission, the Kerner Commission, the Eisenhower Commission, the McKay Commission, and the Knapp Commission, to say nothing of the Watergate hearings—the official point of view is the least disinterested point of view.

## A Short Historical Review of Imprisonment

Considered in historical perspective, the prison seems to have passed directly from infancy to senility in the twinkling of a moment in history. The imposing presence of the American prison conveys the impression of an ancient institution. It is, in fact, a relatively recent historical development, for the procedure of locking people up after they have been convicted has been practiced only during the past two hundred years. Until the end of the eighteenth century, convicted criminals were usually fined, whipped, branded, banished, or executed. The jails that preceded the more modern prisons were used to hold persons awaiting trial, debtors, and a few religious heretics or political offenders. Penal facilities designed for the confinement of persons found guilty at trials did not exist, except in the case of a few of the major cities that were beginning to experiment with workhouses for minor offenders. Imprisonment for large numbers of convicted prisoners, and for long periods of time, was a social invention of the American pragmatic genius shortly after the American Revolution. In less than three-quarters of a century, during the period between 1776 and 1840, most of the states had built prisons for their own serious offenders. As strange as it may seem to the contemporary radical, the new society emerging from the War of Independence was responding to the current of revolutionary ideas of the time. Compared to death, corporal punishment, and banishment, imprisonment was a revolutionary practice.

Eighteenth-century philosophers such as Beccaria, Montesquieu, and Bentham argued from a secular point of view against the brutal and futile system of corporal punishments and ready resort to executions. The Quakers adopted the same enlightened view from religious principles. Thus, while the movement for reform of penal policy was rationalized on humanitarian and utilitarian grounds, the religious belief that solitary confinement and contemplation would lead to penitence (the origin of the term "penitentiary") and reformation also made its contribution. The criminal offender, a human being born in original sin, was also seen as a rational calculator of pains and pleasures who made mistakes in arithmetic. When the hedonistic calculus resulted in the wrong answer, a period of contemplation was in order, in the penitentiary. If that did not improve his mind, penitence might at least save his soul. Probably more important than this utilitarian-rationalist-religious nonsense, was a less spiritual force that fostered the transition to imprisonment. Some recent historical analyses, commenting on the early creation of asylums and prisons, have stressed the notion that prisons were located far away from the cities in order to protect their inmates from the corrupting influences of the urban centers of sin. No doubt, the Augustinian imagery of Carthage, "where there sang all around me in my ears a cauldron of unholy loves," loomed large in the fantasy life of New England divines. It is an interesting rationalization for which documentary evidence can be found, for it comports with the inflamed sentiments of the document-producing classes of that day. More persuasive, however, would be an analysis of the relative real estate values of land located in the city and the country, and of the benefits to be gained by creating employment opportunities in the more remote regions. Religious sentiment and economic opportunities have a way of combining, as Weber and Tawney have indicated, and it would be surprising if the early history of prisons were an exception to such a morganatic arrangement between idealism and materialism, where the former gets all the benefits of causal paternity while the latter has only the pangs of actual childbirth. Thus, while religion and rationalism have their place in the early American development of imprisonment, we should not overlook the opportunity afforded the contract-letters, suppliers, and builders, those who were placed in charge of the new prisons—and those who appointed them—to profit from prison labor, and the local labor and supply markets that the new prisons generated in the remote regions. These are still potent influences in the location of new prisons, as Marion and Vienna, both in Illinois, and Lucasville, Ohio, will illustrate, all the rhetoric about "community-based corrections" notwithstanding.

A number of important conclusions may be drawn from this first stage in the history of American imprisonment for many elements from this stage still survive in the contemporary prison. First, it should be noted that imprisonment was not a carefully chosen policy of dealing with offenders that was rationally selected on its own merits; it was, rather, the residual choice of a lesser evil in comparison to corporal punishments and executions; the reformers knew what they wanted to avoid but were less clear about what they wanted to achieve. The result was a method of dealing with offenders that incapacitated and isolated them from the community for a while in unisexual, age-graded institutions ruled by strict caste relations between keeper and kept. Second, the fact that imprisonment was seen as being a more humane way of dealing with offenders served to shield prison administration from the kind of public scrutiny that had led to public criticism of corporal punishment and execution. Brutal, corrupt, and exploitive practices were thus easily and, for the most part, silently condoned from the very beginning of prison history, and their grip is tenacious. Finally, it was no accident that economic factors played a major role in early penal reform. Whether it is a question of saving tax dollars, exploiting prison labor, creating patronage jobs, or letting contracts for prison supplies and maintenance, the profit motive has been a major determinant of prison policies in the United States. This preoccupation with money values rather than human values also leads to cynicism among prisoners, who see themselves as neglected and exploited victims of a rapacious capitalist system whose values are no better than their own.

The second stage in American prison history, from the early establishment of prisons until about 1930, was largely dominated by the exploitation motive. It took less than half a century for the new prison system to rid itself of the early competition between the "silent-solitary" and "congregate" experimental models which, despite later judgments as to their folly, were serious in theory and intent. From the age of Jacksonian democracy through the Great Depression, wardenships were awarded to persons who made large cash contributions to political parties, or were simply distributed by the state governors as an economic opportunity for their cronies. The labor of prisoners, in turn, was leased to the highest bidder by these worthies. Sometimes even the feeding, care, and discipline of prisoners were delivered over to the contractor. Neglect of human decency, ruthless exploitation, and physical abuse were the inevitable result of this legally condoned form of slavery. The effective opposition to the system of prison contract labor was neither humanitarian nor religious, however, although some such voices were raised; it was, again, economic. Business and commerical interests who wanted to avoid the competition of prison labor and to sell their own goods in those markets, and the free labor outside the prison that wanted the jobs that produced those goods, resented the advantage held by those who controlled convict labor. Moreover, as organized labor became increasingly powerful toward the end of the nineteenth century, with increasing influence over the labor vote, common cause was made among the affected elements of the industrial, commerical, and business establishment to secure passage of state and federal legislation outlawing the sale of prison-made goods and the leasing-out of convict labor.

In the post–Civil War period the dilemma of increasing penal populations combined with increasing rates of idleness became acute. Some of the more enlightened penal administrators, supported by academic scholars and social critics, began to form the view that imprisonment ought to serve some constructive purpose rather than ruination. If the state was to be justified in taking power over a man's life by depriving him of his liberty, the prison experience should serve as a method of treatment, reform, and rehabilitation rather than as an ill-disguised form of class warfare characterized by repression, exploitation for profit, and social ostracism. At the very least, men who were sent to prison as punishment should not emerge morally worse than when they entered. Perhaps the finest early expression of these new sentiments toward reform was the Declaration of Principles of 1870 which gave rise to the "New Penology," encouraged the Reformatory movement and parole, and set ideals for American prisons that they have yet to achieve. Unfortunately, the Reformatory movement was undermined by adhering to most of the assumptions of the earlier period, most of which were "frozen" into the maximum security architecture and staff ideologies of the old institutions. The change from prisons to reformatories and, indeed, to "correctional institutions" required more than a change in nomenclature. Changes limited to nomenclature, however, accord very well with the predominant standard of American corrections, the "standard of custodial convenience." Nevertheless, the rehabilitative ideal embodied in the New Penology represented a new direction in thinking about prisons and prisoners. For the next one hundred years rehabilitation was the main topic of conversation associated with prisons.

At present we are in the third stage of American prison history. While prisoners are no longer exploited and worked to death by private contractors, the pendulum has swung too far in the other direction: inmates are too often completely idle, or they engage in obsolete or uselesss make-work, or are exploited by the state for its own benefit by being grossly underpaid or, more often, not at all. The rehabilitative ideal can now be said to be the dominant ideology of American prisons, but it is still more rhetorical than real for nowhere has it been fully implemented. In some of the prisons, in the more progressive states, serious attempts at educational and vocational training are being made. At a more experimental, and sometimes merely faddish level, programs of group therapy, operant behavior conditioning, transactional analysis, and machine-programmed learning are undertaken. In general, however, "rehabilitation" seems to mean that we lay some stress on academic education to increase literacy, vocational training to increase employability, and group therapy to increase insight and interpersonal skills. Insofar as positive programs exist, these are among the most frequently available in the largest numbers of prisons. The assumption is, of course, that the remedying of these deficiencies has some relationship to the reduction of future criminality; and, perhaps, in a marginal way it does. But that would be of very little comfort if we awoke one night to discover a recidivating burglar in our home who had decided to crack our wall-safe on his way home from his regular job, using the welding skills he had learned in vocational training during his last term in prison, and who, in a burst of inter-personal skill, dissuaded us from raising an alarm until he had made his getaway. The serious point here is the attenuated relationship between these popular prison pastimes and crimi-nality. They are another example of "high school thought" in American penal policy.

If literacy had some significant relationship to legal conduct, we would not have the volume of shoplifting committed by middle-class housewives, nor the volume of tax evasion and expense sheet padding by their white-collar husbands. Similarly, if vocational skill were strongly related to legitimacy, we would not have a serious problem with the theft of tools and supplies, and the diversion of finished goods, among blue-collar workers. Whether corporate groups that seek to restrain trade through the creation of monopolies, or that engage in unfair labor practices and consumer fraud, or that merely pollute the environment, are lacking in insight or could benefit from group therapy, is extremely dubious. The same may be said of their sinister counterparts in organized crime, and of corrupt politicians and venal bureaucrats, for they all score highly on interpersonal skills and have good insight into the groups that protect and support them. The Watergate conspirators were not illiterate, unskilled, mental defectives.

Nor should this be taken as an argument against education, vocational training, group therapy, or, indeed, any other kind of prison program or process thought to have rehabilitative po-tential. It is clear that we may be able to increase the prob-abilities of an offender's future chances to pursue a conventional and legitimate life through such programs if three conditions are present: (1) if literacy, vocational skill, and social competence are successfully imparted to the offender; (2) if opportunities for conventional and legitimate participation are available to him in the free world without his having to acquiesce in his own victimization; and (3) if, all things considered, he then chooses to participate in them. But the delivery of the program content, the existence of external opportunities, and the choice the ex-offender will make are related to quite different sets of values. Unfor-tunately, literacy, vocational skill, and interpersonal competence are morally neutral, they can be used for bad ends as well as good, and no amount of childlike faith in their moral efficacy will redeem them. We cannot coerce men into virtue by supplying them with reading, shop, and social skills. For that matter, we cannot even coerce men into learning such skills, except in a most superficial manner, for the generalized responses to coercion are resentment, withdrawal, and counter-coercion. The use of coercive methods inside of a coercive environment is the least likely condition for the absorption of program content. Penal administrators can coerce a prisoner's body, but they cannot—in the present state of democracy—coerce his mind. There is a difference between influencing a prisoner and having him learn to act as if he has been influenced. The latter response is the one made by the overwhelming majority of prisoners, who call it "going along with the program." The prisons are like drama schools, with the parole boards serving as critics of acting skill. Prisoners, like the rest of us, must give their consent if they are to be influenced constructively. But "going along with the program" is the prisoner's counterpart to the prison employee's "standard of custodial convenience"—the minimum response—and, in combination, they reduce most prison programs to nonsense. Going along with the program in a penal system dominated by the standard of custodial convenience sums up the American experience in penology.

In the light of that experience there is growing doubt among those associated with the criminal justice system, and in the mind of the public at large, as to the efficacy of imprisonment as a means toward any constructive end with human beings. Just as it is all but impossible to train airplane pilots in submarines, so is it all but impossible to train inmates in prisons for the life of free men in the free community. Most of the evidence indicates that prisons, as we now know them, serve mainly to maladjust men and to confirm criminals in their criminal careers. Despite a growing disillusionment on the part of the more enlightened penal administrators, the public, and the mass media, the traditional prisons survive for lack of an acceptable alternative. They represent a tremendous amount of past investment—both economic and psychological—that continues to pay off its beneficiaries, those with an investment in the status quo. Most penologists cling to the belief that minimum security, community-based institutions can play a constructive role in the treatment and supervision of convicted offenders and that the traditional prisons should be a last resort after all possible alternatives have been exhausted. Since nearly all prisoners must eventually return and adjust to society, it is far better never to remove them from it insofar as that can be done even with a calculated risk to public safety. Current practice, however, is still to imprison many more offenders than need to be imprisoned for their own or the public's benefit, and to keep them, far too often, in maximum security prisons for too long a time. The wardens of most maximum security prisons will freely admit that from one-half to three-quarters of their prisoners do not belong in such prisons. Similarly, the wardens of most medium and minimum security institutions openly wonder why half to three-quarters of their inmates are not on probation or in some other community-based program. Most penal administrators, however, prefer to grouse about such matters at the annual meeting of the American Correctional Association rather than take the politically vulnerable role of advocate with the governor, the state judiciary, or the mass media. This is merely the "standard of custodial convenience" at work at a higher level of abstraction: why ask for trouble, even if one knows that something should be done? It's easier to go along with the program than to raise a fuss. It is clear that until the huge, Bastille- and dungeonlike prisons built in the nineteenth and early twentieth centuries are physically razed, Americans will not find their way out of the penal dilemma that imprisons and punishes them all.

## Contemporary Prisons and Imprisonment

The designations "prison" and "jail," like the terms "detention," "incarceration," and "imprisonment," tend to be used generically and interchangeably. This usage is a mark of the relatively unimportant status of all things, human and material, associated with penal phenomena and accounts for the fact that most people make no distinctions where fundamental differences are involved. Prisons, in the broadest sense of the term, come in many organizational forms, serve a large range of functions at every level of government, and are embodied in buildings of all conceivable shapes and sizes. Among the more important public institutions used to confine persons accused or convicted of crime, the following must be distinguished: (1) small, transient police and court lockups, or "bull pens," used for detention; (2) local jails, workhouses, houses of correction, and penal farms and camps holding persons awaiting trial, transfer to other authorities, or on appeal, as well as those sentenced to terms of less than a year; (3) local- and state-operated detention and correctional facilities for juvenile delinquents and dependents; (4) security hospitals or wards, drug and alcoholic treatment centers, and other specialized institutions as, for example, those for defective delinquents or criminal sexual psychopaths; and (5) state and federal farms, camps, reception and release centers, correctional institutions, reformatories, penitentiaries and prisons for adult offenders—those usually convicted of felonies and the more serious misdemeanors and usually sentenced to terms of more than a year.

The term "prison," however, is properly applied only to the last of the five categories enumerated and then mainly to the larger, walled institution. The tendency to stereotype the large, walled, traditional prison as "the prison" has the unfortunate consequence of focusing attention on only the tip of the imprisonment iceberg whenever the question of penal reform is raised. It is important, therefore, to point out that there are fewer than five hundred state and federal prisons, penitentiaries, correctional institutions, and so on in the United States, while there are more than seven hundred juvenile institutions, at least five thousand local jails, and probably thirty-five thousand police and court lockups. Moreover, although the prisons tend to be larger, some of them holding two and three thousand prisoners, they receive and process far fewer inmates over a period of time. The number of commitments made to local county and municipal jails, for example, is by all estimates at least three million, and may be as high as eight million (Illinois jails handled 528,000 commitments in 1972), while the annual commitment to state and federal prisons is less than eighty thousand prisoners. The focus on prisons in the narrower sense of state and federal institutions for adults serving sentences longer than one year should not lead us to neglect the greater importance of all the other kinds of penal facilities, nor should we overlook the fact that they all share the same kinds of problems. Indeed, these other confinement facilities that the public has been taught to view as unimportant because they are said to hold only minor or petty offenders, that is, the jails and lockups, are usually far worse because they are even more invisible, neglected, and misused than state and federal prisons. As inadequate and unstable as prisons may be, they are the "tranquil millionaires" of the penal system compared to the tumultuous, neglected, and abused local jails.

Viewed in terms of organization and structure, the state prisons tend to be specialized in a primitive division of labor. Adult men and women and youthful offenders, convicted of felonies, are usually sentenced to separate facilities, as are misdemeanants who happen to be under state jurisdiction rather than local control. In the smaller and more rural states, fewer separate facilities are available, thus combining some of these inmate populations. Prisons tend also to be crudely graded as to the degree of security they are supposed to represent: maximum, medium, and minimum. These standards are so arbitrary that similar prison facilities are differently classified in different states, and it is not unusual for the same prison to be designated at different levels of security at various times in its career. Penitentiaries have been transformed into reformatories as if the power of defining the latter as medium or minimum security could breach the old maximum security walls. In general, however, there are four prisons classified as medium and minimum for every maximum security prison. Since very few convicted persons are so socially dangerous, or such imminent escape risks, as to require maximum security, this 4:1 ratio is probably on the low side in terms of actual requirements. Moreover, since maximum security prisons are so expensive to build (about $20,000 per cell in 1973), they tend not to be replaced; but they also tend to be kept in use long after they are obsolete. Auburn Prison in New York, described by the McKay (Attica) Commission as "the model and prototype of the American maximum security prison," was opened in 1819 and is still in use today, as are sixty-nine other prisons built before 1900. Until they are finally razed, such maximum security prisons will continue to exhibit the major problems of imprisonment: inflexibility, dehumanization, and demoralization that defeat every constructive effort. They are as problematic to their administrators as they are maladjusting to their inmates, and they do a disservice to all of society.

The 170 prisons, penitentiaries, and major correctional institutions are of special importance, for while they constitute a minority of penal "units" they confine the large majority of those prisoners that the public stereotypes as convicts, giving rise to what Barnes referred to as "the convict-bogey." Many were built in the nineteenth century and reflect the influence of archaic theories of human nature and criminality that are still frozen into their architecture. They were built by architects and engineers associated with foundries, quarries, and bridge-building who were more interested in the sale of steel and stone than human psychology and socialization. About 70 state prisons were built to confine more than 1,000 inmates each, and another 125 have capacities in excess of 500 prisoners. Since there is almost universal agreement among penal administrators that prisons become increasingly unsafe and unmanageable in direct proportion to population capacity (even the conservative American Correctional Association asserts this principle), it is clear that far too many prisons in the United States are designed for trouble. In recent years most penologists have come to the view that the maximum population size for any penal institution should not exceed 500 prisoners, and that optimum size, for the most effective delivery of what are deemed to be rehabilitative services, is less than 300 for adults and even less for juveniles. A quick survey of prisons opened in the last ten years will, however, reveal that the penologists, as usual, have been talking to themselves. The federal prison at Marion, Illinois, and the state prison at Vienna, Illinois—both opened in the 1960s—and the state prison opened at Lucasville, Ohio, in 1972 were built with capacities in excess of 1,000. When sound penal principles conflict with politics and patronage—the spending of public monies for contract-letting, symbiotic relations with union labor, the reelection strategies of governmental incumbents—and other irrelevancies, the evidence is clear as to the controlling interest. It is in the context of the present inappropriate and unmanageable prisons, however, that the current and inadequate efforts at "rehabilitation" must be judged—to say nothing of again compounding the prison problem of the future.

The prisoners that have been selected out of the criminal population to inhabit these maladaptive structures are the residue of the traditional criminal legal process described earlier. In recent years the total population of the adult state and federal prisons has been somewhat less than 200,000, with about 80,000 new admissions and discharges per year. The inmates are overwhelmingly male, urban, and under thirty-five years of age. Minority groups are heavily overrepresented, making up at least one-third of the prison population, a proportion that rises to 70 or

80 percent in the prisons serving metropolitan areas. For this and other reasons some penal administrators have asserted that there is a "new breed of prisoners" in the prisons and that they are the source of recent prison disturbances. The fact is, however, that it is much more a case of an old breed of prison guard and penal administrator, who have been sheltered from social changes taking place in the outer world and who have to be dragged, kicking and screaming, into the last quarter of the twentieth century. The free world cannot afford the luxury of adapting to social changes at the glacial rate of change in prisons. Population shifts in the last one hundred years, and changes in sentencing practices in the last fifty years, have had an impact on imprisonment and disturbances that some of the more obtuse penal administrators and their mass-media public relations "flacks" are still groping to understand.

Geographically, there seems to have been a slow migration of prison violence in a northerly and westerly direction in this country, as white racism has manifested itself in heretofore less tested regions. The Southern prisons of yesteryear had a much greater tolerance for violence and a more apathetic public audience for what went on among the lower classes, including both inmates and guards, in the prisons; while violence that came to public notice in the North tended to generate more moral indignation in passing. Thus, while Northern prisons got blacker and blacker, incident to Negro migration, and more Hispanic as well; and as the increasing use of probation and other alternatives to imprisonment tended to weed out the less violence-prone and more stable prisoners of all races, an exacerbated level of racial conflict was added to the normal level of violence in Northern prisons while Southern prisons were still segregated and able to shield their normal level of violence from adverse public scrutiny. The net effect of these population shifts, changes in sentencing practices, and differences in public attitudes was to increase the actual and perceived amount of violence in Northern and Western prisons, while the amount of violence, actual and perceived, in the Southern prisons was largely masked. Racial conflict between guards and prisoners has a long contributory history to prison violence, with the inmates getting much the worst of it. Contemporary prisoners are more urbanized, have been exposed more to the mass media, and are more socially aware. They are more concerned about civil rights and more ready to assert them, but this too is part of a wider social movement for equality and justice, and even the most secure prison cannot keep it out. As long as prisons do not keep pace with changes in the outer world, every generation of prisoners will seem to be "a new breed." A generation ago, penal administrators were lamenting the presence of a "new breed" of spoiled and overindulged youthful offenders who were the offspring of permissive parents and bemoaning the absence of the old, professional safecrackers, pickpockets and conmen "who knew how to do time."

The nature and quality of prison personnel, even more than the kinds of inmates or age of buildings, can have the determining influence on the impact of penal practices. Of the 50,000 or so persons who work in the prisons, nearly two-thirds are custodial employees who simply guard, process, and escort inmates. Another 25 to 30 percent are administrative, supervisory, or maintenance workers. Only 5 to 10 percent of all prison personnel are primarily concerned with "treatment," as opposed to custody, and this includes nearly all the few medical and counseling employees. Since the ratio of inmates to "treatment staff" is so high, only the most serious and obvious cases receive any kind of "professional" attention, while the rest of the inmates are more superficially processed, if they are noticed at all. About half of this less than 10 percent of the treatment personnel are academic or vocational teachers whose efforts are supplemented by those of paraprofessional inmates. As for the qualifications of the staffs for their work, only a minority of the treatment personnel are employed with the full professional, educational, and character qualifications that are thought to be necessary by their professions (doctors, nurses, teachers, vocational trainers, and group counselors). But the vast majority of prison employees, the custodial, administrative and maintenance staffs, have few minimum employment standards to meet, if we exclude the suspect criteria of political patronage considerations. As recently as 1966, about half the states had no educational or civil service requirements for prison wardens. Such a failure to specify standards of professional qualifications maximizes the chances for political opportunism to dominate the American "correctional" system. The standards for custodial workers are somewhat higher, or at least explicit, but seldom expect more than a high school education. Moreover, the conscientious warden congratulates himself every time he can succeed in hiring a guard who has finished high school. Ordinarily, considering the low starting salaries offered, with a range of $5,000 to $9,000 a year, skewed to the lower end, the prison system settles for what it can get. In-service training, except for a two- or three-day "walk-around" with a more experienced employee, is still the exception rather than the rule; pre-service training, leaves of absence for specialized training, or management training for middle- and upper-level personnel, are simply exotic and not worth mentioning.

Leaving aside the "theoretical foundations" and the ideological tendentiousness of "treatment programs" that have already been subjected to a relatively superficial analysis in an earlier section of this paper, an overview of the actual programs and treatment provided to inmates, by the kind of personnel who have been described, indicates the limitations of current penal practice. In point of fact, most prisons make a serious effort to meet the basic needs of food, clothes, and shelter. (The same cannot be asserted of American jails.) Health and medical services are substandard but can meet emergency situations and maintain minimal survival conditions. (In jails, health and medical services vary from the atrocious to the lethal, if any are present at all.) Academic and vocational instruction is frequently available but insufficient to meet the full range of need, so it is reserved for the younger prisoners and the illiterate. (In jails such programs are almost totally absent.) Some kind of recreational activity is usually available, but, for the most part, it is indoor, passive, and debilitating (board games, cards, comic books, pulp magazines, and radio). The intention to keep inmates "busy" is present, but there is usually not enough work for everyone and much of it is diluted make-work of a useless nature. Moreover, prison labor laws requiring that prison-made goods be sold only to nonprofit or tax-supported agencies (that usually prefer the private market), limit both the amount and the training value of prison industries. There is little demand on the labor market for ex-inmate mail censors, license-plate-makers, or even printers skilled in operating foot-pedal presses filled with hand-set paragraphs of type. Finally, many prisons provide some kind of individual counseling, group therapy, or job placement service. One may wonder how seriously such "programs" are regarded when there is only one psychologist, social worker, or counselor for every two hundred inmates, and some state prison systems do not begin to meet that ratio.

Moreover, the low starting salaries and elastic definitions of "professional workers" often seriously debase what it means to be a psychologist, social worker, or therapeutic counselor. A college dropout who made an unsuccessful attempt to master "English Lit. II" cannot be converted into a therapeutic counselor by undergoing an employment ritual that confers that status. No wonder the inmates see the whole enterprise as essentially fraudulent.

Over the past fifty years there has been a slow but steady increase in the proportion of persons who have been convicted and placed on probation rather than sent to prison. Since a probation officer with a salary of $10,000 and fifty probationers to supervise can save the state at least $90,000 per year, the economic motive is again contributing to "penal reform." As more judges become aware of the recidivism rates produced by prisons today, and as the general public and the mass media become less ambivalent about and more disillusioned with the moral and economic bankruptcy of imprisonment, a greater tolerance for community-based corrections may begin to develop. Thus far, however, the motives for penal reform have been more concerned with saving money than saving human beings, and herein lies a danger. In practice, most probation officers lack professional qualifications, earn less than $10,000, and in some areas of the United States have case-loads for supervision of 200 to 300 probationers. Thus, in an attempt to capitalize on and magnify the economic "saving," the correctional effectiveness of probation is diluted and debased with the consequence that the myth of imprisonment as the safer alternative is perpetuated. The economics of imprisonment and probation, insofar as they can be discerned, represent a perfect example of a "Catch-22" dilemma.

The judgments rendered by Sutherland, Barnes, Sellin, and Tannenbaum more than thirty-five years ago still stand: the major prisons of the United States do not protect society from its criminals; they do not deter criminals; they do not reform and do not rehabilitate criminals. If the prisons, and the method of imprisonment, do none of these things, just what functions do they serve? At the most general level, imprisonment serves at least two functions: one for the prisoners and the other for society at large. By substituting official neglect and abuse for private vulnerability and crime, it serves to confirm prisoners in their criminal careers and maladjusts them for their future life in the free community. Clearly, such a powerfully damaging weapon in "the war against crime" should be sparingly used. As for society at large, the illusion that a serious social problem is being successfully addressed continues to mislead and victimize the public. Everyone—the general public, the mass media, public officials, and even the prisoners themselves—share an ardent desire that something constructive be done about "the prison problem." But wishing will not make it so. As in all fields of human endeavor, if our means are not appropriate to our ends, we will accomplish nothing. This lesson has been learned by science, engineering, medicine, and business; it is time that it be learned in the field of criminal justice.

## Some Reluctant Recommendations for Reform

Throughout this disquisition on "the prison problem" there has been a recurrent theme calling for the physical destruction, the actual razing, of the large, walled, maximum security prisons. That is the only rational, final, solution. It is not, however, likely to happen in the predictable future. There is, therefore, a certain virtue in simply maintaining these malfunctioning institutions, intact, as a strategy for maintaining the level of social criticism and political pressure that might hasten the day of their ultimate destruction. One has serious reservations about proposing "reforms" that simply serve to prop up an evil instrument of misguided social policy. To offer to "reform" the destructive, Bastille-like, prisons is like taking on the assignment of that anonymous German technician whose task it was to perfect and maintain the Nazi ovens at Buchenwald; for the large, walled, maximum security prisons are like the Nazi ovens, except that they burn at a lower rate of oxidation. At the same time, it is clear that the miseries experienced by those who are obliged to function in these prisons, whether as inmates, guards or administrators, will continue into the future. There is, therefore, a certain luxury to preaching the doctrine of increasing misery as an efficient cause of future change, if the preacher of the doctrine does not have to share the misery. These are the horns of the dilemma that the concerned critic of "the prison problem" must thread as he contemplates the future. Given our two hundred years of experience with the prison problem during which it has demonstrated a remarkable resilience; and given no grounds for expecting a sudden burst of enlightenment on the part of those who have permitted and condoned the development and maintenance of the problem by their active complicity; the choice is clear—we must do what we can to ameliorate an indefinite, interim period of misery.

Reform measures that respond to immediate conditions, like the "demands" that tend to surface during prison riots, while useful, are also superficial, for they are addressed to symptoms rather than causes. In dealing with "the prison problem" at the most general level, the first principle that must be established and realized in its full implications is that the criminal justice process is a unified process. Every stage in the traditional criminal legal process, from the time that a crime is defined by law, through arrest and the entire chain to parole, has important consequences for every other stage in that process. Until that fact is fully realized, and taken into account, much that masquerades as reform will be mere tinkering with obvious symptoms of limited importance. While the Watergate revelations, and the fascination of the law enforcement authorities with computer technology, information systems, and surveillance equipment, have given many thoughtful observers pause about the desirability of unifying the criminal justice system under such conditions, it is clear that the policy questions raised at this juncture in history must be addressed at the political level. It is possible to have a rational criminal justice system consistent with the benefits of a free, pluralistic, and democratic society. Thus the necessity for a greater sense of unity, and a better appreciation of the interdependence of the elements of the criminal justice system, despite some current aberrations, is still a desirable goal.

What that means for prison reform is that effective measures for dealing with "the prison problem" may often seem far removed from the prison gate. The traditional "solutions" to the problem are those that were put forth in 1870, in the Declaration of Principles that heralded the New Penology: (1) more money, staff, and buildings; (2) better staff, training, and programs; (3) smaller and more diversified institutions with staffs capable of engaging in individualized treatment; (4) more professionalism and less partisan politics; and (5) more rationality and justice. For the most part, these recommendations are as relevant today as they were then. But they have been resisted by entrenched interests and neglected by an apathetic public. They are, moreover, the time-bound solutions of another era—a time when the industrial revolution and American immigration seemed to imply that more production, more population, more of everything was in the natural order of things; a time when the announcement of the New Penology seemed tantamount to its implementation. The fact that these "solutions," and almost no others, continue to be put forward as contemporary solutions is simply another example of "the standard of custodial convenience" at the policy level. Instead of making a frontal assault on the old, large, walled, maximum security prisons, the "reformers" inside and outside the criminal justice system have increasingly sought ways to outflank or avoid these centers of resistance to social change by beginning to fashion parallel and substitute organizational forms, for example, half-way houses, work-release and probation subsidy programs. The importance of such beginnings should not be denigrated, but, clearly, something more fundamental is required.

The beginning must be made in criminal law reform. The range of human conduct that the law now defines as illegal has a direct relationship to the number of persons who are imprisoned. As earlier remarked, the wardens of maximum and medium security prisons will freely admit that from half to three-quarters of their inmates do not require that level of security. Similar sentiments are expressed by the superintendents of medium and minimum security institutions who wonder why most of their charges are not on probation or otherwise under supervision in some community-based program. Most persons who are convicted simply should not be physically incarcerated. Moreover, probation officers with excessive caseloads actively supervise only a minority of their probationers, while the rest seem to get along in the community as if they were "free men." From such evidence it is clear that entirely too much behavior that could either be reasonably tolerated or otherwise dealt with is now defined as criminal and wends its way into the prisons. The criminal law can be no substitute for adequate social legislation, nor is it particularly effective in controlling all forms of human behavior. The criminal justice system is a poor instrument for dealing with the consequences of deficiencies in education, housing, health, employment and welfare, and frequently compounds the problematic character of a variety of forms of social deviance.

The criminal justice system, including the police, the courts and the prisons, is overloaded with the task of handling what have come to be called "crimes without victims," a more accurate description of which is conduct for which the authorities are the only effective complainant. Human behavior that does not involve the use or threat of violence against others, or fraud, or serious attacks against the property of others, but consists, rather, of willing buyers and sellers coming together to exchange goods or services, or the voluntary consumption of some commodity should, insofar as possible, be removed from the criminal law. The "revolving door drunk," caught up in the treadmill of criminal justice, is only the most obvious example; the gambler, the drug user, the consenting sexual adult, and the vagrant are other likely candidates. The decriminalization of such conduct does not confer social approval, nor does it imply that all such behavior will cease to be problematic once the criminal stigma is withdrawn—although that accounts for much of its problematic character. The criminal law has had these problems in its care for a very long time, and without much visible impact. It is time to turn them over to the agencies of medicine, public health, education, welfare, family counselling, and moral persuasion insofar as they may pose a public or private problem once they are not criminal by definition. The jails and prisons certainly do not have the staffs or resources to address these problems; on the contrary, under present conditions, the jails and prisons actively contribute to precisely these forms of social deviance. Prisoners gamble, intoxicate themselves with whatever chemicals they can get their hands on, engage in homosexual relations or rape, and are as idle as any vagrant on the street could be.

Criminal law reform, in turn, must be supplemented by procedural and administrative reforms designed to divert large numbers of persons from every stage in the traditional criminal legal process. This is not simply a proposal to turn criminals loose on the community (that happens, anyway, as was earlier illustrated in connection with unreported crime, the discretionary and selective nature of criminal justice, and the steep case mortality rates of serious crime known to the police); it is, rather, a plea for more careful screening of appropriate cases that may be released consistent with public safety at the various levels of the criminal justice system. Where the procedures to be proposed have been tried, they have been found to be equal or superior to maintaining unnecessary custody. Beginning with a stricter application of the criteria of arrest, to reduce marginal input into the system and to prevent the careless spoiling of identities of the young, the overload in the pretrial stages can be reduced through: (1) the increased use of the summons rather than physical arrest; (2) a greater reliance on release on one's own recognizance; (3) the lowest possible requirement of cash bail; and (4) mandating the welfare authorities to deposit cash bail for offenders as an "emergency payment" rather than having the offender's family apply for relief. There is no doubt that it is cheaper to rely on such measures than on custody, and that these measures enable persons who are presumed to be innocent under our laws to contribute more effectively to their own defense and the support of their families. At the posttrial level the overload may be reduced by: (1) more use of suspended sentences; (2) a greater resort to graded fines payable on the installment plan— for rich and poor alike—so that the collection of fines becomes a form of periodic supervision and counseling and so that the rich do not simply buy their way out; (3) an expanded use of more adequate probation, preferably on the California subsidized probation plan, to help upgrade probation and to bribe communities to tolerate offenders that they too readily export to state prisons without such subsidies; and (4) partial confinement in community-based half-way houses or other facilities designed to treat special problem groups, for example, addicts and alcoholics. Even the impact of imprisonment can be moderated by sentences that permit work-release, education or vocational training release, incentive furloughs, and parole at the earliest time consistent with a calculated risk for public safety. In short, in every appropriate case and at every stage of the traditional criminal legal process, all forms of custody, and especially imprisonment, should be avoided whenever possible.

A serious effort to effect such a program of law and procedural reforms would go a long way toward reducing the numbers that now overload the criminal justice system and would tend to reduce the current prison population. At the same time, it would enable the existing penal plant and staff complement to deal more rationally with the reduced, residual prison population. Clearly, such a program of reforms would require a redistribution of criminal justice personnel and a more adequate allocation of resources to health, education, and welfare agencies in the community that would take on an increased work level. A greater infusion of due process measures into internal prison procedures— disciplinary hearings, supplemented by external and independent ombudsmen to monitor the conditions of jails and prisons and the treatment of prisoners—would also go a long way toward reducing some of the more blatant forms of injustice. In the last analysis, however, the systematic physical destruction of the older, Bastille-like monster prisons must be accomplished, for they will be used as long as they are available.

# Index

2847